The International Atomic Energy Agency

This volume offers a wide-ranging examination and discussion of the International Atomic Energy Agency's (IAEA) past, present, and future as it enters its seventh decade.

Including contributions from leading experts across the globe, the book assesses the historical record of the IAEA; the issues and challenges it faces at present; and its future prospects. In doing so, it addresses the primary missions of the IAEA outlined in the IAEA's statute, i.e., to safeguard and promote the peaceful uses of nuclear energy, as well as the missions over which it is expanding its mandate, including nuclear safety and security. The volume is divided into two parts: Part I focuses on historical recollections and reflections of participants in key events, ranging from a personal account of the initial negotiations of the IAEA to an account by its chairman on the dynamics of the Board of Governors in recent years. Part II covers current and future issues in the IAEA's role in nuclear safeguards, the peaceful uses of nuclear energy, and nuclear safety and security.

This book will be of much interest to students of nuclear proliferation and arms control, global governance and international security in general.

Joseph F. Pilat is a Program Manager in the Office of National Security and International Studies at the Los Alamos National Laboratory and a Global Fellow at the Woodrow Wilson International Center for Scholars where he co-directs the Nonproliferation Forum.

Routledge Global Security Studies
Series Editors: Aaron Karp and Regina Karp

Global Security Studies emphasizes broad forces reshaping global security and the dilemmas facing decision-makers the world over. The series stresses issues relevant in many countries and regions, accessible to broad professional and academic audiences as well as to students, and enduring through explicit theoretical foundations.

Military Coercion and US Foreign Policy
The Use of Force Short of War
Edited by Melanie W. Sisson, James A. Siebens, and Barry M. Bleachman

Expanding US Military Command in Africa
Elites, Networks and Grand Strategy
Edited by Tshepo Gwatiwa and Justin van der Merwe

Nuclear Weapons Free Zones
A Comparative Perspective
Exequiel Lacovsky

Renegotiating the Nuclear Order
A Sociological Approach
Tarja Cronberg

The Treaty Prohibiting Nuclear Weapons
How it was Achieved and Why it Matters
Alexander Kmentt

The Nuclear Terrorism Threat
An Organisational Approach
Brecht Volders

The International Atomic Energy Agency
Historical Reflections, Current Challenges, and Future Prospects
Edited by Joseph F. Pilat

For more information about this series, please visit: https://www.routledge.com/Routledge-Global-Security-Studies/book-series/RGSS

The International Atomic Energy Agency

Historical Reflections, Current Challenges, and Future Prospects

Edited by
Joseph F. Pilat

Routledge
Taylor & Francis Group
LONDON AND NEW YORK

First published 2022
by Routledge
2 Park Square, Milton Park, Abingdon, Oxon OX14 4RN

and by Routledge
605 Third Avenue, New York, NY 10158

Routledge is an imprint of the Taylor & Francis Group, an informa business

British Library Cataloguing-in-Publication Data
A catalogue record for this book is available from the British Library

Library of Congress Cataloging-in-Publication Data
Names: Pilat, Joseph F., editor.
Title: The International Atomic Energy Agency's: historical reflections, current challenges and future prospects / edited by Joseph F. Pilat.
Description: Abingdon, Oxon ; New York, NY : Routledge, 2021. | Series: Global security studies | Includes bibliographical references and index.
Identifiers: LCCN 2021002541 (print) | LCCN 2021002542 (ebook) | ISBN 9780367749156 (hbk) | ISBN 9781003160205 (ebk)
Subjects: LCSH: International Atomic Energy Agency--History. | Nuclear nonproliferation.
Classification: LCC HD9698.5 .I59 2021 (print) | LCC HD9698.5 (ebook) | DDC 341.7/34--dc23
LC record available at https://lccn.loc.gov/2021002541
LC ebook record available at https://lccn.loc.gov/2021002542

ISBN: 9780367749156 (hbk)
ISBN: 9780367749187 (pbk)
ISBN: 9781003160205 (ebk)

DOI: 10.4324/9781003160205

Typeset in Times
by KnowledgeWorks Global Ltd.

In Memoriam

Yukiya Amano
1947–2019

and

Myron Kratzer
1925–2021

Contents

List of Contributors

Editor

Joseph F. Pilat is a Program Manager in the Office of National Security and International Studies at the Los Alamos National Laboratory and a Global Fellow at the Woodrow Wilson International Center for Scholars where he co-directs the Nonproliferation Forum. He served as Representative of the Secretary of Defense to the Fourth Review Conference of the Nuclear Non-Proliferation Treaty (NPT), and as senior adviser to the US Delegation at the 1995 NPT Review and Extension Conference. Dr. Pilat also served as representative of the Secretary of Defense to the Open Skies negotiations. He has held positions in the Pentagon and the Congressional Research Service, and has taught at Cornell University, Georgetown University and the College of William and Mary. He is the co-editor of the *Handbook of Nuclear Proliferation and Policy* (Routledge, 2015) and the co-author of *The Politics of Weapons Inspections* (Stanford University Press, 2017).

Contributors

Ambassador Nobuyasu Abe is a former Commissioner of the Japan Atomic Energy Commission and former UN Under-Secretary-General for Disarmament Affairs. He has an extensive history of diplomatic service, having served as consul general in Boston, as ambassador to Austria and Saudi Arabia, and for the IAEA and other international organizations in Vienna. At home he served as Director-General for Arms Control and Science Affairs of the Japanese Foreign Ministry. Abe has taught international relations and arms control at Sophia, Doshisha, Tokyo and International Christian Universities and has published numerous papers on nuclear nonproliferation and disarmament. He is currently a senior advisor to the Council on Strategic Risks in Washington, D.C.

Ambassador Yukiya Amano was the Director General of the International Atomic Energy Agency (IAEA) from 2009 to 2019. He previously served in the Japanese Foreign Ministry, where he held many positions, including Director-General for Arms Control and Scientific Affairs and Director-General of the Disarmament, Nonproliferation and Science Department. As Japan's ambassador to the IAEA, he was the Chairman of the Board of Governors from 2005 to 2006.

Massimo Aparo was appointed as a Deputy Director General and Head of the Department of Safeguards at the International Atomic Energy Agency, effective from June 4, 2018. Prior to this, Mr. Aparo was Acting Director, Office for Verification in Iran, since March 1, 2016. Mr. Aparo has been working at the IAEA's Department of Safeguards since 1997. He served as Section Head in the Division of Technical and Scientific Services, as Head of the Tokyo Regional Office in the Division of Operations A, and as Head of the Iran Task Force. Before joining the IAEA Mr. Aparo worked as Director General of an Italian company in the area of radiation detection and monitoring, in the European Space Agency and at Italy's former National Committee for Nuclear Energy.

Ambassador John Barrett served as Ambassador to Austria and Slovakia and as Canada's Permanent Representative to the International Organizations in Vienna, including as Governor on the International Atomic Energy Agency's Board of Governors from 2009 to 2013. He chaired the Board from 2012 to 2013. Previously, he served as Director, Non-Proliferation and Disarmament Division (2005–2006) and Director General, Strategic Planning (2006–2009) in the Department of Foreign Affairs and International Trade (now Global Affairs Canada). Following his Vienna posting, Dr. Barrett was President & CEO of the Canadian Nuclear Association (2013–2019) and is President, Portoloan Global Inc., a consultancy specializing in energy policy, nonproliferation, and diplomacy.

Maria Betti has been Director of the JRC - Directorate G for Nuclear Safety and Security since 2015. From August 2008 to September 2012, she was the Director of the NAEL Division of the IAEA. Before joining the European Commission (EC) in 1991, she served at the Italian National Research Council and the department of Chemistry and Industrial Chemistry of the University of Pisa, Italy, where she lectured until 2012.

Bernard Bigot is the Director-General of the ITER Organization. Prior to his appointment in 2015, he was delegated by the French government to act as High Representative for the implementation of ITER in France, a position that he occupied since 2008. Prior to his appointment at ITER, he completed two terms (2009–2012 and 2012–2015) as Chairman and CEO of the French Alternative Energies and Atomic Energy Commission, CEA. From 2003 to 2009, Bernard Bigot served as

France's High commissioner for atomic energy, an independent scientific authority whose mission is to advise the French President and the French government on nuclear and renewable energy policy and in all the other scientific and technological domains where the CEA intervenes. From 1975 to 2003, he was University Professor in Physical Chemistry at Ecole Normale Supérieure de Lyon (France) and was successively appointed as Deputy Director (1987–1993) and Director (1999–2003).

John Carlson is Non-Resident Senior Fellow at the Vienna Center for Disarmament and Non-Proliferation, a member of the Asia-Pacific Leadership Network and the International Advisory Council of the International Luxembourg Forum, and consultant to the Nuclear Threat Initiative. Carlson was Director General of the Australian Safeguards and Non-Proliferation Office from 1989 to 2010. His concurrent appointments included the chairmanship of the IAEA Standing Advisory Group on Safeguards Implementation, Alternate Governor at the IAEA Board of Governors, Sherpa at the 2010 Nuclear Security Summit and founding Chair of the Asia-Pacific Safeguards Network. He holds the national award of Member of the Order of Australia (AM) and is a Fellow of the Institute of Nuclear Materials Management.

Ambassador Piet de Klerk has worked most of his career for the Netherlands' Ministry of Foreign Affairs, most recently as Ambassador for International Organisations (2018–2019) and Special Counterterrorism Envoy (2014–2017). He is also one of the Co-Chairs of the International Partnership for Nuclear Disarmament Verification. Previously, Mr. de Klerk served as the chief negotiator in charge of preparations for the Nuclear Security Summit held in March 2014 in The Hague, and prior to that as Dutch Ambassador to Jordan, Deputy Permanent Representative of the Netherlands at the United Nations in New York and as Human Rights Ambassador. From 1998 to 2003, he served as the IAEA Director for Policy Coordination and External Relations.

Jean-Paul Glatz is the Head of the Nuclear Chemistry Unit at JRC-ITU, a position he has held since 2007. Previously, from 1996 to 1997, he was deputy head at the same unit, with research programs related to the safeguarding of nuclear materials in support to EURATOM and IAEA, and the measurement of radioactivity in the environment. He was head of the Hot Cells unit from 1998 to 2006.

Pierre Goldschmidt was a nonresident senior associate at the Carnegie Endowment for International Peace from 2005 to 2017, and was the Deputy Director General and head of the Department of Safeguards at the International Atomic Energy Agency from May 1999 to June 2005. Before joining the IAEA, Goldschmidt was director general of SYNATOM, the company responsible for the fuel supply and spent-fuel management of seven Belgian nuclear plants, for twelve years. He was a member of the directorate of EURODIF, the French uranium-enrichment company, for six years. Goldschmidt was a member of the European Nuclear Society's High Scientific Council and has headed numerous European and international committees, acting as chairman of the Uranium Institute in London, the Organization of Producers of Nuclear Energy in Paris, and the Advisory Committee of the EURATOM Supply Agency. Among a number of cultural and scientific awards, he received the 2008 Joseph A. Burton Forum Award of the American Physical Society.

Ambassador James Goodby is Annenberg Distinguished Visiting Fellow at Stanford's Hoover Institution. Goodby served in the US Foreign Service, achieving the rank of Career Minister, and was appointed to five ambassadorial-rank positions by Presidents Carter, Reagan, and Clinton, including ambassador to Finland. During his Foreign Service career, he was involved as a negotiator and a policy adviser in the creation of the International Atomic Energy Agency, the negotiation of the limited nuclear test ban treaty, START, the Conference on Disarmament in Europe, and the Nunn-Lugar cooperative threat reduction program. Goodby is the author and editor of several books, his most recent is *Approaching the Nuclear Tipping Point: Cooperative Security in an Era of Global Change.*

Ambassador Rafael Mariano Grossi is the Director-General of the IAEA. He was Ambassador of Argentina to Austria and Permanent Representative to International Organizations in Vienna. From 2002 to 2007, Mr. Grossi was Chief of Cabinet in the Office of the Director General of the Organization for the Prohibition of Chemical Weapons in The Hague (OPCW) and from 2010 to 2013, he was Assistant Director General for Policy of the IAEA. Ambassador Grossi served as Chair of the Nuclear Suppliers Group (NSG) for two consecutive terms (2014–2016).

Mark Hibbs is a senior fellow at the Carnegie Endowment for International Peace's Nuclear Policy Program. Before joining Carnegie in 2010, he was an editor and correspondent for twenty-five years in the field of nuclear energy, nuclear trade, and nonproliferation, working principally in Europe, the Soviet Union and its successor states, and the Asia-Pacific region. His work appeared in a number of publications, including the *Financial Times*, *Nucleonics Week*, and *Nuclear Fuel.* Hibbs' research is focused broadly on international nuclear trade and nonproliferation governance in four main areas: the multilateral international nuclear trade regime, decision-making at the International Atomic Energy Agency, nuclear safeguards and verification, and bilateral nuclear cooperation arrangements. Hibbs also investigates works on national and international policy issues concerning the generation of nuclear power. His book on *The Future of Nuclear Power in China* was published by Carnegie in 2018.

Ambassador Laura S. H. Holgate is Senior Fellow at the Belfer Center for Science and International Affairs. Previously, she served as U.S. Representative to the Vienna Office of the United Nations and the International Atomic Energy Agency from July 2016 to January 2017. Ambassador Holgate was previously the Special Assistant to the President and Senior Director for Weapons of Mass Destruction Terrorism and Threat Reduction on the National Security Council. She was also the U.S. Sherpa to the Nuclear Security Summits and co-led the effort to advance the President's Global Health Security Agenda. From 2001 to 2009, Ambassador Holgate was the Vice President for Russia and New Independent States Programs at the Nuclear Threat Initiative. Prior to that, she directed the Department of Energy's Office of Fissile Materials Disposition from 1998 to 2001, and was Special Coordinator for Cooperative Threat Reduction at the Department for Defense, where she provided policy oversight of the "Nunn-Lugar" Cooperative Threat Reduction program.

Ambassador Heidi Hulan serves as Canada's Permanent Representative to the International Organizations in Vienna, including the International Atomic Energy Agency, where she currently serves as Chair of the IAEA Board of Governors. She is concurrently accredited as Canada's Ambassador to Austria and Slovakia, having joined Canada's Department of Foreign Affairs and International Trade in 1996. At Headquarters, she has worked in a variety of assignments, including: Director, Non-Proliferation and Disarmament Division; Director General, Non-Proliferation and Security Threat Reduction; and most recently as Director General, International Security Policy. Ambassador Hulan was Canada's "Sous-Sherpa" for the 2016 Nuclear Security Summit (NSS), and served as the inaugural "Convener" of the post-Summit "Nuclear Security Contact Group," which aims to maintain momentum on implementing NSS commitments. Overseas, she has served as Minister Counsellor and Head of Political Section at Canada's Permanent Mission to the UN in New York and was Deputy Permanent Representative of Canada to NATO from 2010 to 2013.

Willem Janssens is Head of Department, Nuclear Safeguards and Security, Directorate for Nuclear Safety and Security, Joint Research Centre, European Commission. He originally joined the EC as nuclear safeguards inspector analyst for the reprocessing facilities at La Hague and Sellafield and started his career at Westinghouse as nuclear safety and licensing engineer. He is the 2019–2020 President of ESARDA (European Safeguards Research and Development Association) and Chair of the Strategic Planning Committee of INMM (Institute of Nuclear Materials Management).

Myron Kratzer joined the U.S. Atomic Energy Commission's Division of International Affairs in 1957. As Director of International Affairs and Assistant General Manager for International Activities, he negotiated numerous Agreements for Cooperation in the peaceful uses of nuclear energy. He was the principal U.S. negotiator of the IAEA's safeguards documents INFCIRCs 26, 66, and 153; and participated in the negotiation of the safeguards provisions of the NPT. He joined the Department of State in 1971, serving as Deputy Assistant Secretary of State for Nuclear Affairs from 1975 to 1977. After leaving government service in 1977, Kratzer continued as a consultant in nonproliferation and safeguards policy publications and has stressed the application of the system to undeclared nuclear materials and activities.

Daniel Poneman is President and Chief Executive Officer of Centrus Energy Corporation. As Deputy Secretary of Energy from 2009 to 2014, his responsibilities spanned the range of U.S. energy policies—hydrocarbons, renewables, nuclear, and efficiency—including cybersecurity, resilience and emergency response, project management, national security, and international cooperation. From 1990 to 1996, he served at the National Security Council as Director for Defense Policy and Arms Control and then as Special Assistant to the President and Senior Director for Nonproliferation and Export Controls. He also advised corporate clients as a Principal at the Scowcroft Group and spent eight years practicing law at Hogan & Hartson and Covington & Burling. Mr. Poneman is a Senior Fellow at the Belfer Center for Science and International Affairs, a Distinguished Fellow at the Paulson Institute, and a member of the Council on Foreign Relations. Mr. Poneman was educated at Harvard and Oxford University.

Laura Rockwood is the Director of the Open Nuclear Network. She was Executive Director of the Vienna Center for Disarmament and Nonproliferation. Rockwood worked for almost 30 years at the International Atomic Energy Agency, where she worked primarily on the negotiation, interpretation, and implementation of IAEA safeguards. She served in the Office of Legal Affairs of the IAEA, from which she retired as section head for non-proliferation and policy making in November 2013. Prior to working for the IAEA Rockwood was employed by the US Department of Energy as a trial attorney in radiation injury cases, and as counsel in general legal matters.

Vincenzo V. Rondinella is Head of the Hot Cells Unit at the Institute for Transuranium Elements.

1 Introduction

*Joseph F. Pilat**

The International Atomic Energy Agency (IAEA) was envisioned in U.S. president Dwight D. Eisenhower's "Atoms for Peace" speech, delivered to the United Nations (UN) General Assembly on December 8, 1953. The IAEA was created in 1957, more than 60 years ago, but its history goes back at least a decade earlier to the *Report on the International Control of Atomic Energy*, written under the auspices of Dean Acheson and David Lilienthal in 1946, and the Baruch Plan that was based on the report. The Baruch Plan was presented to the UN Atomic Energy Commission (UNAEC) on June 14, 1946, by Bernard Baruch, the U.S. representative to the commission. In his presentation, Baruch stated, "We must provide the mechanism to assure that atomic energy is used for peaceful purposes and preclude its use in war."[1] The plan proposed:

> … the creation of an International Atomic Development Authority, to which should be entrusted all phases of the development and use of atomic energy, starting with the raw material and including:
>
> 1 Managerial control or ownership of all atomic-energy, activities potentially dangerous to world security.
> 2 Power to control, inspect, and license all other atomic activities.
> 3 The duty of fostering the beneficial uses of atomic energy.
> 4 Research and development responsibilities of an affirmative character intended to put the Authority in the forefront of atomic knowledge and thus to enable it to comprehend, and therefore to detect, misuse of atomic energy. To be effective, the Authority must itself be the world's leader in the field of atomic knowledge and development and thus supplement its legal authority with the great power inherent in possession of leadership in knowledge.[2]

The Baruch Plan has been seen, at different times, as idealistic and naïve or as cynical, and Baruch has been criticized for focusing on "condign punishment" for violators and for calling for "no veto to protect those who violate their solemn agreement not to develop or use atomic energy for military purposes."[3]

DOI: 10.4324/9781003160205-1

Although the Soviet Union provided two counterproposals to the Baruch Plan, discussions of the U.S. proposal dominated the UNAEC, where the United States and its allies held a 9-to-2 majority. Amid the emerging Cold War, an aggressive Soviet nuclear-weapon program, and Soviet suspicion of U.S. motives, the Baruch Plan languished in the UNAEC as the Soviet Union and the United Kingdom developed nuclear weapons themselves. The Baruch Plan was not realized, and the issue of disarmament was no longer on the table in the same way when the "Atoms for Peace proposal" appeared.

Atoms for Peace was a response to the problems that led to the Baruch Plan, particularly as these problems had worsened over time. In a speech to the United Nations on December 8, 1953, President Eisenhower stated:

> … the dread secret, and the fearful engines of atomic might, are not ours alone.
>
> In the first place, the secret is possessed by our friends and allies, Great Britain and Canada, whose scientific genius made a tremendous contribution to our original discoveries, and the designs of atomic bombs.
>
> The secret is also known by the Soviet Union….
>
> If at one time the United States possessed what might have been called a monopoly of atomic power, that monopoly ceased to exist several years ago. Therefore, although our earlier start has permitted us to accumulate what is today a great quantitative advantage, the atomic realities of today comprehend two facts of even greater significance.
>
> First, the knowledge now possessed by several nations will eventually be shared by others—possibly all others.
>
> Second, even a vast superiority in numbers of weapons, and a consequent capability of devastating retaliation, is no preventive, of itself, against the fearful material damage and toll of human lives that would be inflicted by surprise aggression.[4]

Eisenhower then declared:

> The governments principally involved, to the extent permitted by elementary prudence, should begin now and continue to make joint contributions from their [military] stockpiles of normal uranium and fissionable materials to an international atomic energy agency. We would expect that such an agency would be set up under the aegis of the United Nations….
>
> The atomic energy agency could be made responsible for the impounding, storage and protection of the contributed fissionable and other materials. The ingenuity of our scientists will provide special safe conditions under which such a bank of fissionable material can be made essentially immune to surprise seizure.[5]

The president did not have a clear notion of the new agency he proposed, but he saw the Soviet Union as an essential member in its future:

> The United States would be more than willing—it would be proud to take up with others "principally involved" the development of plans whereby such peaceful use of atomic energy would be expedited.
>
> Of those "principally involved" the Soviet Union must, of course, be one.[6]

He hoped that the relationship would produce benefits that went beyond those related to his substantive proposal. Specifically, he stated that he would support an agency that would "open up a new channel for peaceful discussion and initiative at least a new approach to the many difficult problems that must be solved in both private and public conversations if the world is to shake off the inertia imposed by fear and is to make positive progress towards peace."[7]

This swords-to-plowshares vision of the nuclear future was less dramatic and sweeping than the failed Baruch Plan. Even though it had been intended to facilitate nuclear arms reductions, it was no longer tied directly to disarmament.[8] The Atoms for Peace program, as it became known, nonetheless was received with great fanfare and enthusiasm. It would set the foundation for the international nonproliferation regime that Eisenhower had called for in his speech. Over the next five years, the key components of this regime developed. Along with the IAEA, further negotiations led to the Treaty on the Nonproliferation of Nuclear Weapons (NPT), which was based on the Atoms for Peace bargain of peaceful nuclear cooperation in exchange for a verified pledge to forgo further development of nuclear weapons.

Despite the widespread acceptance and influence of the U.S. initiative, Atoms for Peace did not end the concerns about the dual nature of the atom that had made the proposal possible. It was criticized on nonproliferation grounds by academic and nongovernmental experts, and some states from the beginning. From the outset, there were concerns that the peaceful nuclear cooperation promised would actually facilitate advances in weapons programs. Atoms for Peace did in fact open the floodgates of nuclear information to at least some degree, through declassification and release of research in all areas but enrichment—and, of course, in weapons production. It fostered the spread of research reactors around the world that were unnecessary for many states, posed a security challenge with highly enriched uranium fuel, and in at least one case provided the basis of a nuclear weapons effort.[9] Some of those reactors remain a problem today. Moreover, the bank of nuclear material to be established at the IAEA, a central tenet of the proposal, was never realized. Some states made minimal contributions, but the idea soon fell by the wayside. In any case, the initiative's arms control rationale was based on a flawed assumption: nuclear material production was not as great a bottleneck for weapons production as was originally thought, although it remains the greatest hurdle to overcome for any state with an interest in creating a nuclear arsenal. Finally, IAEA safeguards were slow to develop and limited in application, and almost continuously criticized as being neither safe nor an effective guard. Safeguards would expand once the NPT was concluded in the 1970s, but they continued to be criticized on the same grounds, and the debate on their impact has persisted to this day.

Beyond this inherent ambiguity, there initially was some uncertainty in the United States about how to realize the objectives set forward in the speech, including the proposed agency and the ways to bring the Soviet Union into its creation. The U.S. Atomic Energy Commission and the Department of State drafted a statute for the agency, which was fully consistent with the themes in the speech. Within the United States, thinking about the agency proposed in the speech embodied hope that it could improve relations with the Soviet Union and reduce the dangers of nuclear war. Discussions with the Soviets began shortly after Eisenhower's speech.[10] In these initial discussions, however, the Soviets ignored the U.S. position and focused on the limited role the agency could have in disarmament, and noted that the possibility of creating and diverting materials from peaceful to military uses could actually increase the production of nuclear weapons. This element of the response clearly showed that the Soviets understood the dual nature of the atom, and it has been seen as a warning that the proposal could worsen the proliferation problem by encouraging the spread of nuclear materials, equipment, and expertise worldwide. The response involved a reiteration of the Soviet disarmament proposals. Soviet positions had been evolving since the Baruch Plan was put forward. At this time, the Soviet Union accepted the idea of inspections in principle, but it was concerned about possible interference in domestic affairs in practice. The United States, by contrast, saw safeguards as the means of solving the problem of the dangers associated with the possible military uses of peaceful nuclear energy programs.

Although the Eisenhower speech envisioned the proposed agency as being established under the "aegis of the United Nations," the Soviets at this time called for close relations between the new agency and the UN, with the Security Council as the sole authority to address noncompliance—an arrangement which would allow the Soviets to wield a veto if their interests demanded it. The United States, which was already highlighting the role of the agency in peaceful nuclear cooperation rather than in disarmament, did not believe that the Soviet Union would join the new agency, and made clear to the Soviets that it was prepared to move ahead without their participation. However, the Soviet position changed in September 1954. Soviet negotiators indicated that the issues they raised could be resolved technically and that they were prepared to study U.S. safeguards proposals. This was seen as opening the possibility of Soviet participation in the agency's creation. U.S.-Soviet exchanges on the creation of the agency continued through 1954.

Multilateral negotiations without the Soviets began in December 1954 and, on the basis of an initial U.S. draft, produced a draft statute that was shared with the Soviets on a confidential basis. By 1955, the Soviets formally agreed to enter the negotiations, offered their views on the new agency, participated constructively in the 1955 Geneva Conference on peaceful uses, and engaged in technical meetings with the United States and other states on safeguards. At the same time, they aggressively began to cooperate with China, Eastern Europe, and other socialist allies on peaceful uses of nuclear energy. The negotiations then expanded to include the Soviets and other states in 1956. Based on the existing draft text, and Soviet proposals that supported their interests in tying the agency to the UN and ensuring that it did not operate against Soviet interests, the 12 powers drafted a statute for the IAEA. The Soviet Union's positions were not all adopted, but it accepted the results.

On September 20, 1956, a UN conference was convened to review the draft. Despite the ongoing crises of the Hungarian revolution and tensions over the Suez Canal, there was no East-West crisis at the conference. Nonetheless, the Soviets reiterated their disarmament proposals, and safeguards were a point of contention. The Soviets refused a U.S. proposal to coordinate their positions, and even tried to remove safeguards references from the draft statute in apparent support of the position of India, Iran, and other developing states that were opposed to safeguards. A compromise that effectively retained safeguards in the statute was proposed and accepted. Generally, the United States and the Soviet Union were prepared to cooperate on the goal of creating the agency, and the IAEA's statute was adopted unanimously on October 23, 1956. The IAEA thus came into being on July 19, 1957.

After these complex and difficult negotiations, the early years of the IAEA saw a remarkable growth in the power and nonpower applications of nuclear energy, in part because of the promotional role outlined in the statute. This role has continued over time and continues to evolve to meet Member States' needs. Nuclear power production has been challenged by difficult economics; by concerns about proliferation and terrorism; and by nuclear accidents at Three Mile Island in 1979, at Chernobyl in 1986, and most recently at Fukushima Dai-ichi in 2011. Today, long after Three Mile Island and Chernobyl, and in light of the uncertain long-term impact of Fukushima on global interest in nuclear power, the IAEA has been helping nuclear newcomer states to assess their infrastructure, regulatory, and other needs.

At the same time as the IAEA pursued its promotional mission, its safeguards system was being forged. The emergence of the IAEA safeguards system began a unique experiment in international security cooperation. This system pioneered on-site inspections and involved limited yet unprecedented inroads into Member States' sovereignty. In the early years, progress on developing and implementing safeguards was slow, as both the inspection technologies and techniques, as well as political acceptance of the endeavor, had to be created. The entry into force of the NPT, which designated the IAEA as the inspecting power, vastly expanded the reach of safeguards. The near-universal scope of the NPT and its indefinite extension in 1995 solidified the global importance of safeguards. The IAEA's safeguards system has evolved over the past 50 years to meet the challenges posed by new technologies, new international undertakings, and new threats.

From the earliest safeguards to the early 1990s, innovations in procedures and technologies allowed IAEA safeguards to significantly improve capabilities. Innovations in nondestructive assay equipment, including neutron coincidence counters and gamma spectroscopy, have provided inspectors with rapid in situ determinations of the concentration, enrichment, isotopics, and masses of nuclear materials. Through these innovative tests, inspectors have been able to collect information that would have been expensive and time consuming, and in some cases impractical, to determine by other means. Advances in miniaturizing these instruments also have provided inspectors with more portable measurement methods that are useful for both routine inspections in declared facilities and in-field application during nonroutine inspections. Additionally, video surveillance devices that monitor spent fuel ponds at reactors, core discharge monitors that monitor fuel movements in on-load reactors and electronic seals, and continuous unattended monitoring of activities in nuclear facilities have all improved the efficiency of inspections by reducing the time that inspectors spend at facilities. All of these devices have been important in providing assurances of material integrity during an inspector's absence by recording surveillance data for periodic review. Automated review stations have provided further gains in efficiency, and new IAEA technology for remote transmission of facility data continues to reduce the need for inspectors to be present.

Along with technology advances, the IAEA has made innovations in procedures that enhance effectiveness and efficiency, including application of randomized inspections to verify the material flows at low-enriched uranium fuel fabrication plants; expanded reporting requirements for states, especially in the area of nuclear technology imports and exports; and earlier reporting requirements for design information relating to new facilities. These and other capabilities developed over these critical decades have enabled the IAEA to act rapidly and flexibly to handle unprecedented situations in South Africa, countries of the former Soviet Union, Iraq, North Korea, and Libya.

Today, outstanding issues with Iran and North Korea and concerns about nuclear terrorism both highlight the fact that, despite its evolution, the IAEA was created in a different time to deal with different threats. Even though the Agency was able to respond to the challenges of the 1990s, its leadership recognized that more capabilities and authorities would be needed in the future. For the past two decades, the IAEA has been transforming its safeguards system to address these and other issues, including the burden of noncompliance issues. These changes have been essential to provide confidence that shared nuclear technologies and expertise, as well as nuclear materials themselves, are not being diverted to weapon programs. "Completeness" as well as "correctness" became critical.

Central to this transformation is the Additional Protocol (AP), an important new tool that needs to be universally accepted as the basis for safeguards and as a condition for exports. Implementing the new measures in the AP, as well as integrating new and old safeguards measures, remain a work in progress. The innovative approach to IAEA safeguards is one of information acquisition, evaluation, and analysis along with inspections, designed to evaluate the nuclear program of a state as a whole and not just the condition and use of each of its declared nuclear facilities. The emerging safeguards system thus is more flexible and should be better suited to allocating scarce resources to where they are needed most in countering proliferation risk. In the future, further efficiencies in the IAEA's procedures will be required and could be realized through even greater utilization of information and communication technologies to collect, analyze, and process safeguards-related information, as well as remote monitoring coupled with secure information technologies. However, such efficiencies alone may not be sufficient.

The latest form of the new approach is the state-level concept, which tailors IAEA safeguards activities to the particular needs and capabilities of individual states. Based primarily on the AP, and the view that all the activities in a state need to be taken into account, the use of a state-level approach would, in theory, differentiate but not discriminate among states. In this context, some have argued that it would be desirable to shift safeguards resources away from countries with large nuclear power programs such as Japan, Canada, and Germany. In any case, the state-level approach will require balance. If it were to go too far, it will risk being seen as discriminatory. Moreover, if the resources devoted to safeguarding large nuclear power programs were cut too deeply, the IAEA may lose its ability to make independent judgments on these programs, which could undermine global nonproliferation efforts.

This new state-level approach also requires that the IAEA decide on the path it will take to address weaponization. It currently considers weaponization, among other factors, in its state evaluations. As it pays greater attention to weaponization, the issues raised are serious, involving the capabilities and focus of IAEA safeguards. If these safeguards are not monitored carefully, classified or sensitive information might be spread, worsening the proliferation problem and possibly raising other issues. How well can the IAEA assess weaponization? In addition to its current efforts to detect clandestine weaponization activities, should it determine the status of a state's nuclear-weapon program? Can it under any circumstances be expected to make independent judgments on a state's weaponization? What are the legal authorities on which these activities are based? Could other legal authorities support or raise questions about this activity? The IAEA and its Member States—some of whom have been more critical of safeguards and inspections programs—will need to pay close attention to these difficult, complex issues.

These are major issues that affect the transformation of safeguards. This process is further complicated by the fact that whatever the long-term impact of Fukushima on global interest in nuclear power, IAEA safeguards responsibilities are expected to grow in the coming decades. On the basis of current plans and other factors, the IAEA could be inspecting third- and fourth-generation nuclear reactors, enrichment plants using new technologies, pyroprocessing plants, and other new fuel-cycle facilities, along with multinational fuel-cycle centers and international fuel banks. These ambitious inspections plans are unlikely to be fully realized. However, even limited expansion could place increasing strains on the IAEA. Regardless of growth, old plants will continue to be decommissioned, and growing stocks of plutonium and spent fuel (including defense material declared excess by nuclear-weapon states) will have to be safeguarded.

Beyond the formidable challenges of transforming and strengthening safeguards, other challenges include the uncertain impacts of new technologies and growing politicization in the IAEA, particularly the Board, raised in part by Iranian charges against it over the past decade and the debate over the Joint Comprehensive Plan of Action (JCPOA). Moreover, the IAEA, its Member States, or both have been advocating new and expanding roles in the areas of safety, security, and possibly even arms control and disarmament, as allowed by the statute. Nevertheless, its two fundamental missions enshrined in the statue—the peaceful promotion of nuclear energy and safeguards against proliferation—have remained central to the IAEA's mission for six decades, and continue to be pursued as its role and capabilities have evolved.

The IAEA's rich and continuing history spans the Cold War, the post-Cold War era, and the emergence of what some believe is the end of the post-Cold War era. During the chills and thaws of the Cold War, the IAEA's doors were always open to serious East-West security discussions. With the end of the Cold War, a time of new authority for the UN, revelations about Iraq's nuclear-weapon program after the Gulf War threatened the IAEA and its mandate to administer international inspections of peaceful nuclear activities to help ensure that nuclear materials were not being diverted to military programs. The extraordinary actions taken to address these challenges affirm the history of vision, statesmanship, international cooperation, institution building, and progress in creating the indispensable agency. It is a story of technical adaptation and political evolution in the face of continuous and continuing challenges—technical, geopolitical, and institutional. It is clear that the challenges to the IAEA will continue, as will the need for it to evolve in the future as it has evolved over the past six decades.

To explore these and other issues related to the IAEA and its historical and future missions, the Los Alamos National Laboratory in cooperation with the Woodrow Wilson International Center for Scholars held a conference commemorating the 60th anniversary of the IAEA at the Wilson Center in Washington, DC, on November 6 and 7, 2017. This volume is based on the presentations at the conference, which have been updated and expanded with other contributors. It is divided into two major sections, as outlined below, preceded by an interview with the current Director General.

In an interview comprising Chapter 2, the IAEA Director General, Rafael Mariano Grossi, reflects on the historical record of the Agency; the issues and challenges it faces at present; the roles it is assuming or expanding; and its future prospects. He assesses the impact of COVID-19 on the operations of the Agency, and argues for a greater IAEA role in combatting future pandemics. While highlighting the Agency's uniqueness and its broad influence over wide-ranging mandates, he specifically addresses the safety, security, technical cooperation, safeguards, and new verification missions of the IAEA. He argues that the Agency must be nimble and efficient if it is to continue its vital contribution to, and impacts on, international peace, security, and development.

Part I, comprising Chapters 3 through 7, focuses on historical recollections and reflections of participants in key events, from a personal account of the initial negotiations of the IAEA to an account by its chairman on the dynamics of the Board of Governors in recent years. In Chapter 3, James Goodby reflects on Eisenhower's Atoms for Peace speech, which proposed the IAEA and led to its subsequent successful negotiation. Goodby was involved in the original negotiations, and his chapter highlights the development of the Euratom (European Atomic Energy Community) safeguards and the accommodation between Euratom and the IAEA on inspections, which was critical to European accession to the NPT. Myron Kratzer in Chapter 4 assesses the allure of atomic energy at the time of the IAEA's establishment, and how it affected its founding, U.S. agreements on nuclear cooperation, and the development of safeguards. He focuses on the evolution of international safeguards from their modest beginnings to the negotiation of the Comprehensive Safeguards Agreements (INFCIRC/153), in which he was a major U.S. participant. In Chapter 5, Laura Rockwood reflects on the negotiation of the Model Additional Protocol (INFCIRC/540), in which she played a key role as the Agency's negotiator. She explores the development that led to the negotiations, particularly the revelations of a clandestine Iraqi nuclear program after the Gulf War and the recognized need to strengthen safeguards. Daniel Poneman in Chapter 6 offers his thoughts on the place of the IAEA in the international order, and its role in addressing the multiple challenges that appeared in the 1990s and played out over the next decades, including the need to strengthen safeguards in the aftermath of the Gulf War, noncompliance by North Korea and Iran, and the collapse of the Soviet Union and fears of "loose nukes." To Poneman, who was a high-level White House official during this period, the IAEA's role was very different in these cases. In some cases, it was more prominent than others, as it took the lead in global efforts to address nuclear dangers, but it always played a role. To close this section, in Chapter 7, John Barrett critically assesses the issue of governance at the IAEA from the perspective of his time as chairman of its Board of Governors. He looks at the implementation of the AP, and the IAEA's responses to Iranian noncompliance and to the Fukushima accident. His recounting reveals the importance of little-understood internal dynamics, and the roles of power, influence, and divergent interests in the development of policies and other outcomes.

Part II covers current and future issues in the IAEA's role in nuclear safeguards, the peaceful uses of nuclear energy, and nuclear safety and security. The first three chapters in this section address the question of nuclear safeguards. In Chapter 8, Massimo Aparo, the current head of safeguards at the IAEA, addresses the evolution of safeguards and their central role in deterring the spread of nuclear weapons. He highlights the importance of its technical credibility and political independence at a time of profound challenges to and rising demands for safeguards, notably the demands of verifying the JCPOA. John Carlson in Chapter 9 assesses the evolution of safeguards. He focuses on current safeguards issues, including the state-level approach and the IAEA's role in examining weaponization activities. He also looks at possible future directions for it, including greater transparency and internal cultural change. Pierre Goldschmidt, a former IAEA safeguards head, derives a series of lessons in Chapter 10 from the noncompliance cases of North Korea and Iran. He argues that these lessons, which include the need for prompt and decisive action from the IAEA and the UN Security Council as well as the need for the IAEA to have enhanced authorities during crises, are "not yet learned." This is all the more important as more and more states attain the scientific, technical, and industrial capability to develop nuclear weapons.

The next four chapters explore peaceful uses of nuclear energy and key considerations for the safe use of nuclear power. In Chapter 11, Mark Hibbs examines the IAEA's mandate to promote peaceful uses of nuclear energy, and the efforts over the past six decades to implement that mandate, including efforts to tie the safeguards budget to that for technical cooperation. He addresses the development of nuclear safeguards from this perspective, along with the emergence of the IAEA's nuclear safety and security missions. Finally, he looks at future challenges and opportunities in the arena of peaceful uses. Nobuyasu Abe in Chapter 12 addresses the IAEA's role in promoting the peaceful uses of nuclear energy, from power production to medical, agricultural, and industrial uses. He focuses on power production and assesses historical projections of nuclear power and its uncertain future, given issues such as the prospects of accidents and the struggles of many states to find acceptable waste disposal sites. Observing that the future of nuclear power seems to face the most challenges in open, advanced industrial democracies, he argues that a number of measures might help sustain nuclear power, including subsidies and a carbon tax, but notes their political fate is uncertain. In Chapter 13, Bernard Bigot looks at the prospects of fusion energy and its potential place in the IAEA's mandate for promoting the peaceful uses of nuclear energy. He recounts the international collaboration on fusion research and development, with special attention to the ITER Tokamak project, which he heads. He offers a vision of the future of fusion energy in the context of the Agency's role in peaceful uses. Finally, Joseph F. Pilat in Chapter 14 assesses the changes in nuclear safety and security, especially after Fukushima, and assesses how they could impact the international nuclear order and global attention to and interest in nuclear power.

In the following three chapters, Piet de Klerk, Laura Holgate, and Heidi Hulan discuss nuclear security issues. In Chapter 15, de Klerk explores the growth of interest in nuclear security at the IAEA, beginning in the 1970s. This interest expanded dramatically after the collapse of the Soviet Union and the fears of "loose nukes" it generated, and again following the definitive change in threat perceptions with the terrorist attacks in the United States on September 11, 2001. The importance of nuclear security in the Prague agenda and the institution of Nuclear Security Summits (NSS) by President Barack Obama further increased interest and attention. De Klerk argues that with the end of the NSS, the IAEA's role is growing, and will involve activities like developing guidelines, training, and technical advice. Holgate in Chapter 16 focuses on the role and activities of the NSS, and the IAEA's role in the path forward after the summit process ended. She enumerates post-NSS challenges, including divergent threat assessments, sovereignty, and other issues. She draws lessons from the summits, including the importance and impact of high-level engagement, and highlights mechanisms designed to maintain momentum, including the IAEA Nuclear Security Ministerials and the Nuclear Security Contact Group. Finally, in Chapter 17, Heidi Hulan addresses the Nuclear Security Contact Group, of which she was the inaugural convener, in the post-NSS environment. She recounts the group's origins, objectives, and agenda, and assesses progress to date, reflecting on missed opportunities and future challenges.

In Chapter 18, Maria Betti, Willem Janssens, Vincenzo Rondinella, and Jean-Paul Glatz examine the historical relationship between the IAEA and Euratom. Betti and her colleagues look at the development of IAEA and Euratom safeguards over the past six decades, and address collaboration between these organizations on safeguards, safety, security, and technical cooperation. They also address challenges to security around the world and the increasing difficulties of controlling nuclear and other strategic technologies.

The appendix presents a speech given by the late Yukiya Amano at a conference commemorating the agency's 60th anniversary. Amano, who was then the IAEA's Director General, provided a comprehensive overview of its missions, assessing activities and prospects for power and nonpower peaceful uses of nuclear energy, nuclear safety and security, and nuclear safeguards. In the safeguards realm, he specifically looked at the transformation of safeguards, the IAEA's role in inspecting Iran, the issue of North Korea, and other verification prospects.

Notes

* The views expressed are the author's own and not those of the Los Alamos National Laboratory, the National Nuclear Security Administration, the Department of Energy or any other agency.

1. Statement of United States Policy, presented to the United Nations Atomic Energy Commission (UNAEC) by U.S. Representative Bernard Baruch, June 14, 1946. See "The Acheson-Lilienthal & Baruch Plans, 1946," Office of the Historian, U.S. Department of State, https://history.state.gov/milestones/1945-1952/baruch-plans.
2. Ibid.
3. Ibid.
4. "Atoms for Peace Speech [December 8, 1953]," International Atomic Energy Agency (IAEA), https://www.iaea.org/about/history/atoms-for-peace-speech.
5. Ibid.
6. Ibid.
7. Ibid.
8. Ibid.
9. A Canadian research reactor and U.S. heavy water provided to India were used in its "peaceful nuclear explosion" in 1974.
10. For further discussion of the Soviet role in the negotiations, see, for instance, David Holloway, "The Soviet Union and the creation of the International Atomic Energy Agency," *Cold War History* 16, no. 2 (2016): 177–93; and Elisabeth Roehrlich, "The Cold War, the Developing World, and the Creation of the International Atomic Energy Agency (IAEA), 1953–1957," *Cold War History* 16, no. 2 (2016): 195–212.

2 The IAEA's emerging roles, challenges, and prospects for the future

An interview with the Director General

Rafael Mariano Grossi, interviewed by Joseph F. Pilat

JOSEPH F. PILAT: **With the IAEA now three years into its seventh decade, how do you assess its past record and its prospects for the future?**

RAFAEL MARIANO GROSSI: The past 60-plus years are a testament to the International Atomic Energy Agency (IAEA) and its efficiency and nimbleness in the face of the ever-changing circumstances surrounding it. Progress is rarely linear, and the nuclear field is no exception.

The IAEA has 172 Member States, and that number is growing. Its Member States understand the Agency's vital contribution to international peace, security, and development. But as we celebrate the IAEA's successful past and today's good standing, we need to think about where it will be tomorrow. To do so, we—those who work *at* the IAEA and those who work *with* the IAEA—might ask themselves: what it is that we want this institution to achieve? Is it more of the same? Are there any new areas in which the IAEA should play a role? Are there new aspects of the well-known parts of its mission that call for fresh approaches? Should the Agency simply react to new problems and challenges as they appear, or should it adapt as a result of a rational deliberation on the best way forward amid changing circumstances?

I believe that any dispassionate, objective look at the mission and work of the IAEA would conclude that times have changed, technology advances have accelerated, and the basic conditions underlying the work of the Agency are not those of the 20th century. These changes have raised challenges, but with them come opportunities for the IAEA to become stronger and more efficient and to respond in a timelier manner to the expectations of its membership. I believe the IAEA is up to that challenge.

To get us there, I have endeavored to adopt a more dynamic attitude, not just personally as the IAEA's Director General but all across the work of the Agency. That is because I believe that forging inclusive partnerships—not only with Member States but also by reaching out to

DOI: 10.4324/9781003160205-2

nongovernmental and international organizations, industry, and civil society in general—can help the IAEA maximize its ability to build a better future for everyone.

PILAT: **One of the more dramatic challenges the Agency and the world have faced is the COVID-19 pandemic. How did the pandemic affect the Agency and its activities?**

GROSSI: I don't think the COVID-19 pandemic will soon be forgotten. As we speak, it has developed into the worst pandemic the world has suffered since the Spanish flu, which infected 500 million people between 1918 and 1920. COVID-19 has challenged the IAEA because so much of what we do is practical and requires physical contact. I like to say that the IAEA is where the rubber hits the road; where theory becomes practice.

When the pandemic hit, just as I was taking the helm as the sixth Director General, I had to figure out quickly how I could sustain that mandate without interruption in a world put on hold. The rubber of airplane tires was no longer hitting the runway; borders were closing and people feared leaving their homes in case they caught the virus. Reality was threatening to push us into a box and I knew the IAEA could not discharge its mandate that way, especially when the job was already being complicated by the winds of geopolitical change. Those winds were bringing with them increased unilateral tendencies, exclusivism, and nationalism. Even before the pandemic hit us, we were working in a world where the loss of normative limitations was threatening to undermine several areas of international cooperation, including arms control, that the international community had so painstakingly worked to build over many decades. Multilateral cooperation was faltering not only in arms control, of course, but also in other areas, such as climate change agreements.

COVID-19 made the work of the Agency both more urgent and more difficult. But we managed not to stop for even a second. Through the resilience and inventiveness of our staff, the Agency adapted how it served the Board and assisted its Member States. We continued to deliver our activities with minimal disruption while fulfilling our duty to the health and wellbeing of our staff. Our headquarters are in Vienna, so we followed the guidelines of the Austrian authorities and of our own medical services team. We moved many of our staff members to working at home and much of our work, including conferences, training courses, and meetings, online.

Our inspectors and the teams that support them have shown incredible resilience, and our Member States have stepped up their support. For example, when commercial air travel was no longer an option, we scheduled our first private aircraft to get inspection teams to critical sites. Some inspectors spent weeks in quarantine before being able to get to their destinations. We worked tirelessly to help all our staff to do their jobs and care for their families, and to get the respite they needed when they could. Wherever possible, we continued with physical in-person training, such as long-term fellowships, and of course we responded to the requests for immediate help from Member States. We delivered thousands of consignments of equipment for virus detection and diagnosis and other supplies to countries across the world. This was made possible by staff who went the extra mile and by Member States that contributed the funds that allowed us to meet the requests for emergency supplies.

The COVID-19 pandemic also brought home to us the reoccurring nature of zoonotic diseases and the role of the IAEA, not only in reacting to them but also in detecting and understanding them. From our decades of experience at our VETLABS network, we have learned the critical role that nuclear-derived technology plays in the early detection of zoonotic diseases. We also know how much more the world could learn if we were able to leverage the work we do in some of the world's poorest countries, where these diseases often originate.

Much of the work of the IAEA is in capacity building, and COVID-19 has convinced us that one of our priorities should be to build our capacity to monitor zoonotic diseases at the animal-human interface. In this way, we can increase the chance that we detect the next outbreak and stop it before it becomes a pandemic. This is how we came up with our zoonotic diseases integrated action plan, Zodiac. Zodiac is the way nuclear science, technologies, and applications add value to the ongoing efforts by the international community to stop and defeat COVID-19 and prevent the next pandemic of zoonotic origin. It is the nuclear factor in a winning equation that allows the international community to make the best of its efforts. Zodiac allows us to anticipate the next zoonotic virus, whether it looks like Zika, Ebola, or SARS, rather than waiting to stop it once it has begun down its many paths of death and economic destruction.

One final thing I would say about COVID-19 is that other emergencies didn't stop because we were battling a pandemic and so neither did the IAEA's team of responders. Even as we dealt with COVID ourselves and in the service of our Member States, we also helped Lebanon in the aftermath of the explosion at the Port of Beirut in August 2020 and several Central American countries in the wake of deadly hurricanes, to name just two examples. Nor did we stop our long-term capacity-building work or, of course, our work on safeguarding, security, and safety.

PILAT: **You mentioned that the IAEA's inspections didn't stop because of COVID-19. In fact, your inspectors were able to access additional sites in Iran during that time. How do you assess the situation in Iran?**

GROSSI: My first trip to Tehran happened during the summer of the pandemic and our meetings resulted in Iran voluntarily providing the IAEA with access to two locations the Agency had specified. But it is important to remember that this understanding was about procedural difficulties, not substance. As we speak, the IAEA is still waiting for Iran to address and make progress in our verification work through sustained engagement and cooperation. I hope that soon there will be progress on that end. The issue of Iran's nuclear program has been going on for many years. But international relations are rarely static—events change, positions change, and decision-makers change.

PILAT: **How has the IAEA's safeguarding role evolved and how do you see its future?**

GROSSI: The Agency's safeguards system is, and will be, for as long as the Agency exists, the cornerstone of the credibility of the nonproliferation regime. Its essential value cannot be overestimated. Across more than six decades and amid ever-changing circumstances, the IAEA's Safeguards Department has efficiently discharged the technical and political objectives of the system. When the Nonproliferation Treaty moved from an item-specific approach to one that involves safeguarding all the nuclear material in a state, it opened a completely new phase for the IAEA. This system could operate in a relatively quiet way until the discovery of Iraq's clandestine nuclear activities in 1991. The IAEA community adapted to this watershed moment by strengthening safeguards, and in 1997 the Board of Governors agreed on the Model Additional Protocol, which significantly increased the IAEA's ability to verify the peaceful use of all nuclear material in states with comprehensive safeguards agreements.

The number of facilities under safeguards have risen, as has the amount of nuclear material. As one would expect, this expansion in responsibility has led to a steady increase in expenditures, both in the regular budget and through voluntary extrabudgetary contributions by Member States. Without additional funding, for example, the IAEA would not be able to support Iran and the Joint Comprehensive Plan of Action.

The increase in its scope and breadth of verification activities means the IAEA faces significant potential resource management challenges. Meanwhile, ad hoc funding, by its definition, raises concerns about its sustainability and therefore the reliability of critically important funding streams. Economic downturns, such as those triggered by COVID-19, may mean Member States have to tighten their purse strings.

If IAEA inspectors were able to return to North Korea—welcome as that would be—it would test the safeguards program in significant ways. Unlike Iran, North Korea has become a confirmed nuclear-weapon possessing state in recent years, with a growing program comprising an important number of facilities potentially relevant for any credible verification effort. Verifying the North Korea nuclear program would require us to recruit and equip more inspectors with the technical and operational experience to be able to operate in the demanding environment of countries under special inspection arrangements.

Meanwhile, future years could present the IAEA with new verification missions, as provided for in the Agency's statute. The verification and safeguards program could grow rapidly, demanding fast adaptation of the inspector force, the introduction of new monitoring and detection technologies, and access to adequate funding. Considering the essential nature of this work, I am determined to facilitate a dialogue and constructive engagement with the Board of Governors, whose approval is indispensable for any meaningful programmatic activity to proceed at the IAEA.

PILAT: **Talking of the IAEA's evolving safeguarding mandate, how is the state-level concept developing? Do some states continue to criticize it?**

GROSSI: In the past, some Member States have argued that the IAEA's way of approaching its safeguarding work from the state level, rather than looking at individual sites, infringes on the sovereignty of individual nations. This trade-off that Member States perceive between national sovereignty and the scope of the IAEA's mandate is a reoccurring theme.

Examining the way any organization works can be a valid tool for making improvements. However, it is important that arguments in favor of change, especially of well-established ways in which the IAEA works, are based on sound knowledge about the history and norms of its practices. A misrepresentation of these could risk undermining some of the IAEA's most important work and make it more difficult for our inspectors to establish the facts and trends required to keep the world from having to face the potentially dire consequences of nuclear proliferation.

PILAT: **Let's talk about the IAEA's work in nuclear safety and security and how Member States regard the possibility of expanding its roles in those areas.**

GROSSI: Like nonproliferation, safety and security are prerequisites to all of our ability to leverage nuclear technologies in ways that benefit us. If people fear that they and their communities might be harmed by a nuclear accident, or by nefarious actors accessing nuclear material, they are significantly more likely to oppose the construction of a new nuclear power plant, for example.

But when accidents have happened, they have also led to advances in international safety mechanisms. After the accident at Chernobyl in 1986, two conventions on early notification of radiological emergencies and international cooperation were concluded at the Agency and adopted in record time. The accident at Fukushima Daiichi in March 2011 prompted changes in the way the IAEA works and adjusted existing reporting practices and standards. Events with significant social impact, like nuclear accidents, deserve intense and continuous attention.

To that end, I would like us to have the conviction to hold open, transparent conversations with all sectors of society about how we anticipate, communicate, measure, and mitigate the risks nuclear materials pose. As an international organization that enjoys the confidence of its Member States, I believe the IAEA is capable of taking a leading role not only in the debate but also in the evolution of the international nuclear safety mechanisms.

PILAT: **And what about the Agency's role in nuclear security?**

GROSSI: Side by side with nuclear safety, nuclear security also demands increased attention. For many years, the IAEA has played a role in the physical protection of nuclear materials, even though throughout much of the Agency's existence, some have challenged whether this should be the case. Today, the rapid advances of technology present both an opportunity and a threat for nuclear security. Cyberattacks against facilities are increasing, but so is our use of advanced technologies, such as artificial intelligence.

It was the terrorist attacks of September 11, 2001, which brought to the fore the realization that nonstate actors could use nuclear materials to cause panic and destruction. After all, they had already done so with chemical agents, with the most notable example being Aum Shinrikyo's sarin attacks on the Tokyo underground in 1995.

Even so, nearly two decades after September 11, 2001, the IAEA does not have the same kind of structures and norms in place for nuclear security as it does for nuclear safety. Rather than the set of standards the IAEA has managed to establish in safety, security is governed by recommendations and guidance.[1] Likewise, there are no comparable nuclear security committees and subcommittees to those on nuclear safety. Measures introduced since the September 11th attacks have been limited to the upgrade to divisional status of the Office of Nuclear Security, and the development of Nuclear Security Plans and peer-review and self-assessment tools for Member States.[2]

For years, nuclear security flew under the radar. But in 2010, it gained high-level political attention when President Barack Obama began a series of summits, first in Washington in 2010, followed by similar top meetings in Seoul in 2012, The Hague in 2014, and a closing summit back in Washington in 2016. The summits brought political interest and attention from more than 50 countries to a topic that had previously been seen as a technical issue reserved for practitioners. The focus permitted states to relaunch the slow process of repatriating nuclear material, especially highly enriched uranium (HEU), that was scattered around the world. It also facilitated the reconversion and transformation of many nuclear research reactors from HEU to less-enriched uranium. More needs to be done.

Nevertheless, I believe that Member States' positions could evolve in this regard and that the IAEA has been recognized as the most natural platform for a renewed, more inclusive nuclear security dialogue. As long as we avoid politicizing the debate and concentrate instead on the concrete, tangible benefits countries could derive from strong nuclear security rules and protocols, I believe we can build a more ambitious program on nuclear security with the IAEA in a coordinating role, as many publicly advocate.

It is too early to know whether security measures eventually will evolve from guidance to standards and even further. It will, of course, be a matter for Member States to decide. But I believe nations will gradually recognize it is in everybody's advantage that they all sing from the same hymn sheet and that the IAEA's security and safety mandates evolve. These are not simply idle thoughts. After all, it is the Secretariat's job to make sure the IAEA supports and is part of that evolution and, most importantly, that it is ready to fulfil any additional mandate when Member States decide it is time for it to do so.

PILAT: **We have talked about the importance of ensuring that the risks nuclear materials could pose do not undermine their use for peaceful purposes. Could you talk about the Agency's role in helping Member States use nuclear materials in support of their economic development?**

GROSSI: The IAEA helps make a vital difference in people's lives through the use of nuclear applications.[3] It has been working cooperatively with its Member States in areas such as cancer treatment and human health, food and agriculture, water management, and climate change mitigation. As the IAEA's membership has increased, so has the demand for its technical cooperation projects. The Agency's contribution is especially important in the context of its members achieving the United Nations (UN) Sustainable Development Goals (SDGs).[4] Nine of the seventeen SDGs are directly relevant to the work of the IAEA, and the Agency has an important role in helping countries implement those goals nationally and regionally.

For decades, we have been working with other international organizations, such as the World Health Organization and the UN Food and Agriculture Organization, and yet there is scope for more. For example, the Agency has estimated that low- and middle-income countries lack more than 5,000 radiotherapy machines, 10,000 radiation oncology facilities, 6,000 medical physicists, and 20,000 radiation therapists. Between 1980 and 2016, the IAEA invested €297 million in cancer projects. To allow for access to radiotherapy for patients in low- and middle-income countries, nearly US$97 billion will be needed over the coming 20 years. As nations move to implement the 2030 Sustainable Development Agenda, we ask ourselves: what can we do to help our Member States reach them?

Nuclear technology is not only valuable with regard to cancer. Nuclear isotopic techniques are vitally important in emerging health crises such as Zika, Ebola, and COVID-19. Zodiac, which we touched on earlier, is an example of how we are advancing our work in this area.

We also tackle other major issues affecting developing countries in particular. A very relevant program is our NUTEC Plastic initiative, which uses nuclear technology to control plastic pollution. Through NUTEC, the IAEA aims to help countries around the world address the challenge of global plastic pollution by integrating nuclear technology into national, regional, and global initiatives. This includes using irradiation to improve plastic recycling, getting industrial and private sectors to invest in nuclear technology solutions, and supporting baseline assessments of microplastic presence and its impact. For this kind of work, we use labs, such as those we have in Monaco. In the Austrian town of Seibersdorf, our labs have been going through a refurbishment so that they can serve Member States in a variety of ways, from climate-smart agriculture to food security and from environmental management to cancer treatment. All this of course is only possible through the generous donations of certain Member States.

In the future, the IAEA will need to find new ways to finance some technical cooperation projects. New funding streams could come from a variety of sources, including public-private partnerships and like-minded foundations, as well as international and regional banks.

PILAT: **One of the principal ways nuclear technology drives economic development is by producing electricity. What are the prospects for nuclear energy and the Agency's role?**

GROSSI: One of our biggest challenges today is figuring out how to shift economic growth onto an environmentally sustainable footing within an ever-narrowing window of opportunity. What can we do to limit global warming to 1.5°C above pre-industrial levels so that we avoid the worst effects of climate change? Sometimes the apparent magnitude of the challenge can lead to inaction. But it does not have to be this way. We have the technologies that make it possible for us to move away from burning fossil fuels, a practice that experts say we will have to abandon almost entirely by 2050 if we are to meet our climate goals.

Technologies that capture the wind and the sun to generate power have made great strides in recent years and hydropower remains an important part of the equation. But together, they do not generate enough reliable energy to power our future economic prosperity. Add nuclear power to the mix and you balance the equation.

I have repeated this simple fact in talks with leaders from around the world, including during my first trip as the IAEA's Director General, which took me to the UN Climate Change Conference in Madrid in 2019. Nuclear power emits no greenhouse gases during operations. Over its entire lifecycle, its emissions are on par with, if not slightly lower than, solar and wind energy technologies. And nuclear power is a proven entity. It not only produces around 10 percent of the world's electricity and almost one-third of all low-carbon electricity, it remains the only energy source, along with hydropower, to have demonstrated the ability to decarbonize electricity production on a national scale. France and Sweden have used a mix of nuclear and hydro to bring the carbon dioxide (CO_2) footprint of their electricity production to around or below 50 grams CO_2 per kWh (kilowatt-hour), consistent with the climate objectives of the Paris Agreement. The CO_2 footprint of electricity production is more than ten times bigger in many other members of the Organisation for Economic Co-operation and Development. In other major economies, nuclear plays a key mitigation role. In the United States, nuclear power provides 20 percent of electricity but more than half of all clean power, while in the Canadian province of Ontario, atomic energy has facilitated the phaseout of coal. All told, nuclear has helped to avoid an estimated 55 gigatonnes of CO_2 emissions globally over the past 50 years.

In many countries, solar and wind are providing important sources of new clean electricity, but they are not available around the clock. Variable renewables for the foreseeable future will continue to rely on other sources of energy for backup. The Intergovernmental Panel on Climate Change, the world's foremost scientific body on the topic, foresees a need for an addition of 500 gigawatts of new nuclear capacity over the coming three decades. In fact, its analysis projects a larger increase of nuclear capacity than the IAEA's own high projections.

Beyond electricity, nuclear can help produce hydrogen around the clock without generating harmful emissions. Nuclear utilities, including in Japan, are developing demonstration projects to produce hydrogen with electrolysis for electricity generation and other uses, such as transport. Advanced reactors under development will enable high-temperature steam electrolysis or thermochemical processes to produce hydrogen more efficiently and competitively. Nuclear can also be used to produce heat to replace fossil fuels in energy-intensive industrial processes, including chemical, steel, and fertilizer production.

Economics remains a key hurdle for the greater deployment of nuclear power. But with innovation and learning from repeat builds and design standardization, the cost of constructing and deploying nuclear technologies will decline. For example, in some countries, advances are being made in the development of large and small modular reactors that have enhanced safety features, as well as accident tolerant fuels.

Meanwhile, the issue of nuclear waste is being addressed through the construction of deep geological repositories, the first of which will begin operation in Finland this decade. The volume and toxicity of waste can be further reduced by closing the fuel cycle together with the use of fast reactors and fuel multi-recycling, which will greatly enhance the long-term sustainability of nuclear energy.

Many countries see nuclear power as part of their energy future. The United Arab Emirates and Belarus, which have worked closely with the IAEA in developing the necessary infrastructure for new nuclear power programs, recently connected their first reactors to the grid. At least another 30 countries are seriously considering joining them. Through its Low-Enriched Uranium Bank in Kazakhstan, the IAEA offers an added degree of assurance of supply to those thinking of joining the nuclear power generators' club.

The IAEA helps the world tackle climate change not merely by advocating on behalf of nuclear power, sending teams of its experts to help Member States build power plants, constructing an LEU bank, and assisting with the national regulatory systems that define the rules of engagement; it does so also—and perhaps principally—by working hard to minimize the risks nuclear material poses to people and the environment. To do this, it must remain a firm and fair guardian of nonproliferation and fulfill its different mandates that promote the safety and security of nuclear materials.

PILAT: **Since you became Director General, what have been the issues that most preoccupy you?**

GROSSI: I would say that we have already covered quite a lot of them! But let me expand on the double-faceted nature of the IAEA's mandate. One side of the coin is the job of being the world's nuclear guardian (or watchdog) at a time when nuclear weapons still have a magnetic power for those who believe they can derive security from them. The other is the mandate for which many Member States join the IAEA: our job lies in helping them to use nuclear power and nuclear technology to improve the lives and livelihoods of their people.

The Agency can only manage such an ambitious, interconnected double mandate by responding nimbly to the ever-evolving challenges and opportunities it faces. Its challenges include pandemics, geopolitical headwinds, and tight budgets. Its opportunities include the gradual realization by many key players that nuclear power is a critical factor in avoiding catastrophic climate change; the possibility of harnessing nuclear technologies to detect cancer and the next zoonotic virus; and the chance to play a greater role in nuclear safety, security, and law.

To do its job, the IAEA needs to be a reservoir of excellence that Member States can tap into. To keep the reservoir full of the latest science, technologies, and knowledge, the Agency needs to keep on top of and be part of advances in nuclear science. To achieve this goal, the IAEA must find the brightest people, and then to offer a workplace attractive enough for them to want to join and vibrant enough for them to thrive.

To me, women represent the greatest pool of untapped talent. It is one reason I committed us to gender parity by 2025. To bolster the pipeline of candidates, we need more women to study STEM subjects. In December 2019, I launched the Marie Skłodowska-Curie Fellowship, which funds the master's degree studies of 100 female fellows a year through generous donations by some Member States and others. We are in our first year and each year our community of talented women pursuing nuclear studies and careers will grow, so not only the IAEA benefits, but also all of its Member States and the nuclear sector in general.

An organization only holds on to its best talent if it creates an environment in which everyone can do their best work. That is why we have been focused on developing a culture that is inclusive and enables belonging. But our work promoting "Atoms for Peace and Development" not only requires us to be a repository of expertise and a provider of nuclear technologies, it but also means we need to pass on to our Member States the knowledge we have gathered, whether it is the know-how that goes into establishing a national energy law or into operating nuclear equipment safely. That transfer requires time and training in the field, using the internet, through conferences, via exchanges, and by the work we do at our labs, whether they are in Austria or dotted across our international VETLABS network.

The challenge is this: when the last pundit steps off the stage and the conference hall lights are switched off, the real work falls to us. That is true in the work of our experts in the field on development projects and of course also in the work of our safeguarding inspectors.

The past record of the IAEA has been remarkable and unique, but we must keep moving forward hand-in-hand with our Member States amid geopolitical change, the evolution of international law and cooperation, the growth of economies, and advances in technology. Much as they did in the 1950s, countries still recognize the unique importance of the IAEA today. They understand that working with us and supporting us in our evolving mandate is in their interest. To make sure this continues, neither the IAEA nor its Member States can sit on their laurels. The Secretariat must ensure the strength of Member States' support by brandishing its usefulness and maintaining its credibility. And Member States must work with the Secretariat to ensure the Agency has the commensurate scope and the necessary financial support to fulfill a mandate that anticipates and keeps up with their changing needs. Only together can we maintain the IAEA's unique and effective role in helping to keep the peace and in improving the lives and livelihoods of the people living within its 172 member nations and territories.

Notes

1. See the IAEA Safety Standards at https://www.iaea.org/resources/safety-standards; and the search function at http://www-ns.iaea.org/standards/documents/pubdoc-list.asp?s=11&l=83.
2. IAEA, *Nuclear Security Plan (2018–2021)* (Vienna: IAEA, September 14, 2017), https://www.iaea.org/About/Policy/GC/GC61/GC61Documents/English/gc61-24_en.pdf.
3. IAEA, *Annual Report (2016)* (Vienna: IAEA, 2016), 43–63, https://www.iaea.org/sites/default/files/publications/reports/2016/gc61-3.pdf.
4. "Sustainable Development Goals," IAEA, n.d., https://www.iaea.org/about/overview/sustainable-development-goals-sdgs.

Part I

Historical recollections and reflections

3 Present at the creation

Reflections on 60 years of interactions with the IAEA

James Goodby

The International Atomic Energy Agency (IAEA) was formally established in 1957, but from my perspective, it actually came into existence in 1956. Serious negotiations on controlling the atom began in 1953 after the death of Joseph Stalin. One of the first achievements was the IAEA. Tremendously important issues were discussed in the working-level meetings on the draft statute of the IAEA, which were held in Washington, D.C., from February 28 through June 28, 1956. Those meetings were chaired for the U.S. side by a man named James Jeremiah Wadsworth—Jerry Wadsworth—who happened to be a descendent of George Washington's quartermaster general. Ambassador Wadsworth was a man who understood conciliation and how to compromise. Had he not been in charge, and had the attitude that we took in 1956 been similar to the "America First" attitude that we would later adopt, I am not sure that the IAEA would have materialized at that particular point, and maybe not ever. Wadsworth was able to see that there were points of view strongly expressed by the nations represented in the meetings, in particular India, that had to be accommodated in some way.

Homi J. Bhabha was the representative of India at that time. He took a very, I would say, *fierce* line about Indian independence, and was not interested in safeguards against diversion of fissile material that would curtail India's options relative to other nations. Under a lesser man than James Wadsworth, I suspect there could have been an impasse very easily at that early point in the talks.

Georgy Zerubin, the Soviet ambassador to Washington, was the representative of the Soviet Union in these talks and he took a surprisingly conciliatory line—not all the time, of course, but enough so that between the United States and the Soviet Union there was quite a bit of momentum toward solving the issues that came up.

I was there in that meeting, not as a representative of the United States but as a so-called Technical Secretary. I was there to help the delegates with information they might need and to assist in drafting. The meeting was organized by the Department of State, and was held in the Department of State's conference center. There was a Political Secretary, another Technical Secretary, and a secretary named Richard Wheeler from State's Office of

DOI: 10.4324/9781003160205-3

International Conferences. We basically had the job of trying to keep the things going smoothly and to make the trains run on time. I sat next to the chair, next to James Wadsworth, and had a good view down the room of all these people. To me, they became people—that is to say, individuals with their own idiosyncrasies, not representatives of nations. I suspect that kind of atmosphere crept into those talks. I would mention in particular Homi Bhabha, who I think sat on my right side, and he always began the day by offering me a glass of water. I remember that courtesy to this day, over 60 years on. After that, in 1957, I think Eisenhower was very pleased that the Agency that he had proposed was likely going to come to fruition. I do not think he had too much interest at that point in what it would actually do. Originally, he had described it as a fuel bank, but by 1956, that idea had not garnered the necessary support. It had changed quite a bit since the 1953 speech. The policy was influenced by the Joint Committee on Atomic Energy, a very powerful joint House and Senate group which controlled the funds and dictated the policies related to atomic energy.

I had become a member of the staff of the Atomic Energy Commission (AEC) in June 1954, and had worked at the AEC for two years by the time the meeting on the IAEA took place. I had not spent a lot of time on thinking about the IAEA, but I had been working with a couple of people who had—namely, a man named Spofford G. English, a very good friend of mine who became involved in the technical talks between the United States and the Soviet Union about how to put markers into uranium and try to monitor it that way. I also had some dealings with one of the attorneys in the AEC named Max Isenberg, whom we called "Moose." He was actually the main author of the mutual version of the draft statute. He later asked me if I would do a legislative history of the working-level meetings on the draft statute, which I agreed to do. It took me several months, and the result can be found in the National Archives today if you want to see a blow-by-blow account of the back-and-forth in the talks. My attitude was that the Agency should become a center of scientific excellence. I felt that if it did that, it would gain strength and power and would absorb many of the emerging nuclear issues. The person designated to be the first U.S. representative in the IAEA Board of Governors was Robert M. McKinney.

McKinney had a decisive voice in the early years of the IAEA's existence. He was an ally of Clinton P. Anderson, a senator from New Mexico who at various points was the chair of the Joint Committee on Atomic Energy and therefore a very powerful man in nuclear affairs. The attitude that McKinney had shared with Anderson was that we needed to promote the peaceful uses of atomic energy—that is, nuclear reactors—and that the government should pay for it. That had been an issue for two or three years prior, with some saying that we should not really promote it. If it is economically feasible, then fine, we should do it; if not, we will just not push very far into that area. Anderson helped to organize a panel chaired by Robert McKinney, and that panel came to the conclusion that Anderson wanted, which was that we needed to put a lot of money and resources into developing the civil uses of atomic energy through reactors.

When McKinney was appointed to be the head of the U.S. delegation, some of us at the AEC were invited to go up and talk with him to see if we should go along with him to Vienna. I really wanted to do that at the time. We were asked to bring papers along to tell him what we thought ought to be done with the IAEA. I wrote a paper about my idea of a scientific center of excellence. And I met him—I think it was on a Sunday, in his apartment on Park Avenue in Manhattan—and gave him my paper. We had a brief discussion. Needless to say, we did not get very far. He was making cracks about bureaucrats working on weekends, and that threw me off, too. So, I did not get the job. The emphasis on science was not as strong as it should have been, I thought, but that situation has since changed. Now I am pleased with the Agency's technical competence.

My next experience with helping to create the Agency as we know it today was to help in linking the safeguards program of the IAEA with that of the European Community (EC) late in the 1960s. This coming-of-age of the IAEA occurred when I was the first secretary in the U.S. mission to the European Communities (USEC), as it was called then, which consisted of six countries struggling for an identity and worrying what to do about "Euratom," the European Atomic Energy Community. Euratom was the atomic energy arm of the Community. And my job, of course, having a nuclear background, was to follow Euratom, so early on I got to know some of the people in it very well. One of them who I liked and had a lot to do with, was a man named Enrico Jacchia, who was a Venetian—and the term "fine Italian hand" really suited him. He understood how diplomacy works and how one reaches agreements.

Early in my time there, a fierce struggle was going on within the EC about whether they needed to preserve the possibility of not only a civil nuclear option independently run by them, but also whether they should in fact preserve the option of a nuclear capability—a nuclear-weapon capability. That was the reason why, for several years, the United States had sponsored something called the Multilateral Force—which was something that was not widely liked in Washington but it kept on going for some time because it had the potential of developing into a kind of multilateral nuclear-armed group which would take care of West Germany and other countries' desires for some kind of participation in nuclear deterrence. There was still an issue, in other words, by the mid-to-late-1960s about whether the EC should sign on to the Treaty on the Nonproliferation of Nuclear Weapons (NPT), which had gained quite a bit of momentum over the years and was pretty close to being fully accepted when I arrived at the EC headquarters.

In any case, there was a disagreement about whether the IAEA should be allowed to inspect the facilities of the members of the Euratom group. The Europeans were all saying "we will not take on this sort of obligation at all; we won't join this treaty." Well, Jacchia and I talked about it and wanted to solve it, and the way we did so, I think, was probably due to Jacchia as much as anybody. The idea was to have Euratom's safeguards agency, of which he was the head, inspect the facilities of the Euratom countries and then the IAEA would inspect the Euratom safeguards agency to make sure it was doing the right thing. And so that is the way it worked out, at least at that stage, and that is the proposal we sent to Washington. That was accepted, and was, I think, the last breakthrough that enabled the Europeans to sign on to the Nonproliferation Treaty. I call that a coming-of-age because that enabled the IAEA to have a powerful role in Europe as well as in other countries. It also brought the IAEA more fully into the idea of its safeguards role beyond promoting nuclear reactors.

The Agency now had an important role in safeguards, which to my mind opened the door to many other things that could be done and are now being done by the IAEA. Let me just say a few things about Eisenhower. Eisenhower, I think, very early on, before he became president, was influenced by ideas that he picked up from discussions at which he was present. As the Supreme Allied Commander Europe and during World War II, he knew a lot of people, including many from the Soviet Union. He became convinced, and this is documented, that nuclear weapons could prevent war. They would be so terrible that nuclear weapons would basically abolish war. That was his thinking. To do that, you had to make it credible that you would actually use a nuclear weapon in combat—and, of course, that led to some problems. In 1953, Eisenhower's first full year in office, he was intent on setting up that idea as part of his administration's strategy. He resolved the issue about what strategy to use by getting various people together in the solarium of the White House in 1953 to advocate rollback or containment, or various other ideas. He settled clearly on containment, and on nuclear deterrence as one of the ways to enforce containment. In 1953, when he gave the Atoms for Peace speech at the end of that year, he had pretty much consolidated the idea that nuclear weapons would be the major element of the deterrent capacity of the United States.

The speech, at least the way I read it, was aimed at creating the idea that war really is impossible because it is so horrible. I mean, he did not hide anything about what nuclear weapons would do to humanity, and that is what that speech was about. He made that speech in various forms on other occasions as well. That was part of his strategy. He wanted to make clear that if we ever use nuclear weapons, it would be the ultimate catastrophe for humanity.

The idea of cooperation among nations was the other part of the speech, and he saw that nuclear capabilities could be a way of doing that. To my mind, the speech did two things: it said war is a terrible thing, but we can cooperate; we need to keep nuclear capabilities up front. They were worried in those days that the U.S. public would resist being prepared for war at a moment's notice. We had never been in that position in all our history. But now, we had to prepare for war at any moment because a war could break out through surprise attack.

The speech didn't go anywhere for a time, although everybody liked it to some degree. The Soviets were fairly skeptical, but by 1956, it became clear that there was enough momentum behind it so that it could make some headway. In 1956, however, Eisenhower had a wholly different view of what his job was. He needed to try to take advantage of the change in leadership in Moscow. Stalin had died in March 1953, and there was still some residual back-and-forth about who was going to run the Soviet Union from then on, even in 1956. So, from 1956 on, when you look at what he did, it was really amazing. He had an impressive record of trying to reach agreements with the Soviets and others.

The year 1956 saw not only the working-level meeting, but also the establishment of a United Nations study on the effects on humanity—on people—of ionizing radiation. In other words, he acknowledged that there was a fallout problem which the AEC, my employer, had been resisting for quite a long time. Then, in 1957, there was a six-month-long conference in London that came very close to reaching some agreements. Harold Stassen was the head of the delegation; I was there also as an AEC representative. We managed to get through 1957, with pretty good results in fact, by establishing a relationship between the new management in Moscow and in Washington.

In 1958, Eisenhower proposed two conferences. One was on surprise attacks and one was on a nuclear test ban. I was a member of the U.S. delegation to the surprise attack conference. It didn't go anywhere, but it did spawn a whole host of studies and interest in arms control. It was the foundation of the whole arms control movement in the United States, even though it did not reach any agreements. The 1958 conference on the test ban, of course, did result in what they called a Geneva system for the monitoring of nuclear testing and to a moratorium on nuclear tests.

For the rest of his term in office, from 1958 through the end of 1960, Eisenhower pushed the nuclear test ban—not as vigorously as I would have liked, but he kept it alive through a whole series of efforts to end the negotiations. When he left office in 1961, I think you could say that he came very close to reaching an agreement on a comprehensive test ban treaty of some sort. The reason Eisenhower failed was because of the shooting-down of a U-2 in 1960, so that a summit meeting—which I think would have resulted in a movement toward a test ban, and probably an Eisenhower visit to the Soviet Union—collapsed.

4 IAEA safeguards

From the early years to NPT safeguards

Myron Kratzer

In President Dwight D. Eisenhower's historic address before the United Nations on December 8, 1953, he proposed a qualified end to the post-war secrecy on nuclear energy, opening the door to international cooperation in its peaceful uses. I will focus not on what Eisenhower said, but on what he did not say.

More than 60 years have now passed since Eisenhower's address, and two generations have replaced those who were present at the beginning. As a result, many who are now in positions of leadership in the nuclear community likely may not fully appreciate the stature that atomic energy enjoyed at the time of Eisenhower's proposal and for a number of years thereafter. Perhaps there is no better way to capture this stature than to explain that atomic energy was, at its inception, the space program, the computer age, and the digital revolution all rolled into one. That it had recently, in the view of most, ended the war was another key factor in creating and fostering this perception of its importance. There was, in short, no real competition for the public and official view of atomic energy's role as a key to progress.

Under the U.S. system, legislation was required in order for Eisenhower's proposals to become a reality. This led to a new organic law, the Atomic Energy Act of 1954, replacing the original legislation of 1946. There are several striking points about the transformation of the Eisenhower proposals into legislation. First, by today's standards, the speed of this transformation was remarkable. Eisenhower spoke in December 1953, and by August 1954, the Atomic Energy Act of 1954 had come into being. A second key point is that the new law was not simply the Eisenhower plan reduced to legislative language, but was much broader. As one example, it focused on bilateral types of cooperation, in contrast to Eisenhower's emphasis on broad international cooperation under the aegis of a new international atomic energy organization. In both the speech and the legislation, verification was given a surprisingly light touch, but the term "safeguards" at least appeared in the legislation as a requirement to be met by nations receiving atomic energy assistance, although the nature of these safeguards was not explained. Another point of considerable practical and political importance is that the legislation created a complex, detailed regime for undertaking

DOI: 10.4324/9781003160205-4

important categories of cooperation by establishing a requirement for executive agreements, termed "Agreements for Cooperation." These agreements were required to permit specified types of atomic energy cooperation to take place bilaterally with individual countries, with groups of countries, or with members of the anticipated new international atomic energy organization. Thus, whether deliberately or not, the legislation created alternative routes for cooperation that could be, and indeed became, competitive in some important instances.

A further important feature of the legislation, which of course would have been out of place in the Eisenhower proposal, was its creation of a new joint congressional committee on atomic energy, a departure from the customary U.S. practice of separate committees for the House of Representatives and the Senate. The Joint Committee became, as intended, an exceptionally powerful body. Among many other powers, it had the authority to prevent individual agreements for cooperation from coming into force by a vote of the committee alone. (The Supreme Court later would find this requirement to be an unconstitutional delegation of the legislative power of Congress to one of its committees.) Although the Joint Committee never elected to defeat any signed and presidentially approved agreement, it had the power to do so, which gave the committee great authority over the content of these agreements as well as over the nations or groups with which they could be entered into. Much of the Joint Committee's power was derived from a requirement of the legislation that it be kept "currently and fully informed" of all activities and actions of the U.S. Atomic Energy Commission (USAEC), an organ of the executive branch of the U.S. government. This requirement was rigorously enforced. In combination with the Joint Committee's express authorities, it made the committee a de facto administrative body, along with the USAEC itself, in the management of the U.S. atomic energy program.

Neither the International Atomic Energy Agency's (IAEA) Statute nor the Atomic Energy Act of 1954 required recipients of important assistance, whether from the United States directly in the case of bilateral cooperation or from the IAEA, to give up their right to engage in military applications of atomic energy including the development or acquisition of nuclear weapons. Although the assistance granted by the United States or the IAEA could be used only for peaceful purposes, recipient countries were free to engage in military applications if they did so through their own efforts or with assistance of others who did not place a peaceful-use restriction on their help. Under the new legislation, statutory agreements for cooperation placed a peaceful-use restriction on only two categories of cooperation: the supply of nuclear material and the facilities or equipment to produce or utilize it; and the supply of classified nuclear information. With the rapid declassification of most nuclear power technology, the latter category had little impact except in the area of uranium enrichment, which remained classified as it does today.

The high level of enthusiasm for the peaceful uses of nuclear energy suggests that the promise of assistance in this area may have had sufficient leverage to make a nonproliferation commitment a realistic quid pro quo; however, no serious effort was made toward this goal. To my recollection, only one voice in the entire USAEC, that of a member of the General Counsel's office named Max Eisenberg, was raised in support of this objective. He was not listened to. However, there is no doubt that the underlying attitude of those responsible for the Atoms for Peace program that was embodied in Eisenhower's speech, the new U.S. legislation, and the IAEA Statute was that the spread of nuclear weapons should be avoided. That is apparent in the very title "Atoms for Peace." The thinking seems to have been that the help offered in the peaceful uses by the United States, and to a lesser extent, the other nuclear "have" nations, would be so attractive that recipient countries would simply choose to avoid the difficult course of independent and possibly military development, leading to the desired result of nonproliferation—a term which, incidentally, was not even in use in those days.

To a considerable extent, this outcome was achieved. With the exceptions of Great Britain, the Soviet Union, France, and China—together with the United States, the permanent members of the United Nations Security Council—no additional country became a nuclear-weapon state for a number of years. The acquisition of nuclear arms by the five permanent Security Council members was, if not preordained, at least unavoidable by any policy that might have been attainable at the time of the Atoms for Peace initiative. At the same time, many states did pursue peaceful uses and acquired the underlying capabilities that could have supported a military nuclear program. There is no doubt that the bipolar world of those Cold War years contributed to the avoidance of proliferation. It was widely assumed that the acquisition of an independent nuclear-weapon capability by a member of the Soviet bloc was unthinkable, while adherents to the Western bloc had other restrictions to independent nuclear-weapon development, including in many cases reliance on the U.S. nuclear umbrella.

In addition to establishing the bilateral and IAEA routes for securing U.S. cooperation, the legislation opened the door to other routes of cooperation, especially with international or multinational organizations other than the IAEA itself. These parallel routes were not simply alternatives, but in some cases, they competed with the recognized bilateral and IAEA routes of cooperation. One route for cooperation not explicitly mentioned either by Eisenhower or the new legislation, but implicitly included and soon of great significance in the formative days of Atoms for Peace, was cooperation with the newly created European Atomic Energy Community, or Euratom.

Euratom was a special—indeed, a unique—case. Formally established in March 1957, it took its place with the Common Market of the European Economic Community, along with the earlier European Coal and Steel Community, to form the core of what is now the European Union. It thus preceded the IAEA by several months, but preparatory work was well underway in both organizations by the time of their formal establishment. With its initial membership of six nations, Euratom and its sister European Communities joined France and the Benelux countries with their former enemies of World War II, (West) Germany, and Italy, in a tight economic and political partnership that formed the core of the European integration movement. As such, the Communities, including Euratom, enjoyed the strong support of the United States, especially the Department of State, which saw the partnership of Europe's historic enemies, France and Germany, as the key to the avoidance of future world conflicts. As a junior member of the AEC staff, I recall having some part in the drafting of testimony in support of the agreement for cooperation between the United States and Euratom, and included this obvious point.

Although Euratom was smaller than the Common Market and at the time even the European Coal and Steel Community, it had several supranational features, most notably the ownership of all fissionable material in the community and the exclusive right to procure fissionable material from outside nations. Of greatest importance, it had the authority and responsibility to verify the declared use of nuclear energy through a system of inspections—that is, safeguards. These features made Euratom an especially favorable model for a truly supranational partnership and, as such, a favorite partner of the United States. In recognition of this stature and of the importance of European integration, the Agreement for Cooperation with Euratom accorded it, for the first and only time, responsibility for the application of safeguards in place of the "bilateral" safeguards applied by the United States in other U.S. agreements. Through it, the United States also participated directly in the development of a nuclear power industry in the community through a joint program for the construction of 1,000 megawatts (MW) of nuclear power, which included enriched fuel leasing in place of sale and the possibility of direct U.S. financial contribution to the program. In addition to the political and economic incentives for nuclear power in the European community, the occurrence of the 1956 Suez Crisis, which closed the Suez Canal for a number of months, underscored the hazards of reliance on Middle Eastern oil and provided an additional strong impetus for Europe's nuclear power development.

The U.S.-Euratom Agreement for Cooperation and the Joint Program it encompassed were of major import, as it was immediately apparent that it would compete with the role foreseen for the IAEA. Consequently, the IAEA and its U.S. supporters strongly criticized the agreement. The conflict was especially troublesome for the congressional Joint Committee on Atomic Energy, one of whose former members, Sterling Cole, had been selected as the first IAEA Director General. The Euratom-IAEA conflict became a source of great concern, even though the IAEA was not yet in a position to apply its safeguards or administer the other features of the complex joint program. To mitigate the conflict to the degree feasible, the U.S.-Euratom

Agreement was modified before its adoption by including hortatory language foreseeing a role for IAEA safeguards in due course. That opportunity came much later, with the adoption of the Nuclear Nonproliferation Treaty (NPT) and its assignment of primary safeguards responsibility to the IAEA.

At that time, the U.S.-Euratom partnership was the major source of conflict between the IAEA and the alternative routes available for international cooperation, yet it was by no means the only one. The bilateral route of cooperation with individual countries was the fundamental competitor for international nuclear cooperation, but other multilateral or international organizations were at issue as well. The European Nuclear Energy Agency (ENEA), now the Nuclear Energy Agency (then, as now, an arm of the Organisation for Economic Co-operation and Development), was of considerable importance. The United States was only an associate member of the ENEA at the time, but it cooperated closely with several ENEA projects. Chief among these was Eurochemic, a consortium of 14 ENEA members that built, owned, and operated a chemical reprocessing facility in Mol, Belgium, that was capable of processing one ton of materials per day. This plant was intended to (and did) process low-enriched uranium reactor fuel of U.S. origin. As there was no U.S. Agreement for Cooperation with the ENEA, transfers of U.S. fuel took place under the agreement with Euratom. However, for a number of years, the ENEA had its own small safeguards staff that applied safeguards at Eurochemic, and its findings were reviewed at least informally by the United States.

The United States regarded Eurochemic with favor, as the first concrete example of multinational reprocessing and thus as a possible starting point for a multilateral reprocessing endeavor, in keeping with its preferred approach to conducting this sensitive step in the fuel cycle. During Eurochemic's operating lifetime, the United States cooperated directly with it through technology transfer and the provision of a resident U.S. reprocessing expert. The evolution to a broader-based reprocessing industry, however, did not materialize, and Eurochemic was eventually discontinued and ENEA's safeguards undertaking likewise was terminated. One lasting outcome of Eurochemic was the selection, at U.S. initiative, of its longtime director, Dr. Rudolph Rometsch, as the IAEA's second Deputy Director General for safeguards.

Another non-IAEA multilateral route for nuclear cooperation of major importance was the Geneva Conference on the Peaceful Uses of Atomic Energy. This conference took place in 1955, before the creation of the IAEA, and as such there was no possibility of it being sponsored by the Agency. It was instead held under direct UN auspices. Although it was not a continuing international body, the 1955 Geneva Conference was of major importance in implementing the Atoms for Peace concept, bringing together the world's nuclear energy agencies and their leaders and serving as the stimulus for the declassification of peaceful nuclear technology, a step that was critical to its wider development and adoption.

The Geneva conference was repeated in 1958, and it further strengthened the bonds among the world's nuclear leaders and experts. However, the atmosphere of optimism and enthusiasm for nuclear power that permeated the 1954 conference had largely dissipated by that point, in light of the growing recognition of the technical and economic difficulties of nuclear power technology. The final Geneva conference of 1971 reflected a more balanced view as nuclear power made steady headway, especially in the United States and several other technologically advanced nations, including those of the European Community.

The gap between the availability of the bilateral cooperation route under the Atomic Energy Act of 1954 and the formal establishment of the IAEA was quickly populated by the conclusion of a number of bilateral agreements. Initially, these provided only for the transfer of small research reactors and fuel enriched to a maximum of 20 percent. They included safeguards, but in a simplified form, requiring only periodic inspection visits. These limited agreements, however, were soon supplemented by much more comprehensive agreements providing for the supply of enriched fuel in amounts adequate to support at least a beginning nuclear power program. The safeguards regime was specified in some detail, employing language that, as noted earlier, was closely modeled after that of the IAEA Statute, providing for "access at all times" to the facilities, equipment, and nuclear materials made available by the United States under the agreement. Consultations were held with the other principal nuclear suppliers, namely the United Kingdom and Canada, which adopted similar approaches to their bilateral engagements.

Needless to say, the negotiation of agreements providing U.S. inspectors with such unprecedented access rights was a contentious issue for other states. Only the promise of access to U.S. nuclear assistance in the exciting new field of peaceful uses of nuclear energy made the conclusion of such agreements possible. For the United States, successful conclusion of these comprehensive agreements was a matter of importance for several reasons. These included a desire to assert U.S. leadership in the peaceful nuclear field; the desire to assist cooperating countries, a number of which were U.S. defense allies, in their economic recovery and progress; and a recognition of the commercial and economic benefits that could flow to the United States from a major role in the supply of nuclear technology, equipment, and materials. By far the most important reason for the United States' active efforts to secure as large a role as possible in the supply of peaceful nuclear technology, however, was its desire to foster the adoption of the U.S. low-enriched uranium reactor technology in place of the natural uranium technology then favored and offered by other suppliers, including the United Kingdom, France, and Canada. This objective was based on the U.S. conviction, which has remained to the present time, that this reactor technology is not only inherently more proliferation resistant than the natural uranium approach, but that the U.S. role as the supplier would require adherence to the U.S.

nonproliferation standards and provide an important means of ensuring compliance with these standards through the supply of enriched uranium.

It is perhaps no longer widely recognized that during the early days of peaceful nuclear commerce the competition between the U.S. approach and natural uranium approach was an intense one whose outcome was by no means certain. The first two nuclear power reactors sold internationally were British natural uranium units, of which one each was sold to Italy and Japan. Their sales stimulated U.S. efforts to ensure a different outcome in following selections. The global statistics of power reactor utilization make it clear that the preference for the enriched uranium approach has been adopted, although natural uranium reactors are still favored in a few locations for other than economic reasons.

The role of the agreements for cooperation in the provision of information and technology, as distinct from facilities, equipment, and nuclear materials, is of interest and importance. As noted, the new Atomic Energy Act allowed the transfer of classified nuclear information only under agreements for cooperation. Several such agreements were concluded, but with the broad declassification of information on nuclear power, the provision of nuclear power technology no longer required an agreement for cooperation and could take place through any number of means, even with nations with which the United States did not enjoy close bilateral relationships. One complicating factor, however, was a provision of the new atomic energy act that required the USAEC to authorize any activity by a U.S. citizen or entity that could be considered as participating "directly or indirectly" in the production of fissionable material abroad. To ensure compliance with this broad prohibition, the USAEC adopted a general authorization for the communication of all unclassified nuclear information and technology. This action was essential to the initiation of broad international nuclear cooperation by the United States and, by extension, other nuclear supplier states. At a much later date, the United States modified this general authorization to require specific, case-by-case authorization for significant information in such sensitive fields as enrichment, which in any event remained classified and generally excluded from international cooperation.

With the founding of the IAEA in 1957, the Agency was in principle ready to undertake its functions. In addition to the key roles of nuclear material supply and the verification of its use exclusively for peaceful purposes through implementation of the broad authority of the Statute's safeguards provisions, several forms of technical assistance were effectively implemented. These included training and the exchange of unclassified peaceful-use information through an active program of conferences and publications. The Agency made a quick and generally effective start in these latter functions, but significant obstacles remained to the implementation of its central responsibilities of nuclear material supply and safeguards. These two functions were closely linked by the Agency's Statute, because the Statute made the application of safeguards mandatory if the Agency supplied the nuclear material used or produced, or provided the facilities or principal equipment involved in its use. By the time of the Agency's founding, an active program of bilateral nuclear cooperation was already underway, including the application of bilateral safeguards under agreement provisions closely matching those of the IAEA Statute. According to the conventional wisdom, nations receiving external assistance to their nuclear power programs would favor the application of an on-site inspection regime implemented by an international organization of which they were members; however, this expectation proved to be unwarranted. Instead, Agency Member States insisted that they be given a more detailed specification of the safeguards measures to which they would become subject, and made it clear that these measures would have to be more restrictive than the exceedingly broad "access at all times" regime provided for in the Agency Statute and in bilateral agreements. In asserting this position, Member States relied on the provision of the Agency Statute that it would possess its safeguards rights and responsibilities "to the extent relevant" to the project subject to its safeguards.

The U.S. bilateral agreements did not contain this qualifying language. Nevertheless, the United States was actively undertaking safeguards under these agreements, and it doubtless would have rejected any suggestion that it was required to specify and limit the broad rights to which it was entitled under the bilateral agreement provisions. In the view of U.S. officials who were actively involved in the development of the safeguards language in the IAEA Statute based on "access at all times," the qualification of "to the extent relevant" was not intended to provide for a regime of graduated access and related rights, but only to omit those rights that were not relevant to the project to which the safeguards were to be applied. For example, the provision requiring storage with the Agency of nuclear material recovered or produced would not be relevant to an Agency project in which recoverable quantities of nuclear material were not recovered or produced.

Member States' concerns with what they regarded as the severity of the IAEA Statute's safeguards rights also undoubtedly was influenced by the preparation of two reports in the United States that forecasted a need for hundreds of inspectors to safeguard large nuclear complexes, modeled after the U.S. installations in Oak Ridge, Tennessee, and Hanford, Washington. The relevance of these studies to the IAEA safeguards needs was, to say the least, questionable, considering that the peaceful-use programs of Member States neither had nor intended to have such complexes. Nevertheless, it could be foreseen that some safeguarded nuclear power programs would need facilities devoted to the sensitive areas of reprocessing and enrichment, and that these would indeed call for intensive staffing and implementation of safeguarding activities. Despite serious misgivings, the United States decided that it was essential to meet the demand for specification and limitation of the safeguards measures to be applied. In reaching this decision, a key U.S. decision was made to pursue the implementation of IAEA safeguards on a stepwise basis, beginning with the generally modest safeguards requirements called for by the small research reactors then being made available to nuclear states with beginning nuclear programs. This decision was implemented, resulting in the formulation and adoption of the IAEA's first safeguards system document, Information Circular 26 (INFCIRC/26).

INFCIRC/26 was developed by a committee of the Board of Governors and received final Board approval in January 1961, more than four years after the Agency's founding. The committee was chaired by Gunnar Randers, then-head of the Norwegian nuclear energy program and Norway's IAEA governor. Randers was an excellent, respected, and well-liked chairman, and was called on to head several later iterations of the safeguards committee. In keeping with the stepwise safeguards development concept, INFCIRC/26 was limited to the safeguards applicable to reactors of 100 thermal MW or less, encompassing most research reactors and, if power was produced, perhaps some 25 MW reactors. Although the document appears to be applicable to ancillary nuclear facilities such as fabrication and reprocessing handling nuclear material in amounts consistent with 100 MW reactors, it was never applied to these facilities and generally was viewed as reactor specific.

In addition to fulfilling the key role of opening the door to Agency safeguards implementation, INFCIRC/26 included a number of other features—some of which have proved useful and have remained in use, and some of which were troublesome (if not incorrect) and have complicated safeguards development and implementation. Above all, the document accepts and is dependent on the principle that safeguards access can be graduated on the basis of some measure of the threat of unauthorized use. In the process, inspection frequency was employed, and for many years, it remained the principal measure of safeguards intrusiveness, thus departing from the fundamental statutory provision of "access at all times." Although the document defined inspection frequency as the key measure of safeguards intensity, it introduced the concept of special inspections, which retains in a way the principle of unlimited access, provided that cause is found to require it. (It is likely that neither the document's authors nor its Agency users intended it to have this particular use.) The document makes an important distinction between what gives rise to safeguards and how they are implemented, making use of the confusing nomenclature of "attachment" and "implementation." Fortunately, this troublesome nomenclature has not survived. However, the principle that certain events (such as the acquisition of significant equipment, facilities, or materials) "trigger" a requirement for safeguards, as well as the provisions for how these requirements are to be implemented when triggered, remains and is important to safeguards implementation, even under the NPT.

The document adopts the term "diversion" to characterize a violation of safeguards undertakings. For many, "diversion" implies the physical removal of safeguarded material, but the document makes it unmistakably clear that it is "use to further any military purpose," not its physical removal, that characterizes a diversion and thus a violation. Safeguards implementation often loses sight of this important distinction. It is not entirely obvious from the language of the document itself, yet ancillary documents specify that the basis of the numerical frequency associated with reactors is the estimated maximum undiscovered diversion of the quantity of fissionable material used or produced by the reactor in question. Thus, INFCIRC/26 relies heavily on nuclear materials accountancy as its principal means of safeguards. This reliance continued to dominate safeguards rhetoric for many years, despite a growing reliance in practice on surveillance and containment to detect actual misuse or unauthorized removal of nuclear material.

On balance, given the decision to accept the demand that safeguards be more restrictively defined rather than follow the unqualified language of the Statute, INFCIRC/26 was an acceptable starting point for the safeguards system, even with its unfortunate introduction of limited inspection frequency and heavy dependence on materials accountancy as the central tool of verification. As the installation of nuclear power proceeded, however, the safeguards system's limitation to reactors under 100 MW was not merely quickly exceeded but never met the test. No power reactors of this limited size, subject to safeguards, were constructed. Less than three years later, the safeguards committee under Randers' chairmanship was convened again to extend the system to reactors of any size. Additionally, a U.S. goal was to clarify that the safeguards system followed the principle of "pursuit"; that is, that once material became subject to safeguards, any nuclear material produced through its use was also subject to safeguards from generation to generation. INFCIRC/26 did not rule out this principle, but its applicability was unclear.

At the safeguards committee meeting, both U.S. objectives were secured. Of particular significance, approval was obtained for "access at all times" for 200 MW and larger reactors. This result was achieved after a vigorous debate that extended well into the evening hours and took place as a consequence of a vote in the committee at U.S. request—a rare, if not unique, departure at the time from the Agency practice to reach decisions by consensus. Much more importantly, the affirmative vote included the Soviet Union. This was an important reversal from the earlier Soviet position of seeking minimal safeguards, and it marked the beginning of Soviet support for effective IAEA safeguards that was maintained through the adoption of all further Agency safeguards system documents. On my return from this meeting, I was called on to report to Gerard Smith, who held the position of Special Assistant to the Secretary of State for Atomic Energy, and who was the de facto foreign policy head of the Atoms for Peace program. Smith was a distinguished and exceptionally effective and well-liked member of what is often known today as the "foreign policy establishment," and one who was adept at quickly getting to the heart of matters. He had only one question: did we get "access at all times"? My ability to provide an affirmative answer was a relief.

Once again, what was hoped to be a major shift toward the adoption of IAEA safeguards in place of the heavy dependence on the bilateral route did not take place. This was, of course, attributable in part to the fact that much of the ongoing progress in nuclear power was taking place in Euratom, which in any event was subject to its own and not to IAEA safeguards. However, the European Community then encompassed only six states, and several leading nuclear power countries, including Switzerland and Sweden, were not members of the Community. Japan was active in nuclear power, but alone among the industrial states had followed the conventional wisdom of favoring safeguards implemented by an international organization of which it was a member (namely, the IAEA) rather than bilaterally by its nuclear suppliers. The obstacle to the adoption of Agency safeguards at this stage was the strong preference of Member States to secure their nuclear materials and facilities from the states supplying them—frequently, but not always, the United States. Although it was permissible under the IAEA Statute for parties to have bilateral agreements such as the U.S. Agreements for Cooperation to jointly request the IAEA to apply its safeguards, this was not customarily done, except in the case of Japan. One reason is that the intense competition that had developed in the sale of nuclear power facilities made suppliers reluctant to demand a condition such as acceptance of IAEA safeguards that might prejudice their buyers against their bids.

The continuing failure to make IAEA safeguards the rule rather than the exception clearly called for a revised policy initiative, especially on the part of the United States, the principal supplier. This required two parallel actions. The first was the decision to discontinue efforts to persuade recipient states from securing their U.S. nuclear fuel and facilities through the IAEA, and rather to insist that a condition of bilateral supply would be acceptance of IAEA safeguards on the supplied items. The failure of seeking to encourage procurement through the IAEA may have seemed like the abandonment of one of the IAEA's key roles, but it was concluded that this was not the case. The IAEA function of acting as the principal nuclear fuel supplier was based on the presumption that enriched uranium would be a scarce commodity, requiring an international organization of broad membership to assure that the limited supply was distributed equitably to members upon request. However, the presumption of tight supply simply did not come to pass. U.S. law naturally accorded priority in enriched uranium distribution to U.S. defense needs, as evidenced by an annual presidential determination of the amounts of enriched uranium to be made available to U.S. defense and foreign distribution, yet in reality the U.S. enrichment supply was adequate to meet all requirements, defense and foreign, from the start of the Atoms for Peace program. Under this condition, an IAEA role as a nuclear supplier would not involve arbitration of competing demands for a scarce supply, as envisioned in the Eisenhower proposal, but would entail administrative, paperwork activities that would only delay and increase the costs and risks of acquiring nuclear materials. The real goal was to secure the IAEA as the principal, if not sole, implementer of safeguards, and so making Agency safeguards a condition of bilateral supply effectively would secure this goal. The U.S. preference for IAEA safeguards was not based purely on a generalized policy of preference for international solutions. Rather, it was recognized that if the United States were to be the sole supplier of nuclear materials and equipment, reliance on U.S. safeguards implementation would provide the greatest assurance of effectiveness. With other nations serving as suppliers as well; however, only a uniform system of verification subject to review by the United States and other states could provide the necessary assurance of effectiveness.

To ensure that acceptance of Agency safeguards would be a condition of bilateral supply, it was recognized that this condition could not be achieved if suppliers could freely omit it to enhance the chances of success of their bids to recipient customers. To meet this problem, the United States formed a group of the principal Western nuclear suppler states, in which the acceptance of IAEA safeguards would be a required, nonnegotiable condition of nuclear supply proposals. This group, on which I served as the USAEC representative, came to be known as the Nuclear Suppliers Group, but it is beyond the scope of this discussion.

Having succeeded in deemphasizing the IAEA's supplier role while making IAEA safeguards a condition of bilateral nuclear supply, the United States and other nuclear suppliers proceeded to adopt IAEA safeguards and substitute them for bilateral safeguards without serious disagreement on the part of recipient states. The U.S. approach was not to seek the immediate renegotiation of agreements calling for bilateral safeguards, but to tie the transition to Agency safeguards as existing agreements required amendment to increase the quantities of nuclear fuel needed to meet expanded requirements in recipients' nuclear power programs. Additionally, of course, IAEA safeguards were to be required in any entirely new agreement for cooperation. The litmus test for the new policy arose with the negotiation of an agreement for cooperation when India decided to secure its first nuclear power station, at Tarapur near Bombay, from the United States. India had a long established and deeply held opposition to IAEA safeguards, though it did not object to bilateral safeguards on enriched nuclear material provided by an outside supplier. In conformance with this policy, India, as expected, initially objected to the U.S. requirement for IAEA safeguards at Tarapur. After negotiations that lasted at least a year, agreement was reached on an accord that conformed to the U.S. policy of IAEA safeguards. India was accorded a reasonable time to manage the transition to Agency safeguards, though skeptics forecast that the transition would never take place. Given the U.S. control over enriched fuel deliveries, we were confident that the agreement would be complied with; this confidence was borne out, with safeguards proceeding smoothly under the IAEA.

The 1964 extension of the Agency safeguards system did not, however, terminate activity on the development of Agency safeguards. On the contrary, a number of Member States accepted the extension on the understanding that it would be followed by a general review and updating of the Agency system. India itself took a similar position in its acceptance of the Tarapur arrangement. This review was undertaken once again by a committee of the Board of Governors, but it now was open to any member state. The review resulted in the adoption of a much more detailed safeguards document, INFCIRC/66. Despite its length and detail, INFCIRC/66 did not depart in major respects from the existing safeguards regime, preserving "access at all times" for the inspection of all sizeable power reactors. However, it contained several complex provisions designed to deal with the reality that many reactors subject to safeguards would receive their fuel from unsafeguarded enrichment facilities in other states and would, at least in principle, return this fuel after irradiation to the supplying or other states. The principle of these provisions was to ensure that the supplying state did not improve its fissionable material holdings either quantitatively or qualitatively through the irradiation and return of its nuclear material supplied to another state. This, of course, meant that under some circumstances, the IAEA would have to apply its safeguards in supplier states as well as in recipient states, but in principle the United States would allow safeguards, even if implemented bilaterally by the recipient. U.S. bilateral agreements already ensured that the United States would not allocate foreign-produced fissionable material to its military stocks. In reality, much less of this export and return of nuclear material actually took place, but the provisions for dealing with it had been established.

INFCIRC/66 did include one new principle of substantive importance. This was the provisions authorizing a portion of its inspections to take place without advance notice, an addition introduced at U.S. initiative. Previously, the Agency was required to provide advance notice of all inspections; this requirement was given in the Agency's "Inspectors Document," adopted even before INFCIRC/26. The Agency has made little use of its limited authority to conduct inspections without advance notice, but the provision is vital, especially in relation to safeguards measures that depend on containment and surveillance. For example, if cameras are in use to detect unauthorized movements of material, a state would find it much more difficult to alter the functioning of such cameras if it did not have advance notice of any inspection for which it could reverse the alteration.

A year after the adoption of INFCIRC/66, a further meeting of the safeguards committee took place to extend the system to reprocessing plants. Reprocessing needs appeared to be on the rise as irradiated fuel accumulated at reactor facilities. Once again, in keeping with its original decision to seek expansion of the safeguards system in a stepwise manner, the United States approached the negotiation with an important, long-held objective: to secure agreement on the principle of continuous inspection, with inspections on a daily and, if necessary, round-the-clock basis. In the U.S. view, effective safeguards at reprocessing facilities, in common with other facilities handling large quantities of fissionable material in bulk form, could be accomplished only by intensive application of multiple safeguards measures—including containment and surveillance designed to detect unauthorized movements of material—and not by material accountancy alone. This requirement was especially critical in the case of reprocessing, since fissionable material input was contained in highly irradiated fuel that could not be directly measured by chemical and physical assay until the material was introduced into and dissolved in the reprocessing facility. The objective of continuous inspection was achieved. One year later, a similar extension was made to INFCIRC/66 for conversion and fabrication facilities; like reprocessing plants, these facilities handle large quantities of bulk fissionable material. The material at this stage of the fuel cycle is not yet irradiated, and so sampling and measurement are less difficult than in reprocessing plants. However, once again, continuous inspection was authorized.

As nuclear power grew steadily, Agency safeguards grew along with it, and their effectiveness improved. In this process, the United States' voluntary offer to allow the Agency to safeguard the Yankee Nuclear Power Station in Rowe, Massachusetts, was especially vital. This arrangement helped the Agency demonstrate that the critical time for the safeguarding of reactors was when refueling took place, since this was the occasion when spent fuel containing produced plutonium was physically available for conceivable unreported removal of produced material. It also demonstrated that the use of cameras and seals effectively ensured that the reactor remained sealed between scheduled and reported refueling openings when inspectors were present. Because these devices were susceptible to tampering, occasional inspections for placing new film could provide assurances that no one had tampered with the cameras. Thus, it was clear that when and how inspections were conducted, not how often, were the key to effective safeguards at power reactors that were producing plutonium at rates well beyond any reached in the defense programs of nuclear-weapon states. Containment and surveillance measures, not material accountancy formulas, were the backbone of the inspection system—at least at reactors.

Concurrent with the expansion of nuclear power, intensive negotiations were taking place in Geneva under UN auspices on a nonproliferation treaty which, if successfully concluded, could close the gap that permitted nonnuclear-weapon states to acquire nuclear weapons lawfully through their own efforts or with the help of other states. The treaty negotiations were held in any ad hoc UN body called the Eighteen-Nation Disarmament Commission, which included most major nations but not the Federal Republic of Germany. At the time, West German adherence to the treaty was considered essential to its success, and exploratory discussions with the West German government indicated that one condition of its agreement would be a U.S. agreement to voluntarily subject its civilian nuclear power industry to the same safeguards to which West German industry would be subjected. This condition was acceptable to the United States, and President Lyndon B. Johnson announced its acceptance. The United Kingdom, France, and the Soviet Union would all make similar voluntary offers.

In the U.S. view, it was essential that any nonproliferation treaty be effectively safeguarded (that is, verified), that this could be done most efficiently only by a single organization, and that the IAEA was the appropriate body to perform this function. This position was vigorously opposed by Euratom and its Member States on the Disarmament Commission, and for a time it seemed possible that even the United States would accept an unsafeguarded treaty. The USAEC strongly objected to this weaker position; at a meeting that I attended as the USAEC representative, it was not adopted. The impasse with Euratom was resolved by a surprisingly simple suggestion from the congressional Joint Committee that the IAEA be allowed to conclude the necessary safeguards agreements not only with individual states but with other groups of states as well.

At this stage, the negotiations appeared to be nearing a successful conclusion. However, even though West Germany had publicly accepted the U.S. voluntary offer, it once again objected to the prospect of IAEA safeguards. It felt that these safeguards would expose its nuclear industry to the potential loss of commercially valuable technology through inspections by foreign inspectors from competitive countries, and that the inspectors' demands and activities would interfere with the efficient operation of West German facilities. As a result, the United States and West Germany conducted a side negotiation in which the Germans proposed, among other matters, that the Agency safeguards system be steered in the direction of increased use of equipment to minimize its reliance on human inspection and to adopt the practice of concentrating safeguards on so-called strategic points—the locations in the nuclear fuel cycle where nuclear material could be most easily and effectively observed and measured. The United States concluded that both of these concepts were acceptable so long as they were subject to the overriding principle of safeguards effectiveness, and the treaty text was modified to accommodate them. Soon thereafter, the NPT approved and opened for signatures, which took place concurrently in the United States and the Soviet Union in July 1968. The Euratom Member States signed the treaty, but at a West German initiative, their ratification was made dependent on a review of the safeguards system to bring it into line with what they saw as an acceptable resolution of the problems raised by West Germany.

For some time, the United States opposed the review, believing that Euratom would expect the review to weaken the existing system called for by INFCIRC/66, which the United States viewed as adequate and acceptable for the application of safeguards under NPT. As the 18-month deadline for the conclusion of safeguards agreements with treaty parties approached, however, there was no alternative to proceeding with the review. Once again, the Safeguards Committee (designated the Safeguards

Committee (1970)) was convened. Initially, the committee was chaired by Ambassador Kurt Waldheim, a former Austrian foreign minister and later UN secretary-general and president of Austria. However, Waldheim was in an awkward position, as he was forbidden from entering the United States as a consequence of his activities as a German army officer during World War II. The Safeguards Committee meetings, which extended into 1971, resulted in the preparation of INFCIRC/153, with the unusual title of "The Structure and Content of Agreements between the Agency and States Required in Connection with the Treaty on the Nonproliferation of Nuclear Weapons." The purpose of this title was to preserve the U.S. position that the provisions of INFCIRC/153 were not a new safeguards system to replace INFCIRC/66, but only a rationalization of the latter. In reality, in the hierarchy of IAEA safeguards systems, INFCIRC/153 is in every respect a new system, not merely a modification and rationalization of its predecessor. Moreover, the original concern that dictated the U.S. position of preserving the "system" status of INFCIRC/66—that it would prove to be a gold standard of safeguards—did not come to pass. In almost all important respects, INFCIRC/153 is a more effective system. Additionally, the title carries the important benefit of essentially dictating the provisions of NPT safeguards agreements, instead of leaving room for individual negotiation as did the earlier INFCIRC/26 and INFCIRC/66.

A detailed description of the provisions of INFCIRC/153 is also beyond the scope of this chapter. The remarkable fact, however, is that the negotiation was conducted on a positive basis, with both traditional advocates of restricting safeguards intensity and those favoring greater assurance of effectiveness cooperating to find solutions that would ensure effectiveness. From the outset of the negotiation, the United States emphasized the need for *independent verification.* Such a system went beyond merely assuring that the state or states concerned had an adequate national (or even, as in the case of Euratom, a multinational) system, and made it essential that the Agency be able to verify through its own measures not only the findings of national systems but also compliance with the underlying obligation of avoiding the diversion of nuclear material to nuclear weapon purposes.

Among the numerous concepts of INFCIRC/153 that represent a tightening of the safeguards system, two stand out. One is the basic obligation of the nonnuclear-weapon states to accept safeguards on *all* nuclear material in *all* peaceful nuclear activities, with the term *all* being repeated throughout the document. This provision makes the inability to verify nondiversion, rather than positive verification of diversion, an actionable violation of the safeguards agreement. It also grants the IAEA Board of Governors the authority to require remedial action without delay when such action is necessary to verify nondiversion, explicitly recognizes containment and surveillance measures as vital to safeguards, and allows for special inspections if the Agency merely considers that the information from routine inspections or other relevant sources is not sufficient to discharge its responsibilities. All in all, this is a much lower threshold for special inspections than in previous safeguards documents. Second, the obligation to accept safeguards on *all* nuclear material in *all* peaceful nuclear activities makes it evident that safeguards are intended and required to extend to all material in all peaceful nuclear activities, whether declared or undeclared. (The qualification of "peaceful" is necessary to exclude nuclear materials used in military activities such as naval propulsion, which are not prohibited by the NPT.) The document does not explicitly refer to undeclared nuclear material or activities because the committee immediately rejected a South African proposal to limit the system to declared material. Such limits were never an issue, because they would have invalidated the NPT's basic purpose of prohibiting future nuclear weapon acquisition by nonnuclear weapon parties by any means, declared or undeclared.

As unfortunate activities in such states as Iran, Iraq, Libya, and Syria have demonstrated, nonproliferation officials generally concur that undeclared nuclear activities, not diversion from known and safeguarded activities, is the most probable route to proliferation on the part of NPT parties. It is unfortunate that the most serious weakening of IAEA safeguards took place during a considerable period beginning soon after the adoption of INFCIRC/153, when the system was confined, without Board or Member State approval or even consideration of a system limited to declared nuclear material and activities. This came to the attention of policymakers only after both the Agency and concerned Member State intelligence authorities failed to identify the existence of a sizable nuclear weapons development program in Iraq following the first Gulf War. To its credit, the Agency took prompt action to correct this failure by adopting a Board resolution reasserting the applicability of the Agency's safeguards to undeclared as well as declared nuclear materials and activities. The principal tool for putting this determination into effect is the Agency's special inspection authority, and the Board action also urged the use of this and all other relevant IAEA authority to detect or otherwise deal with undeclared activities.

The Agency's action in reaffirming safeguards on undeclared material and activities was especially timely, since not long after it was discovered that North Korea had not reported all of the fuel reprocessing from its small power research reactor, indicating that it had more plutonium than it had declared. Pursuant to INFCIRC/153, the Agency decided that corrective action was both necessary and urgent, and requested a special inspection of North Korean waste tanks to verify the amount of used fuel reprocessed. When the North Koreans rejected this request, the IAEA declared North Korea in violation of its safeguards agreement, and the issue was referred to the UN Security Council, as provided for in the Agency's Statute. This chain of events was followed by a remedial program, leading to an agreement known as the Agreed Framework under which North Korea undertook to discontinue and dismantle its nuclear weapon activities in exchange for two full nuclear power reactors. North Korea later would violate this understanding as well; the subsequent events, including its withdrawal from the NPT and its development of nuclear weapons, are now well known.

Some have interpreted the outcome of the North Korean dispute as a failure of IAEA safeguards, but this interpretation involves a fundamental misunderstanding of the role of safeguards. The Agency lacks the authority to enforce its safeguards findings by force or other means; its role is to sound the alarm and refer findings of noncompliance to the UN Security Council, where concerned Member States or the UN as a whole can initiate remedial measures if they wish to do so. This was exactly what took place in connection with the North Korean violation, and the safeguards system functioned as intended—the high point of IAEA safeguards implementation to date.

Following the North Korean episode, the Agency took further action to strengthen its ability to deal with undeclared activities, leading to the development of INFCIRC/540, the Additional Protocol. The Additional Protocol contains many useful provisions that under some circumstances can lower the Agency's barrier to secure information on and gain access to otherwise undeclared activities. Contrary to some opinions, including those of particular Agency officials, it does not broaden the Agency's access to undeclared activities; such access is already unlimited pursuant to the special inspection authority of INFCIRC/153. The principal provision dealing with what is termed "complementary access" of the Additional Protocol is an article (5c), that allows the IAEA to access any location it specifies to perform environmental sampling and, if it has questions or finds inconsistencies, to make other observations. Compared to the special inspection authority of INFCIRC/153, this authority has the advantage of not requiring Board approval before becoming a binding obligation on the Member State. At the same time, its limitation (at least initially) to environmental sampling tends to tie its utility to the identification of operating facilities. This state of affairs naturally is preferable to no identification at all, but the Agency's goal should be to detect undeclared activities at the earliest possible stage of their construction, certainly before operation resulting in detectable radiation has begun. In any case, like any other special inspection, a state can reject a request for complementary access under the Additional Protocol. This would result in noncompliance with the safeguards agreement, to be dealt with under its provisions. The reality, as the North Korean episode dramatically illustrated, is that a state with undeclared nuclear-weapon-related activity is unlikely to grant access to its undeclared facilities, but nevertheless the demand serves the necessary juridical function of initiating a UN Security Council inquiry that could result in corrective action. The Security Council is on record as having decided that a serious nonproliferation violation constitutes a threat to peace and security under the UN Charter; ensuing action, if any remains a matter for case-by-case determination.

The Additional Protocol is a useful complement to the Agency's tools for dealing with undeclared activities, but these of course must first be at least suspected before action can be taken under either the basic NPT safeguards agreement or the protocol. Full adherence to the protocol is a desirable goal. Unfortunately, much of the advocacy intended to reach this goal has denigrated the Agency's own substantial and, in important respects, broader authority under the basic safeguards agreement. This has been a mistake, and action to revive the utility of the special inspection authority (as the Board of Governors advocated) is greatly to be desired.

A final thought in relation to the future of safeguards relates to the current emphasis on undeclared enrichment. The proliferation risk of enrichment resulting from the availability of centrifuge technology is a serious risk, but it should not lead to complacency about the proliferation risk of plutonium. Viewed historically, it is probable that of the eight states known to have created and tested nuclear explosives, as well as one additional suspected state, all but two (Pakistan and probably China) have employed plutonium to do so. Reactors and reprocessing facilities can be hidden, and compared even to centrifuge enrichment reprocessing is easy technology. Iran's heavy-water reactor remains a significant proliferation risk, whatever the fate of the Joint Comprehensive Plan of Action, and this concern should not be overlooked.

The nonproliferation regime that has been created, while imperfect, has achieved a remarkable result by restricting the spread of history's most powerful weapon to the small circle of countries in which they are found. This result could not have been achieved without President Eisenhower's bold decision to exchange participation in the benefits of nuclear energy for pledges to refrain from nuclear weapons and to call for the creation of a unique international organization to watch the proverbial door.

5 The model additional protocol

Laura Rockwood

The Model Protocol Additional to the Agreement(s) between State(s) and the International Atomic Energy Agency (IAEA) for the Application of Safeguards (the Model Protocol), reproduced in Information Circular 540 (INFCIRC/540 (Corr.)), stands as one of the seminal legal instruments of IAEA safeguards. It is only the third such instrument to be created in the 60 years of IAEA safeguards, and the first in over two decades to be adopted by IAEA Member States. It is a quantum shift in Agency safeguards, evolving from the original item-specific safeguards of the 1960s based on the procedures set out in INFCIRC/66/Rev.2 (and its predecessor documents), to the comprehensive safeguards of the 1970s and 1980s based on INFCIRC/153 (Corr.), and then to the strengthened safeguards system currently being implemented by the IAEA. This chapter will offer some backstory around the conception, birth, and implementation of the Model Additional Protocol (AP).

The road to the model additional protocol

Most analyses of the AP start with the discovery of Iraq's undeclared nuclear program, but its genesis predated that. In 1990, peace seemed to be breaking out all over. The Soviet Union was on the verge of collapse, the Berlin Wall had fallen, and the two Germanys were negotiating a reunification treaty. Yet, this optimistic outlook soon was tempered by growing concern about the Persian Gulf following Iraq's invasion of Kuwait on August 2. Concern was also increasing about possible undeclared nuclear activities in the Democratic People's Republic of Korea (DPRK) and reported attempts by Iraq to secure sensitive nuclear material and equipment.[1]

In his statement at the opening of the Fourth NPT Review Conference, IAEA director general Hans Blix referred to the need to optimize the utilization of IAEA resources when, as was then the case, "expanded safeguarding duties had to be reconciled with zero real growth budgets."[2] He continued: "Efforts on the part of the Agency had to be matched by maximum co-operation on the part of Member States."[3] Although no final document on the review of the NPT was agreed at the 1990 Review Conference,

DOI: 10.4324/9781003160205-5

positive language and recommendations on safeguards were agreed in Main Committee II and subsequently reflected in the text circulated by the Drafting Committee.[4]

In his opening statement to the IAEA's General Conference on September 17, 1990, the Monday following the conclusion of the Review Conference, the Director General noted that the reasons for its failure to agree on a final declaration had been "completely unrelated to the texts which had been prepared on safeguards and other matters of direct relevance to the Agency." He added that "he was sure that many of the interesting and innovative ideas which had been brought up at the Conference regarding the safeguards system would be introduced by Member States directly in the Agency."[5]

Indeed, shortly thereafter, the Director General tasked me with providing legal advice on the IAEA's right to request access using special inspections to follow up on indications of undeclared nuclear material and activities. The resulting assessment, confirmed through a review of the negotiating history of INFCIRC/153 by Myron Kratzer, was that, given the clear language of paragraph 2 of INFCIRC/153, which refers to the Agency's "right and the obligation" to ensure that safeguards will be applied on "all source or special fissionable material" (a right and obligation included in every single CSA), and the provisions related to ad hoc and special inspections, the Agency indeed had such a right.

Redefining the objective of safeguards, 1991–1993

Following the first Gulf War, on April 3, 1991, the Security Council adopted the cease-fire resolution 687 (1991), in which it tasked the IAEA with mapping out and dismantling Iraq's nuclear weapons program. In short order, the Director General created the IAEA's Action Team, headed by Maurizio Zifferero.

In the meantime, work continued in the Secretariat on measures to strengthen safeguards. During the February 1991 Board meeting, the Director General addressed the question of the effectiveness of IAEA safeguards, noting that the more comprehensively the peaceful nuclear sector was covered by safeguards, the greater their effectiveness. In that regard, he referred to universal reporting to the Agency of exports of nuclear material, broader safeguards in nuclear-weapon states, the safeguards-friendly design of facilities and the submission of design information to the Agency, and the definition of significant quantities of nuclear material.[6] He also expressed a renewed interest in special inspections, and referred to a "preliminary study of which affirmed that the Agency had the authority to make such requests and [that] some special inspections had in fact been undertaken where routine inspections had been deemed insufficient." He added, "[n]aturally, any State which had accepted INFCIRC/153 safeguards might, itself, invite special inspections in order to dispel any doubts which might have arisen."[7]

The Director General also raised the issue of how to reduce the cost of safeguards without reducing confidence. In that regard, he proposed the wider use of computers in the field for analysis, the waiving of visa requirements for inspectors, and the acceptance of simplified procedures for their designation. He noted that he had suggested to the Board simplified procedures for the designation of inspectors in 1988, but that some states still insisted on quotas and others took up to three years to respond to designation proposals. He noted that he had on several occasions expressed the hope that Member States would waive visa requirements for safeguards inspectors, or at least to issue long-term multiple-entry visas.[8]

In May 1991, the Director General presented to the Board of Governors a paper on improved safeguards procedures and efficiency gains.[9] In it, he identified five issues that warranted the Board's attention: special inspections, safeguards in the nuclear-weapon states, design information, universal reporting of nuclear material, and significant quantities. The first two issues were analyzed in the paper. In August 1991, he circulated a paper on the other three issues.[10]

Although the Board's attention already had been drawn to the need to strengthen safeguards, the Secretariat's discovery of Iraq's extensive clandestine nuclear program, and its reports to the Board in July and September 1991 of Iraq's noncompliance with its safeguards obligations, made a real impact. Prior to April 1991, the IAEA had been making twice-yearly inspections of three nuclear facilities and a location outside of facilities on the site of Tuwaitha. After implementing UN Security Council resolution 687 for only a few months, however, the Action Team identified other nuclear activities at the site, including research and development related to almost every stage of a nuclear weapon program, previously unknown to the IAEA.

Iraq served as an epiphany for safeguards. It had hidden much of its extensive undeclared activities by co-locating them with declared activities, it had "gone shopping" for dual-use items and made its own single-use items, and it had been able to carry out significant research and development activities using only small quantities of nuclear material. It also had planned to use a technology for the production of highly enriched uranium that the United States had used in producing its first nuclear weapons, but had subsequently declassified as too expensive and energy-intensive for a nuclear weapons program. In the course of its investigations into Iraq's nuclear program, the IAEA learned many lessons, most of which are directly identifiable in the document that eventually became the Model AP.

The Board continued its deliberations on strengthened safeguards measures at its meeting in September 1991. At that same session, the Board also approved the texts of the CSAs for South Africa and the DPRK. In connection with the South African CSA, the Board adopted a resolution requesting the Director General to verify the completeness of South Africa's declarations regarding nuclear material and installations.[11] In its introduction of the draft resolution on behalf of the sponsors, Egypt stated that "in order not to make a mockery of the safeguards system in the future … the sponsors of the draft resolution wanted the Director General, the Agency and all Member States, including South Africa, to help ensure that the inventory established for South Africa was complete."[12] At the General Conference immediately following that Board meeting, a resolution was also adopted, without a vote, requesting the director general "to verify the completeness of the inventory of South Africa's nuclear installations and material."[13]

In his introductory statement to the September 1991 General Conference, the Director General, speaking of the discovery of Iraq's undeclared nuclear activities, said that the IAEA was "now faced with the challenge of strengthening its safeguards system."[14] He referred to the "keen interest" on the part of the previous year's General Conference "in the many innovative proposals which had emerged at the Fourth NPT Review Conference," and with other proposals analyzed in the Secretariat and discussed by the Board. In his view, "It was clear that the time was ripe for adjustment and change." He spoke of one lesson that had been learned in Iraq: in order to make special inspections under full-scope safeguards effective, three conditions needed to be fulfilled:

> Firstly, the inspectorate must have access to information from other sources besides the State in which the inspections were to be performed, notably from satellites and intelligence organizations… .
>
> Secondly, the inspectorate must have the right of timely and unrestricted access to any location which, according to credible information, might be an undeclared nuclear installation or contain undeclared nuclear material… .
>
> Thirdly, the Agency might need to exercise its right of access to the Security Council if the State in question rejected a request for a special inspection.[15]

Although there was no separate agenda item on strengthening safeguards in September 1991, the General Conference adopted a resolution on "Strengthening of the Safeguards System" under the agenda item "The Agency's Budget for 1992."[16] In that resolution, the Conference underlined "the central importance of effective safeguards for the prevention of misuse of nuclear energy for nonpeaceful purposes and for the promotion of co-operation in the peaceful uses of nuclear energy"; confirmed "its resolve to maintain and strengthen the effectiveness and efficiency of the safeguards system in conformity with the Statute"; and requested the Board and the Director General to continue efforts in this respect. It also took note of the decision of the Board to consider, at its February 1992 session at the latest, measures to strengthen the effectiveness of the safeguards system.

During his opening remarks at the Board meeting on December 5, 1991, the Director General noted:

> [the] crucial element in strengthening the ability of the safeguards system to detect any clandestine nuclear activities in States which had

> accepted comprehensive safeguards was information... . a fundamental modification needed to be made in the Agency's practices: ... making more extensive use of such information as the Agency already possessed and ... being prepared to accept and critically examine information that might be offered to the Agency from the outside... . There was certainly the risk that information might be offered for ulterior motives, and it would be a mistake to rely on it. However, it would be a still worse mistake to refuse to accept any other information than that communicated officially by the inspected State.[17]

At the Board's meeting the following day, he invited the Board to consider, by way of example, what might have happened if the armed action authorized by the Security Council had never happened and the Secretariat had been approached by a group of Iraqi scientists who had left Iraq, bringing with them drawings and photographs. He asked, "Would the Secretariat have been wrong to examine such evidence and, if it had seemed credible, to ask the Government of Iraq for an explanation?" If the answer was yes, he said, he "feared that the Agency's safeguards would soon be regarded by governments and the general public as a 'paper tiger.'"[18]

In February 1992, the Board considered the revised paper on special inspections and the early provision of design information that had been circulated in November 1991.[19] In the case of special inspections, the Board reaffirmed the Agency's right to undertake special inspections when necessary and appropriate as described in CSAs, and to ensure that all nuclear materials in all peaceful nuclear activities are under safeguards.[20] In the case of design information, the Board called on all states to provide information on new facilities and activities and any modifications to existing facilities through the provision of design information as soon as the decision to construct, to authorize construction, or to modify has been taken, and on a continuous and iterative basis thereafter. It also instructed the Secretariat to adapt, where appropriate, the related subsidiary arrangements (effectively, modification of Code 3.1 on the submission of design information).[21]

In June 1992, the Board considered the Secretariat's papers on the provision of information on exports, imports, and inventories of nuclear material (GOV/2588) and on exports and imports of relevant equipment and nonnuclear material (GOV/2589). It was not until the following February, however, that the Board was able to endorse what came to be known as the Voluntary Reporting Scheme for reporting on exports and imports of nuclear material not otherwise required to be reported under safeguards agreements, and for reporting on the export of specified equipment and nonnuclear material (based on the list published in INFCIRC/254/Rev.1/Part 1 as it stood in February 1993).[22] At the same meeting, the Board also considered the Director General's report on Romania's noncompliance with its CSA and the Secretariat's follow-up special inspection that had resolved the matter. As Romania itself had brought the matter to the attention of the IAEA, the Board decided to report it to the United Nations Security Council "for information only."

Prior to the June Board meeting, the Director General had circulated a document (GOV/INF/654) describing the measures already taken to "streamline and rationalize" the safeguards system so as to reduce costs. From June 24 to 26, 1992, a "brainstorming" session was held to discuss measures to reduce costs and enhance the effectiveness of safeguards. Among the subjects considered were "alternative safeguards approaches," problems of detecting undeclared facilities, the use of new technology, the efficient use of available human resources, and the necessity of improving communication between the Secretariat and Member States. As a result, the Director General requested his Standing Advisory Group on Safeguards Implementation (SAGSI) to reexamine how Agency safeguards were being implemented and to provide, as a matter of urgency, advice on a number of the subjects discussed with a view to reducing costs while meeting new requirements and maintaining effectiveness. SAGSI, supported by the Secretariat, eventually submitted its recommendations to the Director General in April 1993.

In 1992, the General Conference agenda included, for the first time, a separate item on strengthening the safeguards system. The Director General's report under that agenda item recalled that the overall objective was to enhance the Agency's ability to detect and have access to any undeclared nuclear activities that should have been declared under safeguards agreements.[23] The Conference adopted a resolution on "Strengthening the Effectiveness and Improving the Efficiency of the Safeguards System," in which it "confirm[ed] its resolve to maintain and strengthen the effectiveness and efficiency of the safeguards system," "note[d] decisions taken by the Board of Governors over the past 12 months to strengthen the safeguards system, and call[ed] upon Member States to co-operate with the Agency in implementing those decisions," and "request[ed] the Director General to continue and intensify his efforts towards improving the effectiveness and efficiency of the safeguards system, taking into account tasks entrusted to him by the Board of Governors and the General Conference as a result of new requirements."[24]

In the closing days of 1992, tensions were increasing between the IAEA and the DPRK. The IAEA was pressing the North Koreans to provide explanations for the anomalies it had identified in their nuclear material declarations under their CSA, and to provide access to locations the IAEA had identified as possible nuclear waste sites.[25] The DPRK was resisting these requests. Following a special closed meeting of the Board of Governors in February 1993, at which the Secretariat made a case for invoking special inspections in connection with the North Korean nuclear program, the Board adopted a resolution, pursuant to Article 18 of the DPRK's CSA, in which it decided (without a vote) that it was essential and urgent for the DPRK to provide the IAEA with access to the requested information and locations.[26]

In that single action, the Board's decision implicitly approved the use of environmental sampling, a powerful new verification technology developed in the course of the IAEA's activities in Iraq. It also confirmed the IAEA's right to request access to undeclared locations and information; affirmed the Agency's right to use all information available to it, including intelligence information (such as the satellite imagery used to locate the waste sites); and confirmed the Agency's right and obligation to verify the correctness and completeness of a state's declarations under a CSA. When the DPRK refused to provide the requested access, the Board, in April 1993, found it to be in noncompliance and decided to report the noncompliance to the United Nations Security Council.[27] In the meantime, in March 1993, South Africa announced that it had manufactured nuclear weapons and had dismantled them prior to joining the NPT.[28]

In April 1993, SAGSI reported its recommendations to the Director General, who conveyed them to the Board for its consideration at the June 1993 meeting of the Board of Governors.[29] The recommendations addressed improvements in cost-effectiveness through the use of new techniques, procedures to detect undeclared facilities, increased cooperation with State Systems of Accounting and Control, and alternative safeguards approaches. Its primary conclusion was that the Agency's safeguards system must be enhanced to provide a high level of confidence as to the absence of undeclared nuclear facilities and activities in states with CSAs. SAGSI was also of the opinion that the principle of a trade-off between the introduction of an enhanced capability to detect undeclared nuclear facilities and a reduction in certain routine inspection activities was valid. The Board chairman's summary of the discussion noted that most governors agreed with the Director General's view that the SAGSI proposals required further "action oriented" analysis, and requested the Director General to submit to the Board in December 1993 concrete proposals pursuant to SAGSI's recommendations, including their legal, financial, and political implications.[30]

In his opening statement to the 1993 General Conference, the Director General spoke of the need to "add further precision" to the formulation of the IAEA's safeguards conclusions in light of the discovery of an undeclared nuclear program in a CSA country (Iraq).[31] Thus, he noted, the Safeguards Implementation Report (SIR) for 1992 (issued in the first half of 1993) contained the following formulation:

> On the basis of all the information available to the Agency, it is considered reasonable to conclude that nuclear material and other items *which had been placed under Agency safeguards* remained in peaceful nuclear activities or were otherwise adequately accounted for.[32]

He further noted that the statement had been deliberately limited to declared nuclear material and other items. The new formulation was also accompanied by a footnote to the effect that the safeguards system was not so fine-meshed that it was likely to detect diversions of less than a significant quantity. In that regard, he added that it was important that the Agency

> should not offer more reassurance than could in practice be obtained from the safeguards system... . All that could be done was to report on the results of the inspection and analysis effort to verify the correctness and assess the completeness of State declarations, to point to evidence which supported or undermined the veracity of the declarations and to note the presence or the absence of any evidence casting doubt on the credibility of the declarations. Even in the case of Iraq, where the Agency had had exceptional means of investigation and rights of access, the task of assessing the absence of further nondeclared nuclear items was difficult.[33]

During its 1993 session, the Conference adopted, without a vote, a resolution in which it reiterated much of the text from the 1992 safeguards resolution and requested the Director General "to continue and intensify his efforts towards improving the effectiveness and cost-efficiency of the safeguards system, and in particular to pursue the effort of re-examination of safeguards implementation, ... in order that a more effective and cost-efficient system may be achieved..."[34]

Key outcomes

The period between 1991 and late 1993 was a demanding time, with Iraq, South Africa, and the DPRK on the agenda, along with negotiations with Argentina, Brazil, and the Argentine-Brazilian Agency for Accounting and Control of Nuclear Materials of a quadripartite CSA and its subsidiary arrangements, and the efforts to strengthen safeguards.[35] The most important outcome of this period, however, was affirmation by the IAEA's Board of Governors and General Conference of the Agency's right and obligation under CSAs to verify not just the correctness of states' declarations, but the completeness of such declarations. The IAEA's legal authority under CSAs did not change; the objective under such agreements was simply redefined, long before the idea of an AP was even conceived.

The other key outcome was the realization by the Secretariat that, in order to achieve that objective, we needed to change the way we implemented safeguards in CSA states. The Agency had to move beyond safeguards approaches focused on nuclear material and facilities *declared* by the state to looking at the *state as a whole*—to move from facility-level safeguards approaches to state-level safeguards approaches taking into account all of the safeguards-relevant information available to the Agency. Although the IAEA had already between 1991 and 1993 identified a number of measures that it could take to improve its ability to verify the correctness and completeness of a state's declarations, it quickly became clear that greater access to information and broader access to locations could achieve that objective more effectively and efficiently.

Programme 93+2

In December 1993, Deputy Director General for Safeguards (DDG), Bruno Pellaud, introduced the Secretariat's "Development Programme for a Strengthened and More Cost-effective Safeguards System," the results of which he expected to be able to present to the Board in early 1995.[36] The DDG named this exercise "Programme 93+2" with a view to conveying the expected lifetime of the programme, intended to be completed by the time the 1995 NPT Review and Extension Conference was set to begin in New York on April 17, 1995. Richard Hooper was tasked with leading the effort.

As described in the first report to the General Conference on Programme 93+2, the core team involved a program manager, six task officers, and representatives from the Legal and External Relations divisions.[37] The work was carried out through a series of internal working groups, drawing from expertise throughout the Secretariat, and extensive support from Member States (particularly in connection with field trials). Six teams addressed six tasks: cost analysis of present safeguards implementation; assessment of potential cost-saving measures; environmental monitoring techniques for safeguards application; improving the effectiveness and efficiency of the safeguards system through strengthening measures and increased co-operation with State Systems for Accounting and Control; improved analysis of information on States' nuclear activities; and enhanced safeguards training. The purpose of the seventh and final team, led by Rich Hooper, was the integration of the results of the others into proposals for more effective and efficient safeguards. A U.S. expert, Frank Houck, provided considerable technical support as a consultant to the Department of Safeguards.

The seventh team also included an analysis of the legal implications of the proposals, addressing the scope of the IAEA's existing authority within the terms of existing safeguards agreements to carry out the measures considered by the task groups; identifying the extent to which additional authority was necessary to permit the IAEA to implement such measures; and describing, where necessary, legal arrangements or instruments for securing the Agency's right to do so. I was responsible for these analyses. Of particular note was the development of "a coherent and comprehensive approach to the acquisition, management and analysis of information" based on the "diversion critical path" and the identification and the evaluation of potential information sources.[38] This approach, now referred to as "acquisition path analysis," involved, as a first step, defining all known pathways for the production of weapon-usable material and subsequent weaponization, and then using the results as a template against which the activities declared by a state, and all other safeguards relevant information about the state, would be compared.

The Secretariat provided three progress reports on Programme 93+2 during 1994, the latter two of which focused on improved information analysis and the acquisition path.[39] At the 1994 General Conference, IAEA Member States requested the Secretariat to present to the Board in March 1995 "proposals for a strengthened and more cost-efficient safeguards system, together with an evaluation of their technical, legal and financial implications."[40]

In February 1995, the Secretariat circulated document GOV/2784, in which it provided an overview of the measures for a strengthened, more effective safeguards system developed under Programme 93+2. These included broader access to information; increased physical access; and measures for optimizing the use of the present system.[41] In his opening statement to the March Board, the Director General introduced GOV/2784, which, as the Board had requested, spelled out the technical, legal, and financial aspects of these measures. The paper described, in the view of the Secretariat, a number of measures that could be implemented on the basis of existing legal authority, and other complementary measures that presupposed new specific consent by the States concerned. He noted that the form in which the complementary authority could best be given would have to be discussed. In responding to some of the Board's comments, the Director General noted that "traditional" safeguards, geared to verification at declared installations and not to the detection of possible undeclared safeguards-relevant installations, were like "a man looking for a lost key near a lighted streetlamp who, when asked whether he was sure he had lost the key there, said 'No, but it's easier to look here.'" The Agency needed also to "look for any keys lying away from the street-lamp in darkness."[42]

The Board endorsed the general direction of Programme 93+2. As noted in the chairman's summary of the discussion, the Board "reiterate[d] that the purpose of [CSAs], where safeguards are applied to all nuclear material in all nuclear activities within the territory of a State party to such an agreement, under its jurisdiction or carried out under its control anywhere is to verify that such material is not diverted to nuclear weapons or other nuclear explosive devices. To this end, the safeguards system for implementing [CSAs] should be designed to provide for verification by the Agency of the correctness and completeness of States' declarations, so that there is credible assurance of the nondiversion of nuclear material from declared activities and of the absence of undeclared nuclear activities." It took note of GOV/2784 and requested the Secretariat to take into account comments made by the Board, and to submit specific proposals for the Board's consideration in June.[43]

In May 1995, the Secretariat issued GOV/2807, which divided the comprehensive set of measures into measures that could be implemented within existing legal authority (Part 1), and those which the Secretariat considered required complementary legal authority and which eventually evolved into the measures included in the Model Protocol (Part 2).[44]

In his introductory statement to the June 1995 session of the Board, the Director General indicated that, with the benefit of discussions at the 1995 regular session of the General Conference and further informal consultations with Member States, the Secretariat would submit the Part 2 proposals, together with a draft legal instrument, for the Board's consideration in December.[45]

The Board had an extensive and wide-ranging discussion, lasting a full day, on the Secretariat's document and proposals. It took note of the Director General's plan to implement at an early date the measures described in Part 1 and urged states party to CSAs to cooperate with the Secretariat to facilitate such implementation. [46]

The model additional protocol, 1995–1997

Between June 1995 and June 1996, the Secretariat carried out regular consultations with Member States, individually and in groups. All parties involved found them to be useful and productive. On the Member States' part, they had a better understanding of the Secretariat's proposals; for its part, the Secretariat had a better understanding of Member States' concerns and could adjust its proposals accordingly.

Drafts and consultations, 1995–1996

An informal Discussion Draft, dated November 21, 1995, was circulated to Member States and introduced at a briefing meeting on December 1, 1995.[47] Based on the discussion in the Board, and subsequent consultations with Member States, the Director General issued Discussion Draft II on February 27, 1996. As with the first draft, Discussion Draft II consisted of a draft report and three annexes, the third of which was a draft protocol.

In preparation for the March 1996 Board meeting, the Director General convened a briefing for Member States on Discussion Draft II. At that meeting, he pointed out the need to "strike an appropriate balance between measures to credibly strengthen safeguards and the need to avoid excessively difficult or burdensome obligations for Member States."[48] The DDG for Safeguards also made a presentation at that briefing, during which he referred to "six essential principles" on which the complementary authority provided for in the draft protocol were premised. As he put it, the authority was—

Not focused on the measures applied to nuclear material as such, but rather on factors that might indicate the presence or production of nuclear material;
Not concentrated on nuclear material accountancy, but rather on the comparison of all available relevant information;
Not committed to a systematic verification of the information collected, but rather to a systematic analysis of that information;
Not focused on containment and surveillance, but rather on visual observation and environmental sampling;

Not aimed at expanding the basic commitments undertaken in CSAs, but rather at providing new tools to ensure that all available information about a country's nuclear activities is consistent with its nonproliferation commitments; and

Not dependent on increasingly sophisticated equipment, but rather on improved collection and analysis of all relevant information.[49]

He also emphasized that the complementary measures would not be implemented mechanistically, bureaucratically, or directly proportional to the size of a nuclear program.[50]

At its March 1996 meeting, the Board welcomed Discussion Draft II, noting that it represented a reasonable balance between the needs of a strengthened safeguards system and the obligations to be undertaken by states. However, as there continued to be divergence, the Board asked the Secretariat to continue to consult with Member States with a view to submitting a formal text for the June 1996 meeting of the Board.[51] The Secretariat thus convened an informal, open-ended consultative meeting on Programme 93+2 in mid-April 1996. In early May, the Director General issued a report on "Proposals for Implementation under Complementary Authority" (GOV/2863).[52] As requested, the Secretariat also circulated a marked-up version of Discussion Draft II indicating where that text had been modified in response to Member States' comments.[53] As had the two previous discussion drafts, GOV/2863 included as Annex III a draft "Protocol Additional to the Agreement Between … and the International Atomic Energy Agency for the Application of Safeguards in Connection with [the Treaty on the Nonproliferation of Nuclear Weapons][and][the Treaty for the Prohibition of Nuclear Weapons in Latin America and the Caribbean]." The Secretariat convened another workshop in mid-May to discuss GOV/2863.

Following these extensive consultations, the Board formally considered GOV/2863 and, on June 14, 1996, decided to "establish a committee with the task of drafting a model protocol basing itself on Annex III to document GOV/2863 and taking into account, inter alia, the explanation of the measures contained in that document and the discussions on the matter in the Board."[54] With that, the Committee on Strengthening the Effectiveness and Improving the Efficiency of the Safeguards System, or Committee 24, was established.

Committee 24, 1996–1997

Over an 11-month period and four meetings of Committee 24—in which some 61 countries, as well as the Brazilian-Argentine Agency for Accounting and Control of Nuclear Materials and Euratom participated—the Board was able, on May 15, 1997, to approve the final text of the AP.[55]

The first session was scheduled to take place over a two-week period from July 2 to 12, 1996. A first review reading of the draft protocol, article by article, took into account the written comments submitted by Member States. It ultimately lasted less than three full days, ending on July 4. Member States were asked to submit to the Secretariat written comments on the draft protocol by August 1, 1996. On September 2, 1996, the Secretariat circulated a "Compendium of Proposed Changes to Annex III of Document GOV/2863 Prepared in Accordance with the Decision by the Committee on 4 July 1996."[56] This document included the proposals made orally during the committee's first session and those submitted in writing to the Secretariat.[57]

At the second session, from October 1 to 11, participants engaged in an extensive second reading of the draft protocol, using the compendium as the main working document. However, the second session did not go much better than the first. Indeed, it seemed that the additional protocol was capsizing. As agreed by the committee, the chairman circulated a rolling text the following week as the basis for the committee's third reading of the protocol at its next session.[58]

Given the diverse, strongly held positions among the participants, many of us thought the protocol was dead in the water at the end of the October meeting. However, at the third session of the committee, held from January 20 to 31, 1997, as the result of a brilliant diplomatic ballet choreographed by the United States and Germany, the chairman's rolling text was used as the main working document.[59] Unbeknownst to almost all of us, an extraordinary turnaround had taken place over the Christmas break as a direct result of a phone call from U.S. president Bill Clinton to German chancellor Helmut Kohl, and one-on-one meetings between U.S. Representative Ambassador Norman Wolf and Reinhardt Loosch, the former governor for Germany on the IAEA's Board of Governors.

Another significant development during the third session of Committee 24 was the statement issued on January 31 by Mohamed ElBaradei, the then-Assistant Director General and Head of the Division of External Relations, setting out the Secretariat's interpretation of the relationship between the Additional Protocol and the relevant safeguards agreement.[60] In his statement, he referred to Article 1 of the draft protocol[61] and the relationship between the protocol and the safeguards agreement, stating that "it [Article 1]did not seek to determine the question of the existence or non-existence of a legal obligation to adhere to the Protocol. Nor did it prejudge the question of prospective parties or the modalities for their adherence; whether States would adhere individually, or as a group, or in conjunction with international organizations was outside the scope of Article 1... . Article 1 simply sought to determine the manner in which the Protocol was to be implemented in conjunction with the Safeguards Agreement."[62] He also noted that the AP was not to be a stand-alone document because no state could adhere to the protocol unless it had previously concluded a safeguards agreement with the Agency, and because the protocol depended in many ways on the underlying safeguards agreement.[63] In his view, "that interrelationship led to one inevitable conclusion: for the purpose of interpretation, the two agreements—once concluded—had to be read and interpreted as one agreement. That was the only way in which the two documents could be implemented together."[64]

As a result of the progress made during the third session, the committee agreed that a consolidated revised text, largely consensus language, would be circulated in February and that the committee would meet again on April 2–3, 1997, to reach an agreement on a draft model protocol for submission to the Board. The committee's February 1997 report to the Board of Governors referred to the considerable progress made during the January meeting and recommended to the Board that it hold a special session on May 15–16, 1997, to consider and approve the draft model protocol.[65]

At its fourth and final session, April 2–4, 1997, the committee discussed the consolidated Chairman's Revised Text of February 5, and was able to agree on the final text of the AP. The committee submitted its final report to the Board and transmitted the text of the protocol to the Board for its review and approval, summarizing the work of the committee.[66] On May 15, 1997, the Board of Governors held a special session to consider the results of the work of Committee 24. In the morning session of that meeting, Germany referred to the need to assign high priority to "integrating the measures foreseen in the Model Protocol and the Part 1 measures already approved by the Board into the classical safeguards system in order to improve its efficiency and effectiveness, while providing protection against unwarranted intrusiveness."[67] The Board finally approved the text of the AP, endorsed the understandings reached in the committee on the relationship between additional protocols and the respective safeguards agreements, took note of the statements that had been made in the Board meeting by states with noncomprehensive safeguards agreements, and approved the draft AP contained in the committee's report.[68]

Each provision in the AP has a story behind it; each has an explanation that can be tied to a lesson learned in Iraq, South Africa, and North Korea. What specifically was new? Additional information, a new kind of access, and simplified administrative measures. What was not new was the IAEA's right to carry out unannounced inspections, to request access to undeclared locations, and fundamentally to verify correctness and completeness. The AP only gave the IAEA more tools to do that job better.

In the words of Reinhardt Loosch, a problem for the negotiations was the widespread concern that new tools would simply be added to those already available and, like those, be applied "indiscriminately and without regard to the particularities of the specific situation in which safeguards were to be administered." He attributed the committee's ability to overcome the problem to textual changes in the most contentious provisions of earlier drafts; the "masterly statement," delivered on behalf of the Director General by Assistant Director General ElBaradei, that "whereas the proposed protocols would be additional to the underlying safeguards agreements, the implementation of both would be based on their symbiotic and dynamic relationship"; and the goal of "higher efficiency" of safeguards being raised to the same level as that of "increased effectiveness." In remarks he made in 2002, Loosch noted that the real test would come when the Agency would actually employ the "improved safeguards arsenal." He queried whether the inspectorate would "use the integrated tool box wisely and in a manner differentiating according to the specific characteristics of the case on hand, or [would] it, in the name of so-called 'non-discrimination,' treat all cases alike which would lead not only to a waste of scarce safeguards resources but also to one of the worst forms of discrimination."[69]

As noted in the committee's final report to the Board of Governors, the other key issues included: the need to ensure that the IAEA had a stringent regime for protecting confidential information; the importance placed by the Committee on undertakings by nuclear-weapon states to conclude additional protocols; and the simplified mechanism for amendment of the AP's annexes.[70]

Looking at the State as a whole and tailoring safeguards

The IAEA has been drawing safeguards conclusions in its annual Safeguards Implementation Report (SIR) in the form of a Safeguards Statement. Today, in the case of states with a CSA and an AP in force, if the IAEA finds no indication of the diversion of undeclared nuclear material and no indication of undeclared nuclear material and activities, it is able to draw the "broader conclusion"—namely, that all nuclear material has remained in peaceful activities. However, this safeguards conclusion has developed gradually since the discovery of Iraq's undeclared nuclear program in terms of its formulation, the findings from which the conclusions were drawn, and the description of the basis for drawing such conclusions.

Prior to the discovery of Iraq's clandestine nuclear programme, the IAEA's formulation of its safeguards conclusions in connection with CSAs provided that, in implementing safeguards, the Secretariat:

> … *did not detect any event which would indicate the diversion of a significant amount of safeguarded nuclear material* … for the manufacture of any nuclear weapon, or for any other military purpose, or for the manufacture of any other nuclear explosive device, or for purposes unknown… . It is considered *reasonable to conclude that the nuclear material under Agency safeguards in [the relevant year] remained in peaceful nuclear activities or was otherwise adequately accounted for.* This statement is *based on all the information available to the Agency, including information derived from safeguards activities conducted in the field and at Headquarters and information provided in reports submitted by States.*[71]

The first major modification occurred in connection with the Safeguards Statement for 1992. As described by the director general in his opening remarks at the 1993 General Conference:

> The discovery of a non-declared nuclear programme in a country [Iraq] having comprehensive safeguards had also led the Secretariat to add further precision to certain important conclusions it had drawn from its safeguards activities. Thus, the Safeguards Implementation Report for 1992 (GOV/2653) contained the following formulation:
>
> On the basis of all the information available to the Agency, it is considered reasonable to conclude that nuclear material and other items which had been *placed under Agency safeguards* remained in peaceful nuclear activities or were otherwise adequately accounted for.[72]

He added:

> [t]hat statement was deliberately limited to declared nuclear material and other items. Even so, it was qualified by a footnote to the effect that the safeguards system was not so fine-meshed that it was likely to detect diversions of less than a significant quantity.[73]

The Safeguards Statements for 1993 and 1994 echoed the language from the 1992 Safeguards Statement, including the footnote to which the director general referred. (However, the 1993 Statement recorded an exception with respect to the DPRK.)

In the 1995, 1996, and 1997 SIRs, the Safeguards Statement referred to nuclear material "declared and placed under safeguards." In the 1998 and 1999 SIRs, the language reverted to nuclear material "placed under safeguards." The conclusion, however, remained the same with respect to such material; that it remained in peaceful nuclear activities or was otherwise adequately accounted for. The 1999 SIR included, for the first time, a reference to "a further conclusion" relating to the "absence of undeclared nuclear material and activities *in the State as a whole*" (emphasis from the text of the SIR) for the two states in which CSAs and APs had been implemented during 1999.[74] The text read as follows:

> Having completed the evaluation of all the information available to the Agency, including the results of activities performed for each State under its safeguards agreement and additional protocol, the Secretariat found no indication of diversion of declared nuclear material or of the presence of undeclared nuclear material or activities in these States.[75]

The following year, the 2000 Safeguards Statement contained a reformulated conclusion: "the Secretariat—having evaluated all the information obtained through activities pursuant to [seven States'] comprehensive safeguards agreements and additional protocols as well as all other information available to the Agency—found no indication either of diversion of nuclear material placed under safeguards or of the presence of undeclared nuclear material or activities in those States." On that basis, it concluded that "all nuclear material in those States had been placed under safeguards and remained in peaceful nuclear activities or was otherwise adequately accounted for." In the Background to the Safeguards statement, this was described as the "broader conclusion."[76]

The formulation of the broader conclusions reflected in the Safeguards Statements for 2001 and 2002 were similar in nature.[77] However, the Safeguards Statement for 2002 included an additional sentence in connection with states with CSAs and APs in force or being provisionally applied, noting that "Only in such States are Agency safeguards 'able to provide credible assurance of the absence of undeclared nuclear material and activities.'" A similar sentence was included in the 2003 Safeguards Statement, but not in those of later years.[78] The 2003 Safeguards Statement also was reformatted, largely reflecting the formatting in current SIRs. However, in the 2005 Safeguards Statement, the word "nuclear" was deleted from the latter part of the broader conclusion for the first time, so that the Agency concluded that "for these States, all nuclear material remained in peaceful activities." That has remained the formulation of the broader conclusion at least through 2019. The IAEA chooses not to draw the broader conclusion unless it has the benefit of the credibility offered by an additional protocol.

Recognizing the inherent weakness of focusing almost exclusively on individual declared facilities and declared nuclear material, as underscored by the Agency's discoveries in Iraq, in the early 1990s, the IAEA Secretariat started revising the way it evaluated the information available to it, and started looking at each CSA state as a whole. It started shifting away from a mechanistic approach of simply complying with the quantitative facility-based safeguards criteria to a more rigorous analysis of all information available to it. The next major evolution was a result of the realization that, if the IAEA were able to ensure itself that there were no undeclared nuclear material or activities in the state, it could consider reducing its inspection effort on less sensitive parts of the nuclear fuel cycle.

This approach was further developed over the course of Programme 93+2. During this time, the Secretariat underscored at every possible opportunity that it did not wish to pile on safeguards obligations and verify mechanistically all of the information provided under APs. Rather, it clarified that, with the increased capability offered by an AP to verify the absence of undeclared nuclear material and activities (in particular, undeclared enrichment and reprocessing), the Secretariat could, for those states in which it was able to draw the broader conclusion, integrate the measures provided for under the CSA and the AP and tailor the way it implemented safeguards under the state-level for that state.

The conceptual basis for "integrated safeguards" and state-level approaches tailored to its implementation were developed during the early 2000s. Although these state-level approaches reflected some considerations relating to the state as a whole, the primary basis for determining safeguards activities at declared facilities in these states remained the safeguards criteria. In 2001, the IAEA began implementing individual safeguards approaches for states (state-level approaches) on the basis of integrated safeguards. In the 2004 SIR, published in 2005, the term "state-level concept" was used for the first time to describe this process. It was intended as nothing more than another way of describing the development of state-level safeguards approaches tailored to the circumstances of the state concerned—which up until that time had been implemented only in states for which the broader conclusion had been drawn. In that SIR, the Secretariat gave the Member States a heads up that that concept would be extended to all other states with CSAs, and that the next step would be the evolution of safeguards to take full advantage of the information available to the IAEA in order to better focus safeguards activities in all CSAs, given the environment of increasing verification demands and a static safeguards budget.

The next reference to the state-level concept appeared in the Department of Safeguards' long-term strategic plan for 2012-2023. The plan stated that, in its efforts to focus its activities and resources where they mattered most in terms of achieving safeguards objectives, the department would further develop the concept and extend its application to all states. Unfortunately, for reasons that appear to have been not entirely related to the actual implementation of safeguards, a number of Member States actively challenged the state-level concept.[79] What followed was a series of papers prepared by the Secretariat and many consultations with and briefings for the Member States. The issue remains contentious.

The next 60 years?

We have come a long way since 1990. As of September 2020, of the 176 States that have concluded comprehensive safeguards agreements, 143 States had either signed or brought into force an additional protocol to their respective comprehensive safeguards agreement.[80] Four other nonnuclear-weapon states had signed an AP.[81] In addition, another AP had been approved by the Board but had not yet been signed. Together, these accounted for almost 80 percent of the NPT nonnuclear-weapon States. The remaining 38 NPT nonnuclear-weapon states that had yet to bring into force an AP included 33 states that already had a CSA but no AP in force, signed or approved, and five other nonnuclear-weapon-state parties to the NPT that had not brought into force their respective CSAs—collectively described by some as consisting of the "unaware, the unable, and the unwilling."[82]

In 2018, the Vienna Center for Disarmament and Nonproliferation published the results of a study on the impact on nonnuclear-weapon states of the implementation of APs.[83] As the study participants noted, implementation of the AP has not only led to a reduction in the frequency and numbers of IAEA safeguards missions in almost all of the participating states and by Euratom, but has resulted in collateral benefits such as better oversight of nuclear material and related activities, better export and import controls, and improved cooperation between state entities. It has also contributed to a strengthening of the legal and regulatory framework for safety, security, safeguards, emergency preparedness, and improved cooperation with the IAEA. A common theme in participant responses was the indispensability of an AP for a transparent nuclear program, which in turn leads to greater confidence on the part of the international community in the exclusively peaceful nature of states' nuclear programs, increased security, and strengthened cooperation in the nuclear field.

There is still work to do. The IAEA cannot wait for crises to happen for it to evolve further. It must make use of the technological developments in verification and be proactive in addressing evolving risks to the nonproliferation regime. We need to inform the uninformed, build the capacity of those who are unable, and allay the concerns of the unwilling.

Notes

1. The Democratic People's Republic of Korea (DPRK) had become party to the Nuclear Nonproliferation Treaty (NPT) in 1985, but had not yet concluded the required CSA with the IAEA. Press articles raised questions about the possible existence of a previously undisclosed reactor and reprocessing plant in the DPRK. On Iraq, see L. Rockwood, "Non-Proliferation Treaty 1990 Review Conference: Looking Towards 1995," *Nuclear Law Bulletin* 46 (1990), 25–35.
2. The conference ran from August 20, 1990, through the early hours of September 15, 1990.
3. NPT/CONF.IV/45/III, paras. 9–33, at para. 17, reproduced at https://unoda-web.s3-accelerate.amazonaws.com/wp-content/uploads/assets/WMD/Nuclear/pdf/finaldocs/1992%20-%20Geneva%20-%20NPT%20Review%20Conference%20-%20Final%20Document%20Part%20III.pdf.
4. Paragraph 28 of the document referred to in footnote 11 above reads in full as follows: "Recognizes that in the event of questions arising about the commitment to the non-proliferation objectives of the Treaty of any State Party, and in particular about the safeguards coverage of its source or special fissionable materials, there are several courses of action open to the Agency. In such circumstances appropriate steps need to be taken by the Agency and by that State Party, in accordance with the Treaty and the safeguards agreement between them, to help restore confidence. The Conference therefore urges the Agency not to hesitate to take full advantage of its rights, including the use of special inspections as outlined in paragraphs 73 and 77 of INFCIRC/153. The Conference notes that as yet no experience exists of such special inspections, and would welcome a study by the Agency of the possible scope, application and procedures of such inspections, including their implications for the information requirements and policy of the Agency."
5. GC(XXXIV)/OR.323, March 7, 1991, paras. 69–73, at para. 69.
6. GOV/OR.743, February 26, 1991.
7. Ibid., at para.8.

8. Ibid., at paras. 14, 22, and 23.
9. GOV/INF/613, May 29, 1991; GOV/INF/613/ Corr.1, June 4,1991.
10. GOVINF/613/Add.1, August 12, 1991; GOV/INF/613/Add.1/Corr.1, August 15, 1991.
11. South Africa's CSA was approved by the Board of Governors on September 12, 1991, and was signed by South Africa and entered into force on September 16, 1991. GOV/2547/Rev.1, September 11, 1991. The vote on September 12, 1991, was 28 in favor, zero against, and six abstentions (Argentina, Brazil, Cuba, India, Iran, and Iraq) (GOV/OR/762, September 12, 1991, paras. 75–78).
12. GOV/OR/762, September 12, 1991, at para. 65.
13. GC(XXXV)/RES/567, September 20, 1991.
14. GC(XXXV)/OR.333, January 8, 1992, paras. 32–87, at para. 41.
15. Ibid., at paras. 55–58.
16. GC(XXXV)/RES/559, September 20, 1991.
17. GOV/INF/646, January 22, 1992, at Attachment 1, paras. 131–32.
18. Ibid., at Attachment 2, para. 59.
19. GOV/2554, November 12, 1991, Attachment 1 on special inspections (GOV/2554/Att.1) and Attachment 2 on design information (GOV/2554/Att.2).
20. GOV/OR.776, at para. 48.
21. GOV/2554/Att.2/Rev.2, April 1, 1992.
22. GOV/2629, January 22, 1993. The list of specified equipment and nonnuclear material used for the Voluntary Reporting Scheme, taken from Part 1 of the Nuclear Suppliers' Group (NSG) Trigger List, was amended by the Board of Governors on two occasions to take into account modifications to the NSG Trigger List: the first time in December 1994 (GOV/OR.856, paras. 84–89) based on the Secretariat's recommendation set out in GOV/2767 (October 19, 1994); the second time in March 1996 (GOV/OR.889, paras, 130–35) based on the Secretariat's recommendation in GOV/2842 (February 14, 1996) and Corr.1 (March 13, 1996). Thus, the list used as the reference point for the Voluntary Reporting Scheme is as described in INFCIRC/254/Rev2/Part 1 (October 1995).
23. GC(XXXVI)/1017, September 15, 1992, at para. 2.
24. GC(XXXVI)/RES/586, September 25, 1992.
25. Access to the suspected waste sites was not requested because of suspicions of the presence of undeclared nuclear material at those sites, but rather because it was believed that the samples of the waste from those sites could help the IAEA resolve the issues concerning the possibility of undeclared reprocessing by the DPRK.
26. This corresponds to paragraph 18 of INFCIRC/153, which provides that that, "if the Board, upon report of the Director General, decides that an action by the State is essential and urgent in order to ensure verification that nuclear material subject to safeguards under the Agreement is not diverted to nuclear weapons or other nuclear explosive devices the Board shall be able to call upon the State to take the required action without delay, irrespective of whether procedures for the settlement of a dispute have been invoked." See GOV/2636, 25 February 1993.
27. GOV/2645, April 1, 1993.
28. GC(XXXVII)/1075, September 9, 1993.
29. GOV/2657, May 1993.
30. GOV/OR.816, paras. 147–48, June 10, 1993.
31. GC(XXXVII)/OR. 353, October 11, 1993, at paras. 108–9.
32. Ibid. (emphasis added).
33. Ibid.
34. GC(XXXVII)/RES/619, October 1, 1993.

35. "The Agreement of 13 December 1991 between the Republic of Argentina, the Federative Republic Of Brazil, The Brazilian-Argentine Agency for Accounting and Control of Nuclear Materials and the IAEA for the Application of Safeguards," INFCIRC/435.
36. GOV/2698, November 3, 1993.
37. GC(XXXVIII)/17, August 29, 1994, at p. 4.
38. Ibid., at paras. 42–49.
39. GOV/INF/729, February 18, 1994; GOV/INF/737, May 12, 1994; and GOV/739, November 23, 1994.
40. GC(XXXVIII)/RES/10, September 23, 1994.
41. GOV/2784, February 21, 1995, para. 107; see GC(39)/17, August 22, 1995, Annex 1.
42. GOV/OR.862, para. 49; see GC(39)/17, Annex 3 at p. 54.
43. GOV/OR.864, para. 49, and GOV/OR.865, paras. 1, 2, 53; see GC(39)/17, Annex 3, at 58–59 and 63–71.
44. GOV/2807, May 12, 1995; see GC(39)/17, Annex 4.
45. GOV/OR.866, para. 24; see GC(39)/17, para. 12 and Annex 5.
46. GOV/OR.869, 871, and 872; see GC(39)/17, para. 13 and Annex 6.
47. Note to Permanent Missions of Board Members, November 22, 1995; Discussion Draft, 1995-11-21 (GOV/____, 1995).
48. GC(40)/17, para. 9.
49. B. Pellaud (Deputy Director General, Department of Safeguards, IAEA), "Briefing on Discussion Draft II." February 28, 1996.
50. Ibid.
51. GC(40)/17, para. 10.
52. GOV/2863, May 6, 1996; GOV/2863/Corr. 1, May 10, 1996; and GOV/2863/Corr. 2, May 17, 1996. See GC(40)/17, August 23, 1996, Annex 1.
53. Note to Permanent Missions, "Strengthening the Effectiveness and Improving the Efficiency of the Safeguards System," May 6, 1996.
54. GOV/COM.24/INF/1, Attachment, June 26, 1996; see GC(40)/17, August 23, 1996, Annex 3.
55. GC(41)/22, September 17, 1997, Annex 4.
56. GOV/COM.24/3, September 2, 1996.
57. GOV/2885, October 23, 1996; see GC(41)/22, September 17, 1997, Annex 1.
58. Chairman's W.P. 2, October 18, 1996.
59. GOV/2893, February 6, 1997; see GC(41)/22, September 17, 1997.
60. GOV/2914, at Attachment 2, reproduced in GC(41)/22, September 17, 1997, Annex 3.
61. Article 1 of the Model Additional Protocol, as finally agreed, reads as follows: "The provisions of the Safeguards Agreement shall apply to this Protocol to the extent that they are relevant to and compatible with the provisions of the Protocol. In case of conflict between the provisions of the Safeguards Agreement and those of this Protocol, the provisions of this Protocol shall apply."
62. GOV/2914, at Attachment 2, reproduced in GC(41)/22, 17 September 1997, Annex 3.
63. Ibid.
64. Ibid.
65. GOV/2893, reproduced in GC(41)/22, September 17, 1997, Annex 2.
66. GOV/2914, reproduced in GC(41)/22, September 17, 1997, Annex 3.
67. GOV/OR.913, paras. 82, 83; see GC(41)/22, September 17, 1997, Annex 4.
68. GOV/OR.914, paras. 66, 67; see GC(41)/22, September 17, 1997, Annex 4.
69. Reinhard Loosch, "The Additional Protocol as an Important Tool for the Strengthening of the Safeguards System," IAEA-SM-367/1/03, n.d., https://www-pub.iaea.org/MTCD/publications/PDF/ss-2001/PDF%20files/Session%201/Paper%201-03.pdf.

70. GOV/2914, at Attachment 3, reproduced in GC(41)/22, September 17, 1997, Annex 3.
71. See e.g., GC(XXXIV)/915, "The Annual Report for 1989," IAEA, July 1990, 102; and GC(XXXV)/953, "The Annual Report for 1990," IAEA, July 1991, 106.
72. GC(XXXVII)/OR.353, October 11, 1993, at paras. 108–9.
73. Footnote 2 to GOV/2653, to which the director general referred, read as follows: "The probability of detecting a diversion of nuclear material in an amount less than one significant quantity is lower than that of detecting a diversion of one significant quantity. The probability depends on the amount of nuclear material concerned and the technical measures and the resources available." The same text featured as footnotes in the Safeguards Implementation Reports for 1993 and 1994 as well.
74. GOV/2000/23, May 12, 2000, Safeguards Implementation Report for 1999, 1.
75. Ibid.
76. GOV/2001/21, May 4, 2001, Background to the Safeguards Statement for 2000, at para. 9.
77. The 2001 conclusion related to "all nuclear material in those States"; the 2002 conclusion referred to "all nuclear material in the State or under its jurisdiction or control"; and the 2003 conclusion referred to "all nuclear material within the territories of those States, under their jurisdiction or under their control anywhere."
78. The full sentence in the 2003 Safeguards Statement read: "Only for such states are Agency safeguards able to provide credible assurance not only regarding the non-diversion of nuclear material but also regarding the absence of undeclared nuclear material and activities."
79. For an analysis of the debate about the state-level concept see L. Rockwood, "The IAEA's State-Level Concept and the Law of Unintended Consequences," *Arms Control Today*, August 2014, https://www.armscontrol.org/act/2014_09/Features/The-IAEAs-State-Level-Concept-and-the-Law-of-Unintended-Consequences.
80. Each of the five nuclear-weapon states and India have also concluded APs, but the scope of those APs varied considerably.
81. Four of these 14 nonnuclear-weapon states simultaneously signed their respective CSAs, which had not come into force as of September 2020.
82. Unknown attribution cited during a public talk by Christopher Ford, U.S. assistant secretary of state for international security and nonproliferation, at the Vienna Center for Disarmament and Non-Proliferation on September 19, 2018.
83. "Evaluation of the Impact of the Model Additional Protocol on Non-Nuclear-Weapon States with Comprehensive Safeguards Agreements," financed and published by the Swedish Radiation Safety Authority, No. 2018:23 (ISSN 2000-0456), 2018 (available at www.stralsakerhetsmyndigheten.se and reproduced in https://vcdnp.org/vcdnp-report-on-the-impact-of-the-model-additional-protocol-from-a-state-perspective/).

6 The IAEA after six decades

Why I still like Ike

Daniel Poneman

> Today, the United States' stockpile of atomic weapons, which, of course, increases daily, exceeds by many times the explosive equivalent of the total of all bombs and all shells that came from every plane and every gun in every theatre of war in all of the years of World War II… . But the dread secret, and the fearful engines of atomic might, are not ours alone.
>
> President Dwight D. Eisenhower
> Address Before the General Assembly of the United Nations
> December 8, 1953

For more than three generations, President Dwight D. "Ike" Eisenhower's "Atoms for Peace" speech has served as the touchstone of U.S. nonproliferation policy. Even today, Ike's vision for peaceful nuclear cooperation remains resonant and relevant, as do his warnings about the catastrophic consequences of failure. From one generation to the next, thoughtful leaders around the world have taken up his call "to find the way by which the miraculous inventiveness of man shall not be dedicated to his death, but consecrated to his life."[1]

The Atoms for Peace initiative stands as one of President Eisenhower's most important legacies. It also represents one of the greatest success stories of the postwar era: almost 65 years later, atomic energy provides more than 10 percent of the world's electricity needs but has never again been unleashed as a weapon of war. To be sure, there have been many near-misses and dangerous moments along the way, but that does not diminish the profound importance and enduring value of what has been achieved.

In March 1963, President Kennedy offered a grim prediction:

> By 1970, unless we are successful, there may be 10 nuclear powers instead of four, and by 1975, 15 or 20… . I see the possibility in the 1970s of the President of the United States having to face a world in which 15 or 20 or 25 nations may have these weapons. I regard that as the greatest possible danger and hazard.[2]

DOI: 10.4324/9781003160205-6

Hindsight might suggest that he was overly pessimistic, but a happier outcome was not foreordained. The scenario he predicted was avoided not through wishful thinking, but rather through clear-eyed strategy driving determined efforts, sustained from one president to the next, with the support of the United States' allies and vital institutions like the International Atomic Energy Agency (IAEA). Of course, the possibility that a tragic miscalculation, nuclear-armed terrorists, or hostile states will unleash the furies continues to be a source of constant danger to all humanity.

Realizing the vision of Atoms for Peace remains an unfinished work, one that demands continued vigilance from governments, industry, nongovernmental organizations, and other stakeholders. For example, in his Atoms for Peace speech, President Eisenhower called for the IAEA to oversee a "bank of fissionable material" that would be "essentially immune to surprise seizure," and would "devise methods whereby this fissionable material would be allocated to serve the peaceful pursuits of mankind."[3] His notion of an IAEA fuel bank was a good idea—one whose time has finally come. On August 29, 2017, the IAEA inaugurated its fuel bank in Kazakhstan, which will provide important fuel security assurances to nations that live up to their nonproliferation commitments. In doing so, it will help remove incentives that nonweapon states might feel they have to build their own indigenous fuel-cycle capabilities that could lead to the diversion of enriched uranium to explosive uses. The fuel bank is only the latest reminder of how the IAEA remains a critical bulwark of the global order, an indispensable institution to the peace and security of the world, and how each generation has an obligation to strengthen the institution.

Like most of the international institutions established in the postwar period, the IAEA has always had critics in the United States. Some argue that international institutions limit U.S. sovereignty and constrain U.S. influence. In a narrow sense, that may be true. The need to act in concert with others necessarily entails compromise from the unvarnished preferences of any one actor, including the United States. But to the degree that the resulting decisions can be enforced through a number of sovereign entities, and can be sustained over the long term because they bear the imprimatur of international legitimacy conferred through collective action, these international institutions can act as a force multiplier. Indeed, most of these institutions—the United Nations (UN), the International Monetary Fund, the World Bank, the General Agreement on Tariffs and Trade (later the World Trade Organization), and many others—initially were proposed by U.S. leaders who realized that the United States could advance its interests more by enlisting support and leveraging its efforts through many other governments than it could ever achieve by going it alone. These institutions, along with security treaties and organizations such as NATO, not only extended the global reach of the United States but also conferred a strong measure of legitimacy that unilateral actions could never attain.

The history of the past seven decades offers ample proof that these institutions have extended, not constrained, the reach of American influence.

The IAEA came a few years later than the others, but it is very much part of that heritage. In the summer of 1957, the U.S. Senate ratified the treaty establishing the IAEA. Ohio senator John Bricker, who advocated a constitutional amendment limiting the president's ability to make international agreements, called the treaty "an act of suicidal folly."[4] So has the IAEA diluted or extended U.S. influence? I had the opportunity to work with the IAEA on several occasions during my time in government, working for Republican and Democratic presidents, in addressing the serious challenges posed by the nuclear programs in Iran, Iraq, and North Korea. In every case, I found that the IAEA served an indispensable role that the United States could not have achieved unilaterally.

When it comes to nonproliferation, the proposition that the United States can unilaterally impose its nonproliferation preferences cannot be supported by the historical evidence. It does not have enough authority to impose that kind of outcome around the world. It can do many things, but not everything. This reality is even more true today than it was in Eisenhower's day, when the United States was the undisputed leader in nuclear technology and the sole supplier of nuclear fuel outside the Soviet bloc. The United States has not maintained its leadership position—indeed, it can no longer meet its own fuel requirements, much less serve as the ultimate nuclear fuel provider for friends, partners, and allies. The United States is no longer the alpha and omega in all things nuclear. Without close cooperation with other countries and governments that have the means to exercise their will and to provide support, U.S. nuclear policies will be doomed to fail on the global stage. And absent an institution with global credibility for independence and strong subject-matter expertise—such as the IAEA—it is hard to imagine the individual preferences of the United States, or any other individual government for that matter, commanding sufficient credibility to sustain the international support, including UN Security Council resolutions, that are critical to imposing the will of the international community upon a state that has fallen out of compliance with its nonproliferation obligations.

The toughest cases will require a watchdog as well as a bulldog—or perhaps a pack of bulldogs. The IAEA's strong technical capabilities in detecting violations of nonproliferation commitments must be backed up through collective action undertaken by a united, determined community of nations. The threat of force can only be credible when those nations agree that there is a strong basis for collective action. The credibility of a neutral arbiter can provide that kind of strong basis, and over its history, the IAEA has attained that level of credibility. So, with six decades of experience with the IAEA, it is worth reflecting on the history of the organization and what lessons we can glean for the benefit of those who come after us. From having worked with the IAEA in several different roles through the years, I would like to recount four particular episodes that should help to demonstrate why the IAEA matters so profoundly.

Iraq

In 1990, soon after I joined the staff of the National Security Council (NSC), which at that time was led by National Security Advisor Brent Scowcroft and Deputy National Security Advisor Robert Gates, I read a front-page article in the *Washington Times* about an intelligence assessment of Iraq's nuclear-weapon capabilities.[5] (This was in the fall of 1990, back when newspapers were delivered to our doorsteps, not to our iPhones.) I had been hired as the first full-time nonproliferation director on the NSC staff in many years, reflecting the growing concern that President George H. W. Bush and his national security team had about the risk of the spread of nuclear weapons. So, I was surprised to be reading in the newspaper about an intelligence assessment in my area of responsibility that had not crossed my desk. Naturally, I called over to the people who would have been responsible for preparing such a document, blithely assuming that because the assessment had been splashed across the pages of the *Washington Times*, surely they would send it to me without delay. Wrong! I was told that because the document had not been fully coordinated, I could not receive a copy.

The gist of the news report was that in the years leading up to the Iraqi invasion of Kuwait, the risk that Iraq's Saddam Hussein might be developing nuclear weapons had been underrated. At the time, the U.S. intelligence community was criticized for "politicizing the intelligence"—that is, of hyping the Iraqi nuclear-weapon threat in the context of building international support for opposing Saddam's actions in Kuwait. But I did not see it that way. To the contrary, when a dictator like Saddam demonstrates such a brazen willingness to flout international law and crush a neighboring country, it seemed reasonable to conclude that perhaps his commitment to the full and faithful compliance with his nation's IAEA safeguards obligations and Nuclear Nonproliferation Treaty (NPT) treaty commitments also might be less than absolute.

Of course, after Operation Desert Storm, the world discovered that Saddam had in fact built a clandestine nuclear-weapon program. By January 1991, it had become clear to the IAEA that Iraq had researched processes for enriching uranium, extracting highly enriched uranium material from research reactors to create a nuclear weapon, and developing crude radiation weapons.[6] Prior to the war, the international community had fallen far short of gaining a clear enough picture of his true capabilities and intentions. The subsequent revelations suggested that the IAEA had placed too much trust in the nation-state being inspected, lacked sufficient authorities and unfettered access to suspect sites, and may have needed a stronger "enforcement culture"—inherently difficult in an organization dedicated to both promoting the peaceful use of the atom and to policing its possible misuse. Similar concerns over the dual mission of the U.S. Atomic Energy Commission—between promoting and regulating the use of the atom—led the U.S. Congress in 1974 to split that agency into the Energy Research and Development Administration (subsequently the U.S. Department of Energy) and the Nuclear Regulatory Commission.

After the Gulf War, the United States joined with other nations to develop a much more aggressive regime of monitoring and inspections. In April 1991, UN Security Council Resolution 687 set terms and conditions for a cease-fire between Iraq and the international coalition formed to oppose Saddam Hussein's invasion of Kuwait. To assist the IAEA in carrying out inspections and implementing provisions of the cease-fire related to nuclear issues, the resolution also established the United Nations Special Commission (UNSCOM), chartered to "carry out immediate on-site inspection of Iraq's biological, chemical and missile capabilities." The resolution also called on the IAEA, with assistance from UNSCOM, to conduct "immediate on-site inspection of Iraq's nuclear capabilities" and develop a plan for "the destruction, removal or rendering harmless" of Iraq's nuclear program.[7] Iraq agreed to give UNSCOM broad rights to "unrestricted freedom of movement without advance notice" throughout Iraq and "unimpeded access to any site or facility" as part of its inspection protocols.[8] UN Secretary-General Javier Pérez de Cuéllar appointed a talented Swedish diplomat, Rolf Ekéus, as the first executive chairman of UNSCOM. Assisting Ekéus would be two veteran U.S. diplomats with long experience dealing with nuclear issues: State Department nonproliferation specialist Robert Gallucci and IAEA inspector David Kay.

In June 1991, Bob Gallucci called me at the White House from a parking lot in Iraq. The inspection team he was leading had obviously caught the Iraqis red-handed, because the team was denied access to the facility for 72 hours while the Iraqis removed nuclear material and crates of equipment from the site. Iraq drew international condemnation for the incident.[9] A few days later, the dogged team traced the crates to a remote site 40 miles west of Baghdad. While waiting to gain access to the facility, Kay sent two inspectors to climb a nearby water tower. When they reached the top, the inspectors could see Iraqi cargo trucks being loaded up with heavy machinery. The pair radioed to Kay, who sent his team in pursuit of the Iraqi trucks, capturing photos and video. Panicked Iraqi soldiers fired some warning shots at them, ensuring that the incident would command worldwide attention.[10] It turned out that the trucks contained massive, 60-ton magnets—the critical component to a calutron, used for uranium enrichment.

Of course, at the same time that UNSCOM was doing its work, the IAEA continued to seek to discharge its own responsibilities. So naturally, a bureaucratic struggle ensued between UNSCOM and the IAEA over who would have responsibility over the inspections that were intended to identify and then eliminate Iraq's nuclear-weapon-related assets and activities. Eventually, an uneasy arrangement for coexistence was achieved.

In 1998, Iraq announced it would no longer comply with the inspections regime, stating that sanctions would not be lifted while Saddam Hussein remained in power and claiming that the U.S. inspectors had been sent as spies. The United States and Britain responded with four days of bombings and cruise missile attacks targeting suspected nuclear sites. This military intervention and the end of Iraqi compliance with the inspections regime prevented the IAEA from definitively confirming what it had suggested in an October 1997 report—that Iraq no longer had the capacity to produce significant amounts of weapons-grade nuclear material, let alone develop a nuclear weapon.[11]

A few weeks after the bombings, the *New York Times* confirmed that U.S. intelligence operatives had indeed "used the United Nations inspection team to send an American spy into Baghdad to install a highly sophisticated electronic eavesdropping system."[12] When inspectors eventually returned to Iraq, their access was limited—and so was any appetite among the international community to enforce a more robust inspection regime. The efforts of UNSCOM and the IAEA were further complicated as their financial resources dwindled after Iraq's "unfrozen assets" ran out. By the end of the 1990s, the IAEA Iraq Action Team received a budget of $3 million, while some anticipated that the IAEA's ongoing monitoring and verification (OMV) efforts would require close to $10–$12 million.[13] In December 1998, UNSCOM Executive Chairman Richard Butler wrote to UN Secretary General Kofi Annan that Iraq "did not provide the full cooperation it promised" to UNSCOM and had restricted UNSCOM's work to the point where the commission was "not able to conduct the substantive disarmament work mandated to it by the Security Council and, thus, to give the Council the assurances it requires with respect to Iraq's prohibited weapons programmes."[14]

In December 1999, the UN Security Council passed Resolution 1284, which established UNSCOM's successor, the UN Monitoring, Inspections, and Verification Commission (UNMOVIC). Formed as a subsidiary body to the UN Security Council, UNMOVIC continued UNSCOM's mandate to disarm Iraq's weapons of mass destruction and maintain OMV efforts. Resolution 1284 also erased limits on Iraqi oil sales and allowed for the easing of international sanctions on Iraq, funneling a portion of these revenues to UNMOVIC and granting it a larger pool of funding than UNSCOM had been able to access. UNMOVIC aimed to recoup the international credibility UNSCOM had lost in late 1998 and reinvigorate international enthusiasm for an inspection regime.[15] Given Iraq's refusal to deal not only with UNSCOM but also with UN nuclear inspectors in general, however, UNMOVIC spent the better part of three years between 1999 and 2002 outside of Iraq, identifying priority sites for inspection, training inspectors, and developing new OMV capabilities. Its innovations included smaller radiation sensors, portable chemical and biological weapons detectors, and ground-penetrating radar.[16] By the time Iraq surrendered to political and military pressures from the UN, United States, and United Kingdom in December 2002, UNMOVIC was well prepared to begin immediate inspections.

Over the 111 days before the United States invaded Iraq in March 2003, UNMOVIC conducted 731 inspections at 411 sites, including 88 sites that had not been inspected in the past. As with UNSCOM, Iraq's cooperation with UNMOVIC was uneven. Although the U.S. invasion cut short many of UNMOVIC's OMV initiatives, UNMOVIC found neither undeclared weapons of mass destruction nor the capability to develop them. The evidence suggested that Iraq had ended its weapons programs in 1991, just before the beginning of UNSCOM's mandate. UNMOVIC did detect Iraqi violations of the 150-kilometer-range limit, but it did not find alleged hidden batteries of Scud missiles.[17] By 2007, with OMV efforts largely turned over to the United States and the United Kingdom, the UN Security Council moved to terminate the mandates of UNMOVIC and the IAEA in Iraq.[18]

Looking back, for the IAEA, the Iraq inspections were a coming-of-age experience. Before 1991, to some degree, the Agency had become a prisoner of a false premise: the notion that all Member States were being forthright in terms of compliance with their NPT and IAEA safeguards obligations. The IAEA likewise played it straight, and was played for a fool by Saddam Hussein. That humiliation drove IAEA Director General Hans Blix and the Agency to formulate a strong resolve to repair its damaged credibility through a more rigorous approach to fulfilling its safeguards obligations, and appropriately rebalancing the IAEA's promotional and regulatory missions.

The former Soviet Union

During the early 1990s, as the IAEA worked to put an effective inspection regime in place in Iraq, it faced another crisis: the breakup of the former Soviet Union, and the question of what would become of its vast nuclear arsenal. Suddenly, the world faced the specter that out of the ashes of the former Soviet Union would emerge *four* nuclear-weapon states: Russia, Ukraine, Kazakhstan, and Belarus. Fortunately, through visionary leadership and skilled diplomacy, all of the former Soviet weapons ended up either being destroyed or sent to Russia. On December 26, 1991, the day the Soviet Union dissolved, Ukraine, Kazakhstan, and Belarus all gave up possession of the nuclear weapons held in their territory.

Each of the former Soviet republics had its unique story with nuclear weapons, and its unique motivations. In the case of Kazakhstan, the story of nuclear weapons is inexorably bound up with the history of the Semipalatinsk test site, where the Soviet Union had conducted 456 nuclear-weapon tests, going back to its first atomic bomb blast in 1949.[19] The people of the region had suffered grievously from these tests. Roughly 1.5 million of them experienced radiation exposure. By one estimate, the rates of cancer, dystrophy, spontaneous abortion, and mental illness were two to three times higher in the surrounding area than in the nation as a whole, and more than 10 percent of children born in the neighboring Karagandy Region had birth defects.[20] History will always honor President Nursultan Nazarbayev's decision on August 29, 1991, to close the Semipalatinsk test site and to agree to send all of the 1,410 nuclear weapons on Kazakh soil back to Russia.

This was a pivotal moment for nonproliferation writ large, and the IAEA played a key role in fulfilling that commitment, starting with negotiating the applicable safeguards agreement.

But the removal of the weapons themselves was not the end of the story. In November 1994, three of the U.S. Air Force's massive C-5 Galaxy cargo planes lumbered down a snowy runway in a remote corner of Kazakhstan. Their high-stakes mission, codenamed Project Sapphire, was a closely guarded secret. The airmen completed several mid-air refuelings so they could fly direct to Dover Air Force Base, a distance of more than 6,000 miles. On board was a precious and potentially deadly cargo: 600 kilograms of highly enriched uranium. The material, enough to produce two dozen nuclear bombs, had been held in a concrete warehouse with a dirt floor, secured by what was described as a "Civil War padlock."[21] With the help and oversight of the IAEA, the material was down-blended into civilian nuclear fuel for peaceful use, ensuring that it could never again threaten humanity.

Many years later, in an effort that spanned three presidential administrations, the United States and Kazakhstan cooperated in moving 3,000 kilograms of plutonium contained in spent fuel from the BN-350 breeder reactor located at Aktau near the shores of the Caspian Sea, almost 1,900 miles across Kazakhstan to Semi (as Semipalatinsk was then known), a far safer location. The plutonium remains there under effective IAEA safeguards to this day, sealed inside massive, 110-ton storage casks. I had the privilege to see these massive casks at Aktau in 2009 before they snaked their way by rail across Kazakhstan, as well as to see them safely located at their final destination in 2011.

The IAEA's decision to select Kazakhstan to host its international fuel bank recognized the strong commitment Kazakhstan had made to nonproliferation ever since its 1991 founding as an independent nation. It sent an important message to the world that nonproliferation is a collective enterprise, reflecting a shared international effort based on the contributions of many nations. Kazakhstan, which is home to 40 percent of the world's uranium resources, has thus become an important global player in both nuclear energy and nuclear nonproliferation.[22] It is worth noting that the president of Kazakhstan has explicitly affirmed that the choice to denuclearize was a strategic decision. He argued that the economic growth that Kazakhstan has experienced since 1991 and the willingness of international oil companies to invest there resulted from this decision, and would not have happened had Kazakhstan not demonstrated its bona fides to be a good global citizen on matters of nonproliferation.

North Korea

The IAEA also played an indispensable role in addressing the North Korean nuclear crisis of the early 1990s. One cannot understand the role of the IAEA, or the approach of Hans Blix, its Director General at the time, without reference to the Iraqi experience. As mentioned earlier, in Iraq, the IAEA had focused on its safeguards responsibilities with respect to Iraq's declared facilities. When Iraq was discovered in the aftermath of the Gulf War to have had a much more elaborate nuclear-weapon development effort that had escaped detection by the IAEA, it led to severe embarrassment. Significant efforts to strengthen the international safeguards system were then undertaken, such as the development of the Additional Protocol, and Director General Blix was determined to be vigilant in implementing its safeguards responsibilities.

When North Korea submitted its safeguards agreement under the NPT to the IAEA in 1992—five years later than requested—IAEA inspectors discovered that that declaration appeared to fall short of disclosing all of North Korea's nuclear activities. In addition to a previously declared small Soviet-supplied research reactor, North Korea's safeguards agreement included "a 5 MW(e) graphite moderated Magnox type reactor, a fuel fabrication plant, a 'radiochemical laboratory' (in reality, a reprocessing plant) and two much larger Magnox reactors of 50 MW(e) and 200 MW(e) under construction."[23] The presence of the three Magnox reactors, which were similar to the ones the United Kingdom had used to produce plutonium for its nuclear weapons in the 1950s, suggested that North Korea was pursuing a nuclear-weapon program.

Further IAEA analysis uncovered more evidence. A small amount of plutonium supplied to the IAEA revealed that North Korea had engaged in several plutonium-reprocessing campaigns, although North Korean officials insisted that they had only conducted one in 1991. This discovery indicated that North Korea may have disclosed less plutonium than it actually possessed. Satellite imagery from the United States also showed two undisclosed nuclear waste facilities in North Korea that had been camouflaged in order to escape detection by the international community.[24]

Hoping to clarify the questions raised by North Korea's safeguards agreement, the IAEA requested access to the two waste facilities. North Korea refused, arguing that the facilities were military installations.[25] This standoff precipitated a February 1993 request by the IAEA to conduct a special inspection in North Korea—which, in turn, precipitated Pyongyang's announcement that it intended to withdraw from the NPT.[26] Thus began a harrowing 18-month effort to persuade North Korea to stay in the treaty; stop its plutonium production program; and place its spent fuel pond containing 8,000 spent fuel rods (holding enough plutonium to make five or six bombs) under seals, camera surveillance, and on-site inspections.

What was the role of the IAEA in this saga? The United States was able to justify its diplomatic engagement with North Korea by citing the IAEA judgment that North Korea had preserved the "continuity of safeguards."[27] Blix had invented this term, which referred to the fact that even though Pyongyang was not fully complying with its current safeguards obligations, it was at least refraining from actions that would prevent the IAEA from one day analyzing North Korea's past nuclear activities and seeking to reconcile its safeguards declaration with the evidence contained in those spent fuel rods. U.S. diplomats had worked hard to sustain the tissue of connectivity between the IAEA and the North Koreans, to enable the Agency to continue to support the proposition that continuity of safeguards was being maintained in North Korea. But talks broke down in March 1994, as the North Koreans refused to allow inspectors access to its plutonium production reactor in Yongbyon and then threatened to engulf Seoul in "a sea of fire."[28]

North Korea then crossed one of the "red lines" the United States had set. It defueled the Yongbyon reactor in a way that prevented Agency inspectors reconstructing the operating history of the reactor. As a result, the IAEA announced that it could no longer confirm the continuity of safeguards. The United States broke off discussions with Pyongyang and began working in the UN Security Council on a resolution to impose sanctions. The Clinton administration also advanced consideration of its options for a massive military buildup in South Korea.

In the midst of this escalating crisis, former U.S. president Jimmy Carter took it upon himself to go to North Korea to meet with President Kim Il-Sung in June 1994. Carter's intervention occasioned significant concern at the White House, as it was clear that the former president's approach to the North Korean nuclear challenge was not consistent with U.S. policy at that time. Carter intended to focus on defusing the confrontation, even at the risk of easing nonproliferation demands on Pyongyang, whereas U.S. policy was focused on bringing Pyongyang back into compliance with nonproliferation norms, even at the risk of intensifying the confrontation. This divergence complicated U.S. efforts to move the issue to the UN Security Council with a view to imposing sanctions against North Korea in response to Pyongyang's flouting of the IAEA and global nonproliferation norms. That said, Carter's personal intervention gave the North Koreans an opportunity to retreat from their defiant posture and, ultimately, to agree to shut down their 5-megawatt reactor, abandon plans to build two larger reactors, abandon plutonium reprocessing, and to place the 8,000 spent fuel rods under the IAEA's requested safeguards. In exchange, the United States, South Korea, and Japan agreed to provide North Korea with two light-water reactors and, until those reactors began operations, 500,000 tons of heavy fuel oil each year to support North Korea's energy requirements.

The Agreed Framework successfully bottled-up North Korea's plutonium-based nuclear-weapon program until 2002, when Pyongyang's pursuit of a clandestine uranium-enrichment program led to a breakdown in diplomacy with the United States, collapse of the Agreed Framework and, in 2006, the first North Korean nuclear-weapon test. To this day, the North Korean nuclear challenge remains among the gravest threats facing the region and the world. If a new and binding agreement can be reached with North Korea to denuclearize, the IAEA will once again play a pivotal role in verifying compliance. In June 2018, as President Donald Trump and Chairman Kim Jong-Un convened their historic summit in Singapore, IAEA Director General Yukiya Amano signaled that the IAEA "stands ready to undertake any verification activities in the DPRK that it may be requested to conduct."[29]

Iran

In 2009, after just a few months on the job as deputy secretary of energy and just weeks after the leaders of the United States, France, and the United Kingdom jointly announced that Iran had been secretly constructing its Fordow enrichment facility deep inside a mountain outside the city of Qom, I was surprised to receive a call from Deputy National Security Advisor Tom Donilon, asking me to go to Vienna to lead negotiations with Iran about their nuclear program. During an earlier round of diplomatic discussions between Iran and the P5+1 (China, France, Germany, Russia, the United Kingdom, and the United States) in Geneva, the Iranians had suggested that they might be willing to allow a substantial amount of low-enriched uranium (LEU) that they had enriched to around 3 percent uranium-235 (U-235) be sent out of the country in exchange for higher assay (20 percent U-235) enriched uranium that would be imported to supply the Tehran Research Reactor, an important source of radioisotopes used for medical purposes in Iran. The IAEA would be hosting the talks.

At first, I demurred, suggesting that it would be more appropriate to send a State Department negotiator to lead the delegation. Donilon replied that Deputy Secretary of State Bill Burns had already been engaged at the diplomatic level, and that the talks in Vienna were supposed to be led at a technical level. The U.S. side wanted Iran to send the head of the Atomic Energy Organization of Iran, the MIT-trained nuclear engineer Ali Akbar Salehi, as the head of delegation. Donilon reasoned that sending a U.S. delegation led by a deputy secretary would deny the Iranians an excuse to send a lower-level representative on the pretext of the rules of protocol. Of course, the White House calls the shots, so I went, though in the end the Iranian side was led not by Salehi (who directed the Iranian negotiating positions from Tehran) but rather by their IAEA ambassador, Ali Asghar Soltanieh.

And so I was sent off to Vienna. The talks were hosted by Mohamed ElBaradei, then serving in his final weeks as IAEA Director General. Aside from the United States, the other parties to the talks were Russia, France, and Iran. The U.S. team included top experts from across the government, including leading State Department diplomats Bob Einhorn and Jim Timbie.

By this time, Iran's centrifuge program had already produced around 1,400 kilograms LEU with an enrichment level below 5 percent U-235.[30] The Tehran Research Reactor operated on 20 percent LEU, below the level needed for nuclear weapons but needing much less effort to further enrich into weapons-grade material.[31] The negotiations aimed to persuade Iran to ship its existing stockpile of less-than-5-percent LEU to an established foreign enricher, where it would be further enriched up to the 20 percent level, rather than expanding its own capabilities to do this domestically. Critically, the fuel would be returned to Iran in the form of metal fuel rods that would be suitable for the research reactor, but that could not readily be fed back into centrifuges for further enrichment into weapons-grade material.[32]

The nonproliferation logic of the proposed transaction was clear. If Iran had enriched its less-than-5-percent LEU to 20-percent LEU, it would be far closer to producing highly enriched uranium (HEU) suitable for use in nuclear weapons. Indeed, when the feed material for centrifuges is 20 percent U-235 instead of the 0.711 percent U-235 found in nature, the amount of work required to produce HEU drops by a factor of more than 10.[33] Reducing Iran's stocks of LEU and removing the pretext to go from less-than-5-percent to 20-percent LEU would directly reduce the proliferation threat posed by Tehran's growing nuclear program. In exchange for agreeing to this transaction, Tehran would obtain the 20-percent LEU needed to refuel the Tehran Research Reactor, and thus to sustain the production of radioisotopes needed for medical diagnostics and treatment in Iran. In addition, it would enable Iran to demonstrate peaceful intentions and perhaps serve as a confidence-building measure that could set the stage for a broader agreement expanding international oversight of its nuclear program.

In welcoming the parties to the talks on October 19, 2009, Director General ElBaradei emphasized that the IAEA was hosting the talks as an honest broker, a neutral arbiter with no mandate beyond facilitating the engagement of the other parties. In the talks, the French quickly offered to supply the 20-percent LEU fuel to the Tehran Research Reactor. The Iranians rejected this offer. They asserted that France was not a reliable supplier, citing the difficult history of their past investment in France's enrichment enterprise. Prior to the 1979 Iranian Revolution, Iran was a co-financing partner of a multinational joint venture called Eurodif. This included a $1 billion loan to the French Atomic Energy Commission by the Shah of Iran, Mohammad Reza Pahlavi, in 1974, for which Iran was entitled to purchase enriched uranium. After the revolution, however, a range of factors (including Tehran's halting of payments to Eurodif and Western sanctions) resulted in Eurodif never delivering any nuclear fuel to Iran. To respond to Tehran's professed concern about France, Moscow's lead negotiator, Nikolay Spasskiy, offered that Russia would backstop the French offer, and step in to supply should the French fail to perform. Still, the Iranians resisted. Then ElBaradei stepped in. Going beyond his initial posture as a mere convener and honest broker of the talks, the Director General took the initiative to offer that, should *both* France and Russia fail to perform, then the IAEA itself would step in and guarantee the supply of material for the Tehran Research Reactor. On this basis, a deal was finally struck.

In diplomatic terms, the Tehran Research Reactor agreement was ad referendum, meaning that the terms agreed in Vienna had to be reviewed by the home governments of each negotiator. In the end, France, Russia, and the United States all accepted the agreement, but the Iranian government did not. Four months earlier, in June 2009, hardline President Mahmoud Ahmadinejad secured a second term in a hotly contested election amid allegations of widespread election fraud, sparking massive protests across Iran. Against a backdrop of continued election-related unrest and political infighting, Ahmadinejad's political opponents denounced the deal, unwilling to allow him to gain a political victory. Faced with a growing backlash, including from prominent conservatives with close ties to Supreme Leader Ali Khamenei (including Majles Speaker Ali Larijani), Ahmadinejad backed out of the deal—even though his own government had been the first to suggest it.[34]

Despite the disappointing result in the midst of Iran's internal turmoil, this early effort showed the constructive role the IAEA could play in dealing with the world's toughest nonproliferation challenges. The IAEA continued to do so in the years between the Tehran Research Reactor negotiations and the ultimate conclusion of the Joint Comprehensive Plan of Action (JCPOA) in 2015, which reduced the Iranian nuclear threat by capping the number of Iranian centrifuges and quantities of enriched uranium, disabling the Arak reactor (and thus blocking the way to weapon-usable plutonium production), and other measures, all to be monitored under the Agency's watchful eye. As a result of the JCPOA, the IAEA's inspectors collectively spend 3,000 days per year on the ground in Iran, and the Agency has installed tamper-proof seals on nuclear materials and equipment. Inspections are backed up by a network of surveillance cameras at sites throughout Iran, which the agency monitors on a daily basis.[35] The Trump administration withdrew from the JCPOA in May 2018, and its future is uncertain. However, because of the robust use of the IAEA's capabilities and authorities, coupled with its unique ability to gain greater cooperation than national governments owing to its credibility as an honest broker, the JCPOA showed that Agency could be an indispensable tool to reducing global nuclear threats.

Conclusion

Each of these four cases provided a front-row seat to the history of the IAEA and the important role it has played in advancing the peaceful use of the atom. President Eisenhower's vision of Atoms for Peace underpins today's global nonproliferation regime. And the IAEA has been indispensable to advancing that vision.

The duality that Eisenhower articulated—the great benefits from the peaceful uses of the atom, coexisting with the incalculable damage that nuclear weapons can inflict—remains one of the greatest challenges facing the planet. And in seeking to maximizing those benefits while minimizing the risks, the IAEA must continue to play a pivotal role in fulfilling the aspiration that President Eisenhower expressed so well: "to help us move out of the dark chamber of horrors into the light, to find a way by which the minds of men, the hopes of men, the souls of men everywhere, can move forward toward peace and happiness and well being."[36]

Notes

1. "Atoms for Peace Speech [December 8, 1953]," International Atomic Energy Agency (IAEA), https://www.iaea.org/about/history/atoms-for-peace-speech.
2. President John F. Kennedy, News Conference at the State Department, March 21, 1963 at https://www.jfklibrary.org/archives/other-resources/john-f-kennedy-press-conferences/news-conference-52
3. "Atoms for Peace Speech."
4. United Press International via *Lead Daily Call* (S. Dak.), June 18, 1957.
5. Bill Gertz and Rowan Scarborough, "Saddam Close to Nuclear Weapon," *Washington Times*, November 28, 1991.
6. Gary B. Dillon, "The IAEA in Iraq: Past Activities and Findings," *IAEA Bulletin* 44, no. 2 (June 2002), https://www.iaea.org/sites/default/files/publications/magazines/bulletin/bull44-2/44201251316.pdf.
7. United Nations Security Council Resolution 687, April 3, 1991, sections 8–14, http://unscr.com/en/resolutions/doc/687.
8. "UN Special Commission (UNSCOM)," United Nations Special Commission, December 1999, https://www.un.org/Depts/unscom/unscom.htm.
9. "Iraq Moved Nuclear Material While Delaying Inspection, U.S. Charges," Associated Press, June 26, 1991.
10. "Saddam's Secret Bomb," *Sunday Herald Sun*, December 8, 1991.
11. "Note by the UN Secretary General, October 8, 1997," https://www.nci.org/i/iaea-779.htm.
12. Tim Weiner, "U.S. Used U.N. Team to Place Spy Device in Iraq, Aides Say," *New York Times*, January 9, 1999, https://www.nytimes.com/1999/01/08/world/us-used-un-team-to-place-spy-device-in-iraq-aides-say.html.
13. Dillon, "The IAEA in Iraq."
14. "Letter, dated 15 December 1998 from the Secretary-General addressed to the President of the Security Council," S/1998/1172, December 15, 1998, https://www.un.org/Depts/unscom/s98-1172.htm.
15. United Nations Security Council Resolution 1284, December 17, 1999, sections 15–32, https://www.un.org/Depts/unscom/Keyresolutions/sres99-1284.htm.
16. Trevor Findlay, "Looking Back: The U.N. Monitoring, Verification, and Inspection Commission." Arms Control Association, September 2005, https://www.armscontrol.org/act/2005-09/looking-back-un-monitoring-verification-inspection-commission#note04.
17. Findlay, "Looking Back."
18. United Nations Security Council Resolution 1762, June 29, 2007, http://unscr.com/en/resolutions/1762.
19. Rachel Oswald, "Fifty Years After Above-Ground Blasts, A Sense of Calm at Kazakhstani Nuclear Site," Global Security Newswire, Nuclear Threat Initiative, September 3, 2013, https://www.nti.org/gsn/article/fifty-years-after-blasts-kazakhstani-nuclear-site/.
20. Facility profile of the Semipalatinsk Test Site, Nuclear Threat Initiative, accessed September 9, 2019, https://www.nti.org/learn/facilities/732/.

21. David E. Hoffman, "How U.S. Removed Half a Ton of Uranium from Kazakhstan," *Washington Post*, September 21, 2009, http://www.washingtonpost.com/wp-dyn/content/article/2009/09/20/AR2009092002881.html?sid=ST2009092002315.
22. Jonathan S. Landay, "U.S., Kazakhstan complete secret transfer of nuclear materials," McClatchy Newspapers, November 16, 2010, https://www.mcclatchydc.com/news/nation-world/world/article24600817.html.
23. David Fischer, "The DPRK's Violations of Its NPT Safeguards Agreement with the IAEA." Excerpted from *History of the International Atomic Energy Agency,* International Atomic Energy Agency, 1997, https://www.iaea.org/sites/default/files/dprk.pdf.
24. Fischer, "The DPRK's Violations of Its NPT Safeguards Agreement with the IAEA."
25. "Fact Sheet on DPRK Nuclear Safeguards." International Atomic Energy Agency, n.d., https://www.iaea.org/newscenter/focus/dprk/fact-sheet-on-dprk-nuclear-safeguards.
26. Joel S. Wit, Daniel B. Poneman, and Robert L. Gallucci, *Going Critical: The First North Korean Nuclear Crisis* (Washington, DC: Brookings Institution Press, 2004), 409–10.
27. See, e.g., Mitchell Reiss, Bridled Ambition: Why Countries Constrain Their Nuclear Capabilities (Washington, D.C.: Woodrow Wilson Center Press, 1995), p. 258
28. See, e.g., Joel S. Wit et al., Going Critical: The First North Korean Nuclear Crisis (Washington, D.C.: Brookings Institution Press, 2004), pp. 118–161 at www.jstor.org/stable/10.7864/j.ctt1gpcd97.9.
29. Statement by IAEA Director General Yukiya Amano, IAEA News Center, June 12, 2018, https://www.iaea.org/newscenter/statements/statement-by-iaea-director-general-yukiya-amano-12-june-2018.
30. Report of the IAEA Director General, "Implementation of the NPT Safeguards Agreement and Relevant Provisions of Security Council Resolutions 1737 (2006), 1747 (2007), 1803 (2008), and 1835 (2008) in the Islamic Republic of Iran" (Vienna; IAEA, August 28, 2009), https://www.iaea.org/sites/default/files/gov2009-55.pdf.
31. Natural uranium contains around 0.7 percent of the Uranium-235 isotope when found in nature; highly enriched uranium (HEU) suitable for weapons must typically exceed 90-percent U-235.
32. David Sanger, "Iran Deal Would Slow Making of Nuclear Bombs," *New York Times*, October 21, 2009, https://www.nytimes.com/2009/10/22/world/middleeast/22nuke.html.
33. Enrichment is typically measured in Separative Work Units (SWU); the number of SWU required to produce a given amount of HEU depends on two factors: the starting U-235 concentration, or assay, of the feed material, and the final U-235 concentration of the waste stream, or the tails assay. Assuming that the tails assay is set to 0.3 percent, producing 1 kilogram of HEU (90-percent U-235) requires 193 SWU if natural uranium is used as feed material, versus just 18.5 SWU if the feed material has previously been enriched to 20-percent U-235.
34. Trita Parsi, *Losing an Enemy: Obama, Iran, and the Triumph of Diplomacy* (New Haven, CT: Yale University Press, 2017), 97.
35. "Iran Is Implementing Nuclear-related JCPOA Commitments, Director General Amano Tells IAEA Board," IAEA News Center, March 5, 2018, https://www.iaea.org/newscenter/news/iran-is-implementing-nuclear-related-jcpoa-commitments-director-general-amano-tells-iaea-board.
36. "Atoms for Peace Speech."

7 Travails of governance

A view from the board chair

John Barrett

In the International Atomic Energy Agency (IAEA), as in any organization, any one of the main constituent actors—Member States, the Board of Governors, the Director General, the Secretariat, individual personalities—can be the protagonist in an unfolding drama, requiring diplomatic means to resolve. The outcomes can be good or bad for the organization. They can arise from Secretariat obduracy or be "politicized" through the gamesmanship of individual diplomats and delegations. To understand the IAEA better in this regard, it is helpful to draw back the curtain a bit. As a member of the Board of Governors from 2009 to 2012 and as the Chair of the Board from 2012 to 2013, I had ample opportunity not only to look behind the curtain, but also to become enmeshed in some of the dramatic scenes going on there.

This chapter focuses on how governance occurs in an international organization through a variety of interactions and influences, often depending on the issue at hand. It identifies several issues that show the Agency not as a reified organization functioning strictly according to statutes and procedures, but rather as an organism with its own governance flaws and dramatis personae. Each issue puts a different light on the term *governance* and what this concept means in the Agency. The case of Iran's nuclear program illustrates the limits of the Board's ability to resolve concerns over noncompliance with peaceful uses obligations. The creation of the Nuclear Safety Action Plan following the Fukushima disaster shows the limits of common purpose. The concerns over negotiating procedures for Regular and Technical Cooperation Budgets highlight the ways in which the role of the Board Chair is not adequately integrated into supporting the organization's aims and objectives. Finally, the State-Level Concept for Strengthening IAEA Safeguards (SLC) depicts how procedures and Secretariat obduracy raise the question of authority within the organization. Together, these governance-related issues have at times prevented higher-level achievements through common endeavor from coming to fruition—and as such, they are teaching moments for the Agency and for international organizations in general.

DOI: 10.4324/9781003160205-7

Governance and the IAEA

The IAEA looks at first sight to be an organization whose purpose is well understood and whose activities are largely scientific and technical in nature. Its mandate is to promote the peaceful use of nuclear energy, while acting as a watchdog to verify compliance of states party to the Nuclear Nonproliferation Treaty (NPT) through a system of legally binding safeguards against proliferation.

How does this work in theory? Like any international organization, the Agency's membership consists of countries with different interests, sometimes allied and sometimes competing. These member states are represented by diplomats—people who are trained to carry out the instructions of their governments, yet who also work in common purpose with other members to uphold the mandate of the organization and further its objectives. Into the mix comes a bureaucracy (in this case, a secretariat) that brings the Member States together through a legally grounded establishment with activities, programs, meetings, and procedures. The Secretariat staff carry out many of these actions or otherwise render support to the members. At the top of this large, costly pyramid sits a Director General and the senior management cadre of six Deputy Directors General. Finally, there is a Board of Governors made up of 35 Member States, of which 22 are elected in rotation from their regional groupings on a two-year basis. The Board is the Agency's central policymaking body: its policies and decisions, coupled with the resolutions of the full membership through the annual General Conference, are the expression of the members' will and intent.

So much for the basic governance structures of the IAEA. How does the Agency work in practice?

Iran

Iran's nuclear program shows the limitations of the Board of Governors and the Director General in tackling and resolving issues of major national security importance for many members. Sufficient, effective pressure on Iran to abide by its undertakings with regard to the Agency and its fellow members could be neither mustered nor applied. It is therefore instructive to look at how the Agency (Board and Secretariat) reached the limits of effectiveness in resolving Iran's inconsistencies and noncompliance with respect to its nuclear program.

Shortly after I arrived in September 2009 to take up the position as Canada's Permanent Representative to the IAEA and Governor on the IAEA Board of Governors, news broke regarding the existence of a hitherto unreported uranium enrichment plan in Iran, located near the village of Fordow, northeast of the city of Qom. This effectively brought the issue of Iran's nuclear program back into open discussion.

In November 2011, the Secretariat prepared and publicly released 19 questions relating to the possible military dimension (PMD) of Iran's nuclear program. In the document, the Secretariat distilled bits and pieces of information, intelligence, and hard fact into questions for the Board to put to Iran over activities that could be construed as elements of a dedicated nuclear weapons development program.[1] By early 2012, the Agency's investigation into the PMD had not made any progress, despite two high-level IAEA visits to Iran. Both the Board and the Secretariat focused on how to respond to the ongoing lack of cooperation by Iran in addressing the substantive outstanding issues raised at the November 2011 Board meeting. Iran would not agree to the Agency's "Structured Approach based on Agency verification practice." Nor would Iran provide the Agency with appropriate access to the Parchin site, one of the key PMD sites.

At the March 2012 meeting of the Board, the Director General said that the Agency was seeking a holistic, iterative process, one that included prioritization of outstanding issues, identification of initial actions, and agreement on modalities. Iran's response was that it sought a work plan limited to a finite list of questions. Further, once a specific question was addressed, the issue should be closed with no follow-up questions or revisiting of that particular issue. Iran would not accept any actions related to elements of the Additional Protocol or Code 3.1. The Director General treated these demands as inconsistent with IAEA verification principles. The Non-Aligned Movement (NAM) of developing world countries, for its part, reiterated its "principled positions" regarding the pressure being put on Iran, including concerns about document sharing and confidentiality, and also highlighted areas where Iran was cooperating. However, the NAM did call on Iran to cooperate with the Agency, provide Modified Code 3.1–related information, and take steps to address PMD concerns.[2]

In a novel development, the Board meeting was delayed so that the five permanent members of the United Nations (UN) Security Council plus Germany (P5+1) could have time behind closed doors to negotiate a draft resolution, "Implementation of the NPT Safeguards Agreement and relevant provisions of UN Security Council Resolutions in the Islamic Republic of Iran," to put before the Board.[3] Although the United States said that the P5+1 "process" and the IAEA investigation were separate, once the resolution emerged, it was presented to the Board as a fait accompli. This intervention of the P5+1 would later have consequences for the Board's capacity to deal independently on the issue of Iran's noncompliance.

At the Board meeting of June 4-6, 2012, Iran again escaped sanction, largely because the Iranians successful played the Agency against the P5+1 process. Iran dangled the possibility of a June 8 visit to Vienna by Foreign Minister Ali Akbar Salehi and the potential that it would sign the "structured approach" document with the Director General. The prospect of the Salehi visit dampened any criticism of Iran during the Board. Yet, in a bait-and-switch move, Salehi's visit was called off once the Board was finished, while the meeting on the "structured approach" was downgraded in level and broke up with no progress made. Meanwhile, the P5+1 could not agree a joint statement on Iran, with Russia playing the spoiler.

In the run-up to the Board meeting of September 10–14, 2012, the Agency's technical briefing laid out the ways in which Iran was failing to cooperate with the Agency, including its continued noncompliance with resolutions from the IAEA Board of Governors and the UN Security Council. In violation of UN Security Council resolutions, Iran had suspended neither its enrichment-related activities nor its heavy water-related activities. Iran had now produced 189.4 kilograms of uranium hexafluoride (UF6) enriched to just under 20 percent uranium-235 (U-235). This amount of nearly 20 percent enriched uranium far surpassed the amount necessary for fueling the operation of the Tehran Research Reactor—the reason given by Iran for producing the enriched uranium—for a decade. Production continued to increase with no signs of abatement. At the September Board meeting, the Director General reported that Iran had still not implemented the provisions of its signed Additional Protocol to its safeguards agreement with the Agency. Further, Iran was the only IAEA member state with significant nuclear activity that refused to implement the modified Code 3.1 of its Safeguards Agreement. Without compliance with these provisions, he said, the Secretariat could not verify effectively the design and purpose of the IR-40 reactor (a heavy water reactor near the city of Arak), nor could it determine the intent behind the Fordow Fuel Enrichment Plant and the Natanz nuclear facility or the purpose of Iran's heavy water program.

The Director General's "structured approach" on Iran's PMD

At this point, Canada was next in line as Chair of the Board of Governors.[4] As Canada's Permanent Representation to the IAEA, I assumed the position during a short Board meeting following the IAEA General Conference in early September 2012.

At the November 2012 Board meeting, the Director General noted that, in the year since the Secretariat's revelation of the PMD to Iran's nuclear program, no substantive progress had been made and Iran remained in noncompliance with numerous Board and UN Security Council resolutions. In 26 out of 29 interventions, significant concerns were raised about Iran's noncompliance and lack of cooperation in answering outstanding questions about its nuclear program. Some NAM countries, including Costa Rica, Indonesia, Libya, Mexico, Saudi Arabia, South Africa, Thailand, were becoming more critical of Iran in their statements. By contrast, Iran's statement and those of its like-minded allies (namely Syria, Cuba, and Algeria) evaded the substantive questions and focused either on process-related issues or on more general issues of NPT membership and disarmament that were outside the Board and Agency's authority.

On December 13, 2012, Iran and the IAEA held discussions in Tehran. The participants included Assistant Director General of Policy Rafael Grossi and Deputy Director General for Safeguards Herman Neckaerts. They were there to continue negotiations on a "structured approach" to the Agency's investigation into Iran's noncompliance. The structured approach was now intimately connected with the unanswered questions raised in the PMD document of November 2011. Iran objected to the Agency's text on issues of access, foreign documents, procurement and organization matters, conclusions, clusters vs. topics, and closure. Regarding closure, Iran's view was that this meant a return to normalcy and IAEA membership in good standing. However, given that Iran excluded both *correctness* and *completeness* as well as the Additional Protocol from the structured approach, there was little possibility of Iran's putative normalcy. Moreover, to Iran, closure meant an end to investigations into PMD; the Agency was not ready to agree to this condition, and the matter remained unresolved.[5]

Through early 2013, the tug-of-war between the Agency's structured approach and the P5+1's separate negotiations continued. The Agency proposed that the two sides meet on January 6, 2013, in an attempt to sign an agreement. Iran, the Secretariat feared, was going to "play it long and play it complicated," seeking to discredit the PMD document upon which Agency concerns were based. In any case, the Secretariat reported no progress by the time of the March Board meeting.[6] Meanwhile, some Member States were awaiting the outcome of P5+1 meeting with Iran in Almaty on February 26–27, 2013. However, the timing of the Almaty meeting—chosen by Iran—meant it would be difficult to craft a P5+1 resolution in time for the Board meeting, scheduled for March 2–6, 2013. NAM countries said they needed time to consult with their capitals in the event of a new resolution being placed before the Board.

At the March 2013 Board meeting, the P5+1 described their intent to carry on with Iran "a constructive diplomatic process, which will be pursued actively in the months ahead on the basis of reciprocity and a step-by-step approach and restores international confidence in the exclusively peaceful nature of Iran's nuclear program consistent with the NPT. We seek tangible results in this diplomatic process at an early stage." Although the P5+1 commended the Secretariat for its "intensive efforts over many months, including nine meetings with Iran over the last year, to clarify unresolved issues in connection with Iran's nuclear program" and encouraged the Agency to continue its efforts, the conclusion was clear: the lead in the negotiations with Iran was now out of the Agency's hands.[7] According to the P5+1, the IAEA "must play an essential role in establishing international confidence in the exclusively peaceful nature of Iran's nuclear program." This role was now effectively to continue urging Iran to take "substantive steps, as requested by the Agency, toward resolving outstanding issues related to possible military dimensions to Iran's nuclear program, applying the modified Code 3.1, and implementation and prompt entry into force of the Additional Protocol." In practical terms, the P5+1 agreement with Iran created a six-month dialogue process which effectively preempted the possibility of another resolution at the March Board.[8]

By now, many Member States told me they were losing faith both in the Secretariat's efforts to reach an agreement on a structured approach *and* in the separate P5+1 process. The prospect of Board action on the Iran issue had disappeared once the P5+1 and Iran had agreed to meet again in March and April. The absence of a resolution added to the uncertainty to the Agency's immediate next steps, and diminished the sense of effectiveness of any potential guidance provided by the Board to the Secretariat in the meantime. Uncertainty reigned regarding what to do next, beyond focusing on the Director General's report to the Board on Iran.[9] Frustration was clearly rising, as testified by the number of ambassadors who told me in our pre-Board consultations with the Chair that they planned to make strong statements of concern about Iranian intransigence and lack of cooperation with the Agency.[10]

Theatre time

With this discontent in mind, I opened the Iran agenda item at the March Board meeting by noting that the Agency had been unable to verify both the correctness and completeness of the peaceful nature of Iran's nuclear program. Without due verification from the Agency, this lack of completeness would have a negative impact on the NPT. I also recalled the surprise of the Board in 2009 when the Fordow/Qom enrichment plant was discovered, because Iran had kept it hidden and undeclared.

My remarks were greeted with diplomatic theatre, reflecting the tension in the Board over the Iran stand-off and continued Iranian stonewalling. Iran, prior to speaking first on behalf of the NAM, said that it was unprecedented for the Chair to speak on this topic.[11] Only China remarked on my opening statement, stating that the rules and procedures of the Board should be followed. I responded that Rule 23 of the Provisional Rules of Procedures of the Board of Governors called upon the President Officer to "direct the discussions" of the Board agenda—and that I believed I was doing so.

What transpired illustrates how "politicization" occurs. No sooner had I spoken than I could see signs of bustle among the phalanxes of first and second secretaries (political) sitting behind their ambassadors. This was the moment the activist NAM delegations had anticipated. The Chair had said something critical about Iran; he was now open for attack. The activists were ready to divert attention from Iran's foibles. The Sudanese chargé (Sudan was the current chair of the G-77 plus China) read a statement criticizing me for my opening remarks on the Iran agenda item. I repeated the statement I had made in response to China: my role as Chair was "to direct the discussions," which I had done. If Board members did not want this to happen, then I would follow their wishes and say nothing further on such vital matters as the Iran nuclear issue.[12]

The P5+1 takes over

By September 2013, both the Board and the Secretariat had reached the end of their efforts as major players in resolving the international security issue caused by the Iranian nuclear program. Nothing had really changed; Iran had not admitted guilt regarding the past military-related aspects of its nuclear activities, or explained why it was using sophisticated centrifuges in specialized cascade arrangements that would allow uranium enrichment far beyond its legitimate needs to potential weapons-grade levels. The Iranians provided no satisfactory explanation or real investigation into the PMD of their activities over the previous decade and more. The Agency's "structured approach" was finished. Instead, Iran achieved what it wanted: a separate deal that closed the book on its past activities. The negotiation moved away from the Agency and fully into the P5+1, which had both real power and concrete offers for ending sanctions. Two years later, the Agency's role was essentially to help monitor the Joint Comprehensive Plan of Action negotiated between the P5+1, concluded on July 14, 2015.

Whether this was a good deal, or the only deal, is not the issue here. From the point of view of governance, the Iran case showed the limits of the Agency's ability to judge noncompliance and of its powers to restore compliance. These limitations naturally have an impact on general confidence in the Agency's capacity to ensure that IAEA Member States are not diverting peaceful nuclear activities to weapons development. When faced with a skillful, artful dodger, the watchdog was toothless.

The post-Fukushima nuclear safety action plan

The Agency's initial reaction to news of the Great Eastern Japan Earthquake on March 11, 2011, and its consequent seismic and tidal wave impact on the Fukushima Dai-ichi nuclear power plant site, was a lesson in what not to do in a crisis. The earthquake and tsunami happened on a Friday, but it took until the following Wednesday for the Director General to authorize an expert from the Secretariat to describe to Member States what appeared to have happened at the destroyed reactor. Even this statement only appeared as the result of certain states' insistent prodding of the Director General.

A rehearsal of such missteps in those early days of the crisis is beyond the scope of this review. The accident, like many crises, in fact presented an opportunity to reinforce and expand international safety standards. That opportunity unfortunately was restricted in its ambition and impact owing to Agency governance issues, notably the negotiating procedures to which the Director General and Secretariat chose to adhere.

In the aftermath of the Fukushima accident, the IAEA convened the Ministerial Conference on Nuclear Safety in Vienna in June 2011. The Conference directed the Director General to draft an "Action Plan on Nuclear Safety" to strengthen the global nuclear safety framework. However, in preparing the Action Plan, the Director General's procedure was as follows: the Secretariat would hold several rounds of consultation collectively with delegations, invite comments from the floor, and then prepare a draft based on those comments. The procedure would be repeated until a consensus text was reached. Unfortunately, this procedure meant the Secretariat had to abandon activities and language where consensus was not forthcoming, even if only one country (for example, Pakistan) were to say "no." A more effective approach would have used line-by-line negotiation, through which delegations could see who was objecting over what part of the text and demand explanation for why a country was blocking consensus. This approach yields greater pressure for creative solutions and overcoming resistance, especially if the majority are in favor of bolder, more far-reaching actions. Instead of reaching up, the Director General's procedure reached down.[13]

On September 1, 2011, I conveyed this concern to the Deputy Director General for Nuclear Safety and Security. I indicated that draft Action #2 still lacked effective transparency measures such as timely, public provision of information via IAEA peer reviews of nuclear safety. The language in the draft action still required host-country consent to publish information stemming from IAEA-led peer reviews of that country's implementation of higher nuclear safety standards. This requirement would gut the Action Plan of fundamental transparency and contradict the goal of enhancing public trust in nuclear energy. The Director General's procedure, I argued, allowed a small group of states—Argentina, China, India, Pakistan, and Russia—to insist on a state's prerogative to block transparency. On the evening before Board approval of the Action Plan, I met with the Director General to reiterate Canadian concerns about watered-down commitments on transparency and strengthening safety culture. It was important to keep the Plan "evergreen" and open to future improvement. He defended the procedure, pointing out the Action Plan was formally under the Director General's purview, so it would stay as it was. The opportunity to build higher ambition and continuous improvement thus passed.

What does this say about governance? It signified the inability of the organization to exercise leadership in advancing an objective at the moment of opportunity. In this case, there existed a rare opening for raising global standards of nuclear safety to a new level. Instead, the Secretariat and the Director General adopted an approach that merely collected views and saw which ones enjoyed consensus while rejecting those that did not. Such faulty decision-making is a matter of governance. Member States were tied to drafting procedures guaranteed to reduce the possibility of greater things. They were left without hands-on negotiation and, importantly, direct ownership of the outcome. It is a governance weakness that allows the Director General and Secretariat to dictate procedure—and thus accept the least ambitious goals for fear of entering choppy political waters. The reality was that, for nuclear safety after Fukushima, the waters were relatively smooth, with a strong majority of Member States ready to sail further and achieve more.

Budget negotiations and the discord of faulty procedures

Before looking more closely at governance issues affecting the Agency's two major budgets—the Regular Budget (obligatory for all members) and the Technical Cooperation Fund (TCF), which was voluntary, though allotted to the donor countries on the basis of the UN system of assessment—it is important to provide some context.[14]

An old style of management persisted in the Agency. Complacency had taken root. Effective results-based management, transparency, and accountability were absent in its programs and budget. The attitude, best exemplified by the then-Deputy Director General of Management and Finance, was that Member States were to pay their assessed contribution in full and on time without looking too carefully at how it was spent. At the time, however, major donor Member States were still reeling from the 2008 global financial crisis. National budgets were being cut drastically, treasuries were imposing austerity measures, and funds available for international organizations were taking a battering. Yet, the Agency's senior management, led by the Director General, remained indifferent. Undaunted, the budgets prepared by the Secretariat continued to grow annually and relentlessly. Some delegations pressed the Director General and staff to end the egregious budget increases—for instance, the Secretariat requested an 11 percent increase in the 2008/2009 budget—and reform the Agency's financial and program management. These requests were to no avail.[15]

In addition to weaknesses in budgetary management, a built-in governance weakness hampered the budget negotiation process. Nobody seemed to challenge or even notice it. Simply put, the Director General and the Secretariat would draw up their desired budget figures and present them to the Board as the Director General's proposal. However, the Board Chair would be responsible for negotiating the successful outcome—Board consensus and approval—of this proposal. What would happen if the Board Chair, on the basis of consultations with the Geneva Group and the G-77 plus China, were to conclude that the Director General's figures are not pegged at the right level to secure Board agreement?[16] What if the Director General were to refuse to listen to input from the Chair on the most likely path to agreement? The Secretariat made it clear: the Chair was expected to go out, like a knight into battle, and fight for the Director General's budget regardless of its quality or negotiability. Yet, this procedure is flawed, for without a mechanism or the disposition to accept the Chair's input, a battle can—and did—ensue.

The Director General's draft Program Budget for the 2014/2015 biennium was foreshadowed at an informal meeting of the Agency's Program and Budget Committee, which I chaired on February 11, 2013. The proposal was for a 2.1 percent real growth in 2014 (plus 1.4 percent inflation/price adjustment) for a total increase of 3.5 percent, to be followed by 0 percent real growth for 2015. This was a disappointment. I had emphasized to the Director General in our earlier informal meetings that the "psychological threshold" for many Geneva Group members would be a 2 percent total increase. Pitching the real growth at 0.5 percent, plus 1.4 percent for price adjustment (a 1.9 percent increase) would be more negotiable and give me, as Chair, a strong platform on which to advocate acceptance of the proposal. We talked about this for a while. In the end, he said no—he would stick to his opening figure. At that point, it was his budget, not mine.[17] The Secretariat formally released the draft budget on March 5.

For the next two months, we—that is, myself and four fellow ambassadors who acted as "facilitators" on the Regular and TCF Budgets—conducted nearly 60 meetings with delegations. On May 3, 2013, I met with the Director General and his senior management to brief them on what we had heard. Regarding the Regular Budget, the message was clear. The Director General's 3.5 percent increase was unacceptable to the Geneva Group, with some accepting Zero Real Growth (ZRG) and others demanding Zero Nominal Growth (ZNG). The Director General confirmed he would reduce the level of increase in his revised Regular Budget proposal. I suggested the new figure to be close to ZRG. With this, I could achieve consensus at the next Open-Ended Working Group scheduled for May 31. In a separate one-on-one meeting with the Director General, I went a step further, pleading for the revised figure to come in under 2 percent, ideally at 1.9 percent (i.e., real growth of 0.5 percent plus 1.4 percent price adjustment for inflation).[18] I then added what seemed (to me at least) to be the clincher: the United States, for the first time in my experience, was heading toward a ZRG budget.[19]

Perhaps I was finally getting through to the Director General and the management. On May 10, 2013, the new Deputy Director General for Management and Budget presented the Director General's revised budget proposal.[20] It offered an increase of 0.5 percent over 2013 for the Regular Budget, accompanied by a price adjustment for inflation of 1.4 percent, for a total increase of 1.9 percent—exactly the figure I had fruitlessly argued for two months previously.

This obduracy caused considerable difficulties for me in securing eventual agreement on the Regular Budget. Moreover, it would cause further problems in achieving agreement on the TCF Budget, now that "synchronization" was supposed to occur between the two budgets.

"Synchronization" of budgets

A separate weakness in governance came from previous decisions by the Board—specifically, the Board's decision in 2005 to "synchronize" the two Regular and TCF Budgets, even though the two were fundamentally different in nature and legal basis. Four years later, the Board indicated that the earlier decision provided "a framework *beginning in 2012* to consider appropriate increases to the resources for the TC program, including the TCF target."[21] Moreover, "Such adjustments would take into account the changes in the level of the regular operational budget from 2009 onwards, the price adjustment factor in the corresponding years, and all other relevant factors."

This change was significant from a governance perspective. Who was responsible for implementing this new relationship between the two budgets? The Director General had no real influence or interest in TCF target figures or the indicative planning figures (IPF) that shaped Agency budgeting. Because the TCF was voluntary, the Director General left this part of the budget process entirely in the hands of the Chair to figure out and reach an agreement. With no precedent available, and no guidance or support from the Secretariat, the relationship between the two budgets would be fought out between donor and recipient groups—with the Chair caught in between. G-77 countries realized they now had an instrument of leverage over the donor countries.[22] They could withhold their support for the Regular Budget, covering the Agency's main programs and operations, until they got what they wanted in the TCF Budget. Previously, the two budgets had been separate enough to weaken this leverage.

Now I had two intertwined problems, both created by weaknesses in budget governance. First, there was the impasse in the Regular Budget caused by the Director General's original budget increase, followed by his equally rejected revised proposal. Second, there was a real potential for G-77 budget intransigence, thanks to the new "synchronized" relationship that demanded "balance" and identical rates of increase between the two very different budgets.

In an attempt to pull these two strands together in a way that might promote compromise and consensus, on May 30 I circulated my "Chairman's Non-Paper." It read (in part):

> … I have concluded that the Budget figure that would command the widest and strongest support from Member States should: take into account the views expressed by a number of Member States that the current financial crisis warrants a Zero Nominal Growth budget or a figure close to ZNG; hold firm the level of the Technical Cooperation fund target to at least $90 million—a figure that many Member States noted as having particular importance for the TCF; reflect the relationship, identified in the 2005 decision, between the Regular Budget and the TCF, such that the former is taken into account in determining the target figures of the latter; and preserve the integrity of the programs set out in the Director General's initial and revised budget proposal, including the balance and structure established therein, which has gained wide support by Member States throughout the course of Budget discussions.

I also noted, "in order to achieve a consensus that reflects the 4 points, compromise will be required. There is no perfect outcome or special advantage to accrue to any one Member State. The Vienna spirit guides us in this matter." Following this Chairman's Non-Paper, I circulated "Proposal by the Chair of the Working Group on the Programme and Budget and the TCF targets for 2014–2015" at the opening of the Board on June 3.[23]

However, G-77 activism was already on the rise. At the outset of budget consultations in March, the G-77 Chair presented the group's proposal to increase TCF targets by 12.6 percent. This, he said, would correspond to the cumulative 12.6 percent increase of the Regular Budget between 2009 and 2013. In response to my Chair's proposal of June 3, the G-77 put forward its "initial comments," which restated its earlier position from March, citing the "accumulated deficit in the TCF Target vis-à-vis the Regular Budget since 2009" and the "lack of balance between the Regular Budget and the TCF target." The Group then said it wished for "more time to continue consultations" and "invited the chairman to present a revised proposal that takes into account the Group's concerns."

Throughout the Board week, I sought to turn this G-77 gambit into a realistic proposal that the Geneva Group would accept, while bringing an increase to the TCF Budget commensurable with that of the Regular Budget—thereby instituting synchronicity if not full equality between the two.[24] When the Board reconvened on Friday, June 7, the final deal was taking shape. But late that evening, the G-77 rejected the compromise. What was driving this inability to close the deal? Was it a desire by some in the G-77 caucus to stretch out the negotiations and cause discomfort to the Geneva Group members and the Board Chair? Was it personality driven? Or was it entirely delaying tactics to increase pressure on the Chair, believing that I was obliged to reach an agreed outcome by the end of the June Board—which was desirable, but not obligatory?

By now, the Secretariat regarded both budgets as entirely mine and was awaiting Board agreement. No longer was it the "Director General's budget"—it had not been so for some time. I was left on my own. From the June Board onward, I conducted a solo effort to bring all the intransigent players together and reach agreement. Time was running out as the August 5, 2013, deadline approached: the last date on which the Board could bring decisions and matters to the IAEA General Conference for approval. And people were leaving for summer holidays.

Final obstacles and resolution

I continued my discussions with the Sudanese G-77 Chair on the basis of the revised July 1 proposal. He consulted the Group and came back to say that the TCF and IPF figures were still not high enough. On July 8, 2013, I circulated a "non-paper" in which I sought to address the G-77 concerns by upping the TCF and IPF increases, though not substantially. On July 11, I received the G-77's "Amendments to the Chair's Non-Paper." In it, the Group accepted the figures I proposed, but wanted the word "approximately" replaced by "not less than." Could I get the Geneva Group agree both to the figures and the suggested wording? We were now quibbling over whether the term "not less than" meant a floor on which the G-77 could demand additional increase to the TCF. We were debating whether the term "working group" implied financial resources, whereas "informal working group" would not. It was all increasingly surreal, and I was stuck in the middle, having to shuttle back and forth between the Groups because of their protagonists did not trust each other.

In the end, on July 22, I was able to secure Geneva Group agreement to the G-77 Amended Text, on the condition that this would trigger agreement on the Budget as a whole (Regular and TCF). The next day, July 23, I asked the G-77 Chair (as he was boarding the plane for his holidays) whether he could assure me that this was the basis for agreement. He assured me it was. Later that afternoon, his chargé reaffirmed this, saying that the Secretariat could proceed immediately to convening a special Board meeting to approve the overall budget, perhaps as early as the following week. We were finally there.[25]

Reflections on budgets and governance

What does the budget exercise show from a governance perspective? First, there should be a mechanism to permit the Board Chair to work with the Director General and Secretariat on achieving a first budget proposal that is more negotiable and less reflective of what the Agency management desires. The budget therefore would be co-owned and Secretariat support of the Chair would remain throughout the negotiating process, right through to Board approval. Second, the Agency should exercise greater care with respect to the relationship between the Regular and TCF Budgets. What makes this tricky is that the former is obligatory and the latter is voluntary, which means they are de facto unequal. Making them "synchronized" was bound to result in differing interpretations. Some Member States felt that this meant that any numerical or percentage increase in the Regular Budget had to be replicated in the TCF Budget. Others disagreed. These differences of interpretation were bound to infect the negotiation process—as I found out, being the first Board Chair to preside over the newly synchronized relationship. Furthermore, it gives an attractive opening for all those members who see the Agency as politically and regionally divided, with a clash of interests always at hand.

All this notwithstanding, as Board Chair I secured agreement on the two budgets on the penultimate day of July, six days before the deadline for submitting Board documents to the General Conference. The agreed increase for the 2014 Regular Budget was 1.7 percent, not far off the 1.9 percent I proposed to the Director General at the beginning of the year. It was the Agency's first full biennial budget presided over by the Board Chair via the single budget working group. It recognized a "relationship" between the Regular Budget and the TCF Budget, and it created the working group that would continue important discussions on what this relationship would look like in future.

State-Level Safeguards: The Secretariat under attack

There are times when a seemingly routine matter evolves into a contested and politicized debate. Fueled by conflicts involving delegations or personalities or both, it bursts into a firestorm in the Board. From a governance perspective, do the Board and Secretariat have adequate means to detect an approaching conflagration and quell it beforehand? The case of State-Level Safeguards—also known as the State-Level Concept, or SLC—shows, unfortunately, that they do not.

The SLC, in essence, is aimed at using a variety of means to produce assurances that a country is fully complying with its safeguards agreement with the IAEA. These means can reinforce such assurances while reducing the cost of extensive on-site monitoring by IAEA personnel. The SLC is applied only to countries that have Integrated Safeguards, an Additional Protocol, and a clear nonproliferation record. The Secretariat draws from alternative, risk-based, and information-driven techniques to form a broad picture of the country's compliance with its safeguards obligations. Through this methodology, the Secretariat is able to determine whether the country continues to have a clean record.

At the September 2013 Board meeting, Russia, Argentina, South Africa, and Brazil took the floor to chastise the Director General over the SLC. They accused it of being a tool for the IAEA to gather intelligence at the behest of Western countries. In addition, as they saw it, the SLC had come out of nowhere and had been foisted by the Secretariat upon unsuspecting Member States.[26] The Director General and Secretariat were clearly taken aback by the ferocity of the attack. Where had these charges come from? And, more importantly, could we have seen them coming and done anything to defuse them?

In answer to the first question, Russia was at the forefront of this sudden bad-tempered attack. Russia had flagged its growing opposition to the SLC during the Safeguards Resolution negotiation at the 56th General Conference in 2012. Russia questioned the SLC's claim to be nondiscriminatory; moreover, it decried "information-driven safeguards," apparently equating the word "information" with "intelligence." The SLC, Russia said, was a new approach being implemented by the Secretariat without proper oversight by the Board, and therefore requested the Director General to prepare for the Board a detailed report on the State-level Concept. NAM leadership was generally supportive of Russia.

The answer to the second question was, yes, there was opportunity to stop the impending train wreck at the Board. But there was neither mechanism nor disposition on the part of the Director General or Secretariat to take notice of the advance warning flags of such discontent—another governance weakness.

From my position as Board Chair, I could see the storm clouds brewing. Once again, my consultations in advance of Board meetings warned that some delegations were unhappy. They were upset with the SLC, but more importantly, they were upset with how the Director General and Secretariat had handled its implementation. However, I had no way to formally warn the Director General of the coming political storm, nor was there a mechanism for my feedback to produce a common approach or action plan devised by the Director General with direct support from the Chair.[27]

Partway through the September Board agenda lay the seemingly innocuous agenda item: "Conceptualization and Development of Safeguards Implementation at the State Level." It began with the Director General reading a report (which had been requested in the 2012 General Conference resolution) that concluded with the invitation to the Board to "take note" of it—that is, that no action would be needed. In the pre-Board consultations, I had encountered some members who queried the meaning of "taking note" and wanted much more information from the Secretariat on the SLC. The Director General, however, had not listened to my recommendation that he should do more to respond to members' concerns rather than simply report. Now he was going to witness the growing irritation firsthand.[28]

The SLC became the most contentious item at the 2013 September Board meeting. Russia, supported by several activist NAM countries, decided the Director General and the Secretariat needed to have their wings clipped. The Director General's reaction was stubborn resistance: he decided that he would consider comments and views of Board members, provided "it did not set a precedent"; otherwise, the Secretariat would proceed as planned.[29] This did not go down well with Member States already gearing up for a fight. With the SLC thoroughly politicized, we were entering the realm of "who's in charge?" Is it the Member States or the Director General and Secretariat?[30]

As Chair, there was little I could do to stop the imminent collision. I focused instead on explaining matter-of-factly the UN General Assembly definitions of "to note" and "to take note of." The rest of the time I tried to keep order as the piling-on began, starting with Russia, followed by South Africa, Iran, Brazil, and other NAM stalwarts.

The defiance shown by these Member States forced the Director General and Secretariat to adopt the following actions. First, the Director General issued a statement in which he committed to preparing a "supplemental report" addressing all the main issues raised by Member States in the Board discussion. Second, this report was to be issued to members before the 2014 General Conference. Third, the Director General committed to hold consultations following the upcoming 2013 General Conference, to ensure all issues addressed in the supplemental report were clearly identified. My summing-up confirmed the Director General's surrender by putting it on the record. This brought the fireworks to an end.[31]

With hindsight, the SLC could have been handled differently if all of the "intelligence-gathering" possibilities in the hands of the Director General had been utilized. One of the most important of these options was none other than the Board Chair. The absence of defusing mechanisms, such as more systematic analysis by the Secretariat of the Chair's input from consultations with Member States, is another weakness in governance. Such a mechanism would help temper the inevitable shifting balance between Member States' prerogative and the Director General's leadership responsibilities. It could prevent future Directors General from remaining blind to growing irritation among Member States regarding issues that risk being exploited for political and ideological purposes.

Conclusion

Any analysis of the rules, procedures, and structures of an international organization must recognize that such organizations are living organisms. They move, evolve, and act dynamically, because behind the nameplates and formal meetings are real people. As diplomats, they are attuned to political issues and interactions; they may be motivated by personal ambitions or follow instructions from their capitals to pursue specific policy ends. Sometimes, they are encased in ideology and act accordingly. At the same time, an organization functions on the basis of collective will. In the case of the IAEA, this will is expressed through the resolutions and decisions of the General Conference and the Board of Governors. This means that the structures and procedures are aimed at producing consensus and agreement, which then authorizes the activities of the Director General and the Secretariat. (Most of these functions can be seen by examining the IAEA Statute and the Rules of Procedure for the Board and General Conference, or by visiting the IAEA website.)

However, when it comes to governance, reference to documents alone does not provide a full picture of the dynamics within the organization. It does not tell the story of how debates, differences of interest, power, and influence steer outcomes and policies. A fuller understanding can be found if there is an effort to examine more closely instances where the governance mechanisms are weak or not adequately used, or review the points where Member States, Board procedures, and Secretariat responsibilities interact on key issues. I have sought here to use my experiences as a member of the IAEA Board of Governors and Chair of the Board to provide detail, color, and behind-the-scenes insights, focusing on areas where strengthened governance mechanisms could assist in achieving the aims and objectives of the organization.

Notes

1. See "Possible Military Dimension to Iran's Nuclear Programme," Annex to Director General's Report to the Board, GOV/2011/65, November 8, 2011.
2. Modified Code 3.1 of the Subsidiary Arrangements to a Safeguards Agreement requires countries to submit design information for new nuclear facilities to the IAEA as soon as the decision is made to build one or authorize its construction. See for an explanation of the key elements of IAEA safeguard

provisions, see Arms Control Today, https://www.armscontrol.org/factsheets/IAEAProtocol.

3. On Resolution GOV/2012/48/Rev.1, there were 31 yes votes; 1 no vote (Cuba), and 3 abstentions (Ecuador, Egypt, and Tunisia).
4. The Board Chair position rotates annually among the eight regional groupings at the IAEA.
5. If the structured approach had allowed the Agency sufficient flexibility to fully investigate the possible military dimension (PMD)—such as by returning to clusters, revisiting sites or individuals, or asking new questions—then such a request could have been possible. The Agency simply could have withheld closure until it had completed its investigation. If this were combined with an insistence, as found in the UN Security Council resolutions, that Iran would implement the Additional Protocol, any future concerns could have been brought up as part of the regular Additional Protocol process and not as a specific PMD investigation.
6. According to the Secretariat after its meeting with Iran on February 13, 2013.
7. The P5+1 went on to "reaffirm our /2011/69 and support for the resolutions adopted by the IAEA Board of Governors addressing the Agency's efforts to implement its responsibilities under Iran's Safeguards Agreement, recently GOV/2012/50."
8. This outcome was further reflected in the Director General's February 13 statement that "some time is needed now to reflect on the way forward"—in particular on how the outcome of the P5+1 meeting in Almaty would impact the Secretariat's discussion with Iran on a structured approach.
9. GOV/2013/6, February 21, 2013.
10. Of the 33 interventions made during the Board, 8 could be called neutral—that is, calling on both parties to cooperate or calling on Iran to comply with its obligations, but defending its right to nuclear energy and enrichment. Five statements were favorable to Iran: the Non-Aligned Movement statement (written and read by Iran), joined by Cuba, Venezuela, Syria, and Iran itself. The remaining 20 statements blamed Iran for lack of progress and called for compliance and cooperation from Iran, along with full implementation of Iran's international obligations.
11. The expectation of the Secretariat and certain members was that the Chair should simply read out scripts written by the Secretariat, thank the speaker, and give the floor to the next speaker on the list. The Chair would then summarize the prepared statements and ask for Board approval of the summary. Both Board and the Secretariat had fallen into a pattern of procedure where no debate or exchange was expected or encouraged.
12. Many United Nations (UN) WEOG (Western European and Other States Group) delegations were outraged by the cavalier, offensive words used by the Sudanese chargé in his remarks on behalf of the G-77 plus China. They took the floor to defend my opening words and the constructive intent behind them. The Chilean ambassador, a member of the G-77 plus China, registered his strong disagreement with G-77 procedure as well as with its statement. Moreover, he sent a blistering formal diplomatic note addressed to the G-77 Chair to remonstrate that his country (and other G-77 countries) had not been consulted over the Sudanese statement and they had not agreed to it.
13. Governance presupposes leadership. There are moments when the choice of procedure harms the objective and squanders the opportunity before one. All views should be reflected in a consensus Action Plan, but always to a point. The art and skill of diplomacy is to judge where that point lies; leadership takes us past it to consensus.

14. The Technical Cooperation Fund (TCF) is a development and capacity-building fund for less-developed Member States. It is voluntary, but contributions from donor states are expected, and so it is often referred to (seemingly illogically) as a "voluntary assessed contribution." In essence, there is no legal obligation for states to contribute, but their "assessed" notional share is calculated on the basis of the UN assessment formula, which is used to determine legally required contributions to a UN organization or agency's budget.
15. I joined several ambassadors from the major donor states to plead with the Director General and Deputy Director General for Management and Finance for greater discipline in program spending and financial management. Eventually, our demarché had an effect, but not until the Secretariat realized the major donors fully intended to refuse the Director General's large budget increase and demanded "Zero Real Growth."
16. The Geneva Group consists of major donor countries. It began in 1964 and is permanently co-chaired by the United Kingdom and the United States. The 18 members hold generally similar positions on administrative and financial matters within the UN family (including the IAEA). The G-77 was founded in 1964 to create enhanced joint negotiating capacity in the UN. China has associated itself with the Group since 1994, hence "G-77 plus China".
17. The Director General went ahead with his budget proposal in the "white book" (see GOV/2013/1, March 5, 2013)
18. Geneva Group members, particularly the Europeans (Belgium, France, Germany, Italy, Spain, Switzerland, and the United Kingdom), were insistent on Zero Real Growth.
19. In Washington, D.C., there were tough and ongoing discussions on cutting funding for international organizations, arising from the situation of sequestration between the federal government and Congress. The U.S. delegation at the IAEA, while awaiting formal instructions, now joined the chorus of Member States calling for additional efficiencies and savings in the Agency budget.
20. Document 2013/Note 32,
21. As set out in paragraph 7 of the 2009 Budget Package (GOV/2009/52/Rev.1) (emphasis added).
22. The relevant texts include "Proposal submitted by the Co-Chairs of the Open-ended Working Group on TCF targets for 2012–2013 and Indicative Planning Figures for 2014–2015" (GOV/2011/37, June 6, 2011); the "Agency's Draft Budget Update for 2013" (GOV/2012/22 Annex 2, May 8, 2012); and "Strengthening of the Agency's technical cooperation activities" (GC(56)RES/11, September 21, 2012, Section 4).
23. GOV/2013/30, June 3, 2013.
24. I raised the second year (2015) of the TCF Target to $91.5 million, which gave the biennium 2014/2015 a 1.7 percent increase from 2013 to 2014 and an additional 1.7 percent increase from 2014 to 2015. I set the indicative planning figures as approximately, but not less than, $92.8 million for the biennium 2016/2017. Taken together, this represented an increase of 1.4 percent (price adjustment) for each of the two years.
25. On July 26, 2013, I circulated a "Note by the Chair of the Board of Governors" to Board members announcing the convening of a special Board meeting on July 30, 2013, with a view to taking action on the Agency's Programme and Budget and the Technical Cooperation Fund targets for 2014/2015 (GOV/2013/44). I also circulated the "Chair's Non-Paper on the Programme and Budget and TCF targets for 2014–2015, as adjusted" with the accompanying note: "With these adjustments to the original non-paper, the text reflects the acceptance in full of the amendments from the G-77 dated 11 July 2013.

The Chair intends to incorporate this text into his revised proposal for approval by the Board of Governors" (see GOV/2013/30/Rev.1).

26. At the September Board meeting, South Africa was indignant about the lack of information from the Secretariat, even though a South African technical delegation was at that moment working on preparatory documents for South Africa to join other countries benefiting from the State-Level Concept (SLC) approach. The accusation that countries were being kept in the dark over the SLC was contradicted by reality.
27. The Board Chair is supported by a small group of capable, experienced officials in the Secretariat's Policy-Making Organs section. They produce for the Director General a distillation of points raised by member states in the consultations. However, without a means to incorporate (not merely convey) the Chair's feedback, there is no way of ascertaining whether the Secretariat is listening to or will accept advice from the Chair.
28. How to defuse the tension? In my pre-Board briefing to the Director General and his staff, I pointed out that a number of Board members wanted a fuller discussion of the SLC. "Taking note" of the Director General's report was not, in their view, a sufficient course to take. They wanted more explanation from the Secretariat, as well as to have their comments taken into account. The storm was predictable; and it could have been avoided.
29. Logic and precedent were on the Director General's side. He pointed out to the Board that the SLC was first introduced to the Board in 2004. It involved giving consideration to a state as a whole, rather than focusing primarily on declared nuclear material and facilities, as was done in the past. The SLC was already being implemented in a significant number of Member States, following extensive consultation with each of them. Importantly, the approach did not change, or go beyond, the existing legal framework for safeguards, nor did it alter any state's legal obligations with respect to safeguards. Rather, the concept improved efficiency of safeguards implementation while strengthening its effectiveness by improving the ability to detect undeclared nuclear material and activities.
30. The first rule of multilateral diplomacy is that Member States are ultimately in charge. They will accept leadership of the Secretariat in operational matters—but on points of principle, ignore them at your peril.
31. "The Board also noted the Chair's clarification that the recommended action by the Board to take note of the document on the conceptualization and development of safeguards implementation at the State level did not represent approval or disapproval of that document. The Board also noted the Director General's statement at the end of the discussion, as well as the comments made. With this understanding, may I take it that the Board takes note of this report as contained in document GOV/2013/38? It is so decided."

Part II

Current and future issues and prospects

8 The IAEA and the evolution of safeguards

Massimo Aparo

Deterring the spread of nuclear weapons remains a top priority of the international community, and International Atomic Energy Agency (IAEA) safeguards on nuclear material make an indispensable contribution to this effort. Effective safeguards provide assurances to the world that nuclear material remains in peaceful use and is not being diverted to make weapons. The IAEA is respected worldwide for the technical credibility of its work and its political independence; the international community supports its efforts and wants it to succeed. That support is extremely precious, and it needs to be nurtured and preserved.

The demand for these safeguards continues to rise. Currently, around 1,300 nuclear facilities and locations outside facilities are under IAEA safeguards and the amount of nuclear material under safeguards is now over 215,000 significant quantities. In recent years, there has been a significant growth in the number of additional protocols in force, and the Agency also is conducting more verification-intensive activities. For example, there are now many more spent fuel transfers to medium- and long-term storage and facility decommissioning to monitor than there were previously.

The accelerating pace of technological change and globalization profoundly shape the IAEA's operating environment. The volume and diversity of relevant data available are growing exponentially, increasing the demands on analysts to keep pace. In parallel, new technologies have been developed to efficiently process, store, and effectively extract information for further analysis. Globalization has also led to more scientific cooperation across borders, which poses certain challenges. And advancements in information technology have forced the Agency to enhance its cybersecurity capabilities so that it can protect the sensitive information that the IAEA Member States provide to the IAEA in confidence.

In recent years, discussions in the Agency's policymaking organs on safeguards matters have been intensifying, with Member States increasingly wanting to better understand *how* safeguards are implemented, and have been requiring new levels of communication and transparency from the

DOI: 10.4324/9781003160205-8

Secretariat. I firmly believe that we need to maintain that active dialogue with our Member States.

Another looming challenge to the Safeguards Department relates to human resources. There is no pool of well-qualified IAEA inspectors outside of the Agency from which it can draw to replenish its ranks. The majority of IAEA inspectors need to be trained from scratch. It takes approximately two years of training and mentoring for a new inspector to become self-sufficient in the field. Under the Agency's rotation policy, many inspectors have to leave after seven years of service. Owing to a combination of factors, their departures will present a particular challenge in a few years' time. The Safeguards Department estimates that if the seven-year rotation policy is not amended, it would lose around 100 inspectors to retirement or contract completion between 2022 and 2024. This represents about a third of its inspectorate in just two years, and so the Agency would need to manage such a massive turnover with care. That is why the Agency is considering extending the seven-year period within the rotation policy. In addition to inspectors, the IAEA has to ensure that it is able to retain experts in other areas of safeguards implementation, including technology experts and information management specialists. Naturally, the importance of retaining experienced and specialized staff needs to be balanced with the need to constantly revitalize the organization with fresh blood, new ideas, and the latest know-how. But for inspectors, the IAEA will need to find a way of forestalling a problem that otherwise will present a major operational headache quite soon.

Extraordinary events, whether positive or negative, also complicate the effective management of safeguards implementation. Three types of such events come to mind. First, disruptive security events—for instance, a state's loss of control over part of its territory in which the IAEA applies safeguards—are already occurring. The Agency is being required to safeguard nuclear material located within areas in conflict, and this has disrupted its normal ways of operating. Second, widespread disasters such as pandemics, earthquakes, or floods can damage nuclear facilities or compromise the Agency's field activities, or both. To cope with the recent COVID-19 pandemic, the Agency had to implement a series of mitigating actions, drawing from business continuity and disaster recovery measures. Third, diplomatic events, including the Joint Plan of Action (JPOA) and Joint Comprehensive Plan of Action (JCPOA) on Iran, obviously can affect the Agency's workload. For instance, a diplomatic breakthrough on North Korea's nuclear program almost would certainly require the Agency to develop novel and modified monitoring and verification approaches that probably would need to be implemented at short notice in a very challenging environment.

The JCPOA, or Iran nuclear deal, has posed particular challenges for the IAEA. Clearly, it was a gain for verification in that the combination of the comprehensive safeguards agreement, additional protocol, and further transparency measures created a robust verification system overall. The deal also led to a significant reduction in Iran's nuclear activities. Although the IAEA played a key role before, during, and after the JCPOA negotiations, it is not a party to the agreement. Despite the United States' withdrawal from the agreement and Iran's subsequent decision to reduce adherence, the IAEA continues to measure Iran's nuclear activity, and is verifying and monitoring Iran's implementation of its nuclear-related commitments under the JCPOA. Agency inspectors are on the ground at all times. The Agency also monitors Iran's nuclear facilities and centrifuge manufacturing and testing locations, using permanently installed cameras and other sensors. It has regular access to more locations under the additional protocol, which has provided the Agency with further information about Iran's nuclear program.

IAEA inspectors now spend around 3,000 days in the field in Iran each year, twice as many as in 2013. They have taken hundreds of environmental samples and placed around 2,000 tamper-proof seals on nuclear material and equipment. The Agency collects and analyzes hundreds of thousands of images captured daily by its sophisticated surveillance cameras. It collects and analyzes several million pieces of open-source information each year. Furthermore, all of its activities are supported by state-of-the-art technology, including data collection and processing systems. The IAEA's current verification capability is much stronger than it ever has been. Having the latest technology is indispensable.

A number of features of this experience required a significant, swift, and innovative Agency response. In other words, in order to succeed, the Agency had to be agile while still acting within its legal mandate. Many of the things the Agency was requested to do under the JCPOA (and the JPOA before it) required it to develop new, robust approaches and ways of working and even to develop new equipment with little time available. In such cases, there were no "baseline" documents to consult, and no precedent to help it. Here are only a few of these new challenges that the IAEA met successfully:

- Verifying in real time that the enrichment levels of uranium hexafluoride (UF6) never exceeded 3.67 percent uranium-235 (U-235), which required the deployment of a new instrument, the online enrichment monitor;
- Measuring the production and inventory of heavy water, which the Agency rarely had done on earlier occasions;
- Monitoring and verifying centrifuge research and development and manufacturing activities, which required new, innovative, and robust solutions;
- Putting together a realistic budget, a particular challenge considering that at least initially the JPA and JCPOA had to be funded entirely through extrabudgetary contributions; and

- Modifying the resource allocation process, notably by giving temporary assistance contracts and hiring external experts. As experienced staff moved back into frontline JCPOA-related positions, the Agency had to backfill its vacant posts with temporary staff as it waited for new recruits to arrive and be trained.

The demands on the safeguards system have grown, and the resources that the IAEA needs to meet these demands have been squeezed. Of course, it is the Agency's legal obligation to implement these safeguards: it is not a matter of choice. Our legal obligations determine our workload, and our workload continues to increase. However, the budget that Member States provide each year for safeguards does not rise at the same rate as the demands.

To address these trends and ensure that the Agency remains a state-of-the-art, highly productive, and lean verification organization, the IAEA Safeguards Department is doing a number of things, including improving its processes to ensure the delivery of desired outcomes, maximizing collaboration through teamwork within the department and ensuring an efficient distribution of resources. Such enhancements are vital if the Agency is to bridge the gap between demand and resources, and demonstrate to Member States that it is using their resources wisely and effectively.

One of the ways in which the Safeguards Department is improving its effectiveness is by continuing to strengthen information collection and analysis. Recently, it established the Collaborative Analytical Platform (CAP), a project that integrates the use of big data collection and analysis software tools into safeguards work. CAP collects and sorts open-source information according to the steps of the nuclear fuel cycle, and makes this information available in a network analysis platform available for IAEA staff to analyze.

The modernization of safeguards IT through the MOSAIC project has helped to ensure that the department's IT system supports all safeguards implementation processes. Through MOSAIC, which was completed in May 2018, the IAEA developed software and applications that helped staff across the entire safeguards department be more effective and efficient. The introduction of new and improved IT applications and their integration with existing software has allowed for better planning, conducting, reporting, and quality assessment of safeguards activities. The department conducted this upgrade using in-house expertise, but relied heavily on extrabudgetary support from Member States. There is also a maintenance cost, which needs to be met on an ongoing basis. One important benefit of the MOSAIC project was an increased ability to defend against cybersecurity threats. The Department of Safeguards has taken important steps to improve the cybersecurity of information in its possession, including moving safeguards confidential systems and files into a secure environment, raising staff awareness about cyberthreats, and complying with international best practices in this area. Despite this major IT upgrade, the Agency is acutely aware of the need to stay ahead of the game in this area, and it will need to secure additional funding to pay for future upgrades.

Environmental sampling and nuclear material analysis are important for safeguards. The department will continually improve its capabilities in this field to ensure a high level of sensitivity, reliability, and timeliness in its measurements and analysis. As capabilities in this area progress in the rest of the world, the IAEA's analytical laboratories in Seibersdorf and the Agency's Network of Analytical Laboratories (NWAL) will remain tightly coordinated. The Agency is examining ways of improving the timeliness of its analysis, including reducing sample sizes, applying more in situ analysis, or working with states to reduce packaging and shipping time. The IAEA is also improving its quality assurance and quality control program for the NWAL, in particular in the area of particle analysis.

The Agency is constantly working to ensure that inspectors have easy-to-use equipment for measurement and containment techniques. Equipment developed for and deployed in the field has to be usable for staff with a wide range of technical capabilities. It must be rugged enough to be shipped around the world and flexible enough to be used in many different environments. The Agency is constantly monitoring the commercial technology environment to identify and exploit innovations that could enhance its capabilities. In January 2020, the IAEA hosted its latest Emerging Technology Workshop, at which a range of new technologies were discussed with experts from around the world. The aim was to see which innovations might be applicable to IAEA safeguards. The Agency is keen to select promising technologies for further testing and, if such tests are positive, move expeditiously to deploy them in the field.

The IAEA believes that State-Level Approaches (SLAs) are a vital tool for it to improve efficiency and effectiveness. They are part of a process that is based on detailed procedures, and allows for a more consistent definition of technical objectives and safeguards measures. Much has happened since the SLA updating process began back in 2013/2014, when the Supplementary Document was produced. The Agency has improved the procedures and developed more detailed guidance over the years; it remains a work in progress.

Moving forward, our immediate efforts should concentrate on ensuring that our SLA processes are applied consistently and uniformly across all operations divisions. The department is developing additional guidance and tools to support the work, and reviewing the SLAs that have been updated and developed to date to make sure the process is fully followed. It is using a robust internal review process for this to ensure that safeguards approaches are objective and nondiscriminatory and that the processes are applied consistently across the department. The initial focus has been on improving the SLAs for states under integrated safeguards, so that our experience with these states can be improved over time.

The Safeguards Department's main product to the IAEA Board of Governors is the annual Safeguards Implementation Report. But inside the department, its main product is the State Evaluation Report (SER) produced for each country under safeguards through application of the state evaluation process. To improve the Agency's effectiveness, it needs to be rigorous in its state evaluation process, ensuring that its analysis is thorough and that the results are soundly based and well documented. One of the ways in which state evaluations are being strengthened is through the introduction of a peer review process. This involves the use of peer review teams, which conduct a full review of the evaluation. These reviews have generated some constructive results and proved useful in making sure that Safeguard Evaluation Groups consistently use the best approaches and tools in preparing SERs. It is important to highlight the need to implement a holistic approach to the analysis of safeguards-relevant information. In this respect, the Agency has introduced the CAP, referred to earlier. One of my priorities is to strengthen teamwork between our analysts and our inspectors, using these state-of-the-art tools, to create high-quality SERs across the board. Inspectors and analysts are being trained to use the CAP and work together as an integral part of state evaluations.

The challenges to the safeguards system are more profound and varied today than they have ever been. To succeed, the IAEA will need to be agile in response to the unexpected, while maintaining the credibility of the safeguards conclusions it draws. I am confident that by working together with Member States, we can meet those challenges, uphold our credibility, and continue to make the world a safer place for future generations.

9 The evolution of IAEA safeguards

Technical, political, and cultural dimensions

John Carlson

The 60th anniversary of the International Atomic Energy Agency (IAEA) and the 20th anniversary of the IAEA's safeguards Additional Protocol occurred in 2017. These anniversaries offered a key opportunity to reflect on the importance of the Agency's safeguards system to national and international security, and the importance of the Additional Protocol in ensuring the effectiveness of the safeguards system. It is also timely to reflect on lessons learned in the evolution of the safeguards system and how the safeguards system might progress in the future.

IAEA safeguards can be described as a comprehensive set of technical and legal measures to verify the undertakings of states, given in treaties such as the Treaty on the Nonproliferation of Nuclear Weapons (NPT), not to use nuclear material and technology to manufacture nuclear weapons. The objectives of safeguards are twofold:

- At the technical level, to ensure that safeguards measures are effective to detect any violation of nonproliferation undertakings, and to provide timely warning of any violation; and
- At the political level, to provide states with assurance that others are complying with nonproliferation undertakings, and to deter violations through the risk of early detection.

Safeguards have political as well as technical dimensions. The technical dimensions relate to the *practice* of safeguards: approaches, procedures, technologies, and the like. The political dimensions relate to strategic, diplomatic, and legal factors. These include a number of considerations. What are the expectations of states? Do safeguards outcomes meet these expectations? Are states fully cooperative in the application of safeguards? In any assessment of the safeguards system, the technical aspects cannot be considered in isolation from the political context. At the technical level, safeguards have undergone substantial evolution since their inception, but political and cultural development lags behind.

IAEA verification underpins the nuclear nonproliferation regime. Without confidence in the nonproliferation regime, substantial nuclear arms

DOI: 10.4324/9781003160205-9

reductions and eventual nuclear disarmament will not be possible. Nuclear-weapon states and nonnuclear-weapon states alike have a vital interest in ensuring that new nuclear threats do not emerge. IAEA safeguards thus make an essential contribution to national and international security. Safeguards both provide states with assurances about the nuclear activities of others and give states a mechanism for resolving any suspicions that others may have about their nuclear activities. To realize the full benefits of safeguards, however, states must be prepared to change their perspective from an emphasis on national sovereignty to an emphasis on international collaboration, in which safeguards become a cooperative mechanism that advances both international and national interests simultaneously.[1]

The early years: Item-specific safeguards

The concept of safeguards was first expressed formally in the Agreed Declaration on Atomic Energy issued on November 15, 1945, by the leaders of the United States, United Kingdom, and Canada. This declaration called for the establishment of an atomic energy commission to make proposals for "effective, reciprocal and enforceable safeguards acceptable to all nations" in order to protect states from the consequences of noncompliance.[2] Regrettably, the major powers could not reach an agreement on the international control of atomic energy. Safeguards first took the form of bilateral arrangements established by nuclear suppliers, under which officials visited nuclear facilities in recipient states to observe that supplied nuclear items were not being used for nuclear weapons. These safeguards, being limited to supplied items (or facilities or materials), were item-specific and had no application to other nuclear activities and materials in the state concerned.

Following the establishment of the IAEA in 1957, an IAEA safeguards inspectorate was developed and bilateral inspections gradually were replaced by IAEA inspections. The IAEA built on the approach of the bilateral agreements, requiring declarations from the state that then would be verified through inspections. The first IAEA safeguards procedures were introduced in 1959 to cover the transfer of a research reactor and its fuel to Japan. Subsequently, the IAEA's item-specific safeguards system developed progressively, starting with research reactors.[3]

An important influence in the development of IAEA safeguards was the European Atomic Energy Authority (Euratom) safeguards system, which was established following the conclusion of the Euratom Treaty in 1957. Safeguards developed from simple observations by bilateral inspectors to nuclear accountancy and supporting measures, including sampling and analysis, probabilistic analysis, and use of containment and surveillance methods and equipment. This was accompanied by the development of techniques for evaluating safeguards effectiveness. The current form of item-specific safeguards was set out in a model agreement published as

IAEA document Information Circular 66 (INFCIRC/66/Rev.2.) in 1968. This is still applied today to specified facilities and materials in the three states that are not parties to the NPT: India, Israel, and Pakistan.

The NPT and the introduction of comprehensive safeguards

With the conclusion of the NPT in 1968, IAEA safeguards were given a key role in international security. The original focus on item-specific safeguards changed to full-scope safeguards, later renamed comprehensive safeguards. Comprehensive safeguards are applicable to all the nuclear material in a state. Under the NPT:

> Each nonnuclear-weapon state party undertakes to accept safeguards, as set forth in an agreement to be negotiated and concluded with the (IAEA) in accordance with the Statute of the (IAEA) and *the Agency's safeguards system*, for the exclusive purpose of verification of the fulfilment of its obligations assumed under this Treaty with a view to *preventing* diversion of *nuclear energy* from peaceful uses to nuclear weapons or other nuclear explosive devices… . The safeguards required by this Article shall be applied on *all source or special fissionable material* in all peaceful nuclear activities within the territory of (the state), under its jurisdiction, or carried out under its control anywhere.[4]

Safeguards to be applied to all the state's nuclear material

This new role for safeguards had far-reaching implications, perhaps not fully appreciated at the time. The requirement to apply safeguards to all the nuclear material in a state, or comprehensive safeguards, carries with it the obligation for the state to declare *all* its nuclear material to the IAEA, and the responsibility for the IAEA to verify that the state has no *undeclared* nuclear material. As the procedures for comprehensive safeguards were developed, however, the focus was primarily on verifying declared nuclear materials and activities, applying procedures broadly similar to those developed for item-specific safeguards.

Preventing diversion

The NPT's reference to preventing diversion is particularly significant. Safeguards as such cannot prevent diversion, except through the deterrent effect of the risk of detection. Prevention is likely to require the intervention of the international community; however, the opportunity for effective intervention depends on timely warning. The IAEA's responsibility to the international community is, where possible, to provide warning before a nuclear-weapon program has proceeded beyond the point where intervention can be effective.

Diversion of nuclear energy

The reference to nuclear energy, rather than nuclear material, indicates that the IAEA's verification responsibilities are not limited to nuclear material. For practical reasons, the development of safeguards focused on nuclear material because the manufacture of nuclear weapons requires nuclear material and nuclear material is readily categorized and quantified. These facts helped establish the accountancy-based verification approaches already in place by the late 1960s. The prevailing view at the time was that an attempt to manufacture nuclear weapons would necessarily involve diversion of declared nuclear material or the misuse of declared nuclear facilities, or both. It was thought the NPT objectives could be met through verifying declared nuclear material and facilities. However, verification also needs to encompass relevant *nonnuclear* materials and items in order to be able to draw valid conclusions about the absence of undeclared nuclear material.

The agency's safeguards system

Nonnuclear-weapon states that are parties to the NPT are required to accept the Agency's safeguards system. This system is not frozen at 1970, when the NPT entered into force—indeed, the model comprehensive safeguards agreement (INFCIRC/153) had yet to be negotiated then—but evolves over time. This evolutionary aspect is essential for safeguards to adapt to new challenges, changing circumstances, and changing expectations.

The procedures for comprehensive safeguards were negotiated by a Special Committee of the IAEA's Board of Governors in 1970-1971 and published as INFCIRC/153. Two inhibiting factors influenced this work. First, a number of states saw safeguards as a derogation of national sovereignty and sought to limit the IAEA's access to places and information accordingly. Second, several states with major nuclear industries were concerned about the possible costs of safeguards and the perceived potential for industrial espionage, and insisted on limiting routine inspector access to specified strategic points at declared locations. This limitation, later shown to be a major weakness, reflected two major assumptions:

- An attempt to manufacture nuclear weapons would necessarily involve diversion of declared nuclear material and/or the misuse of declared nuclear facilities.
- Development of fuel-cycle capabilities independent of declared facilities would be beyond the resources of most states, and would be readily detectable by national intelligence.

It was considered that intelligence agencies were in a better position than the IAEA to detect any undeclared facilities.

Safeguards growth, consolidation, and vulnerability

The period until the early 1990s was one of major growth and consolidation for IAEA safeguards. Nuclear power programs, and the number of states with nuclear research activities, both grew substantially, as did NPT membership and the number of states under comprehensive safeguards. By the time of the 1995 NPT Review and Extension Conference, the NPT had become almost universal. The Agency had considerable success developing and implementing a safeguards system that appeared able to deal with growing workload and complexity.

However, the system had a serious flaw. The emphasis on declared material and facilities, together with uniformity in safeguards implementation, meant that the same inspection activities were applied at similar facilities regardless of state-specific factors. This led to the concentration of inspection effort in those states with the largest fuel cycles, with insufficient attention given to areas of higher proliferation risk.

Strengthening safeguards: From correctness to completeness

The discovery of Iraq's clandestine nuclear-weapon program in 1991 prompted the IAEA and supporting states to thoroughly review how safeguards were designed and applied. Contributing factors to the Iraq situation were the weaknesses in safeguards practice and the emergence of an extensive black market in nuclear technology. It became evident that if a state has undeclared nuclear material or activities, it is quite likely there will be no obvious links between these and its declared nuclear program. International attention turned to how to strengthen the safeguards system, with particular emphasis on the need to develop capabilities to detect undeclared nuclear material or activities. Central to these efforts are the effective use of information, involving its collection and analysis in ways that enhance the IAEA's knowledge and understanding of nuclear programs, and providing IAEA inspectors with more extensive rights of access to nuclear and nuclear-related locations, including for the resolution of questions arising from information analysis. Two broad areas were addressed:

- Technical: The procedures and technologies needed to detect undeclared nuclear material or activities.
- Legal: Whether any additional formal arrangements were required to cover new safeguards activities.

A number of experts considered that the provisions in comprehensive safeguards agreements for special inspections were sufficient to support the new safeguards procedures under consideration, and simply needed to be put to use. Special inspections may be conducted where the IAEA does not consider that the information made available by the state is adequate for the Agency to fulfil its responsibilities. Because special inspections rarely had been used, however, there was a major political inhibition against using them.

Other experts maintained that an ad hoc approach based on special inspections would not be the best way for the IAEA to obtain the information and access it needed to effectively fulfil its responsibilities. This view prevailed, and it was decided to develop a standard set of reporting requirements and procedures, applicable to all states. Hence the concept emerged of a protocol additional to a state's safeguards agreement, broadening the information reported to the IAEA and the access given to inspectors.

The additional protocol

The Model Additional Protocol was negotiated by a Special Committee of the IAEA's Board of Governors. It was approved by the Board in 1997 and published as INFCIRC/540. Before the Additional Protocol (AP), the principal task of safeguards was generally seen as being to confirm the correctness of states' declarations: that nuclear material declared was present and correct. With the AP, the emphasis turned to confirming the completeness of states' declarations: that there are no indications of nuclear material or activities that the state has not declared.

The AP has extended safeguards from an almost exclusive focus on nuclear material into a number of areas where nuclear material would not normally be present, such as manufacture of centrifuge components, heavy water, nuclear-grade graphite and shielded flasks, as well as the construction of hot cells. The rationale for this is clear. The IAEA can and should look at broader information that strengthens its ability to draw valid, timely conclusions regarding nuclear material in the state concerned. This encompasses procedures to find indicators of undeclared nuclear material and nuclear activities, and indicators of diversion or proposed diversion of nuclear material.

Today, 23 years after the Board of Governors' approval, the great majority of states have accepted the AP but it is not yet universal. Such protocols are in force in 136 states and have been signed by a further 14—a total of 150 states, three-quarters of the international community.[5] It is concerning, however, that five nonnuclear-weapon states with significant nuclear activities have still to sign an AP, and a further four such states have yet to ratify the APs that they have signed. The program to strengthen safeguards has led to fundamental changes in safeguards practice and thinking, outlined as follows.

State-Level Concept

Safeguards planning and conclusions for each state have moved from an accretion of measures applied under a facility-by-facility approach, to the application of a state-level approach based on the relevant characteristics of each state.[6] Information collection and analysis have become key, guided by questions such as the following: What are the avenues available to a state to acquire nuclear material for weapons (acquisition path analysis)? What are the possible indicators of undeclared nuclear activities? What is the optimal safeguards strategy for detecting such activities?

Risk-informed or information-driven safeguards

At one time, it was said that safeguards inspectors have changed from accountants to detectives. This is somewhat simplistic, and does not accurately convey how safeguards work, but it does highlight that the IAEA's methods have moved from technical detection techniques to a combination of such techniques and information collection and analysis. Information is especially important. It includes data the IAEA can directly gather for itself (by inspectors in the field or other technical means), data submitted by the state (including accountancy data and design information), data the IAEA can draw from open sources (including satellite imagery and the application of data-mining techniques), and data supplied by third parties (including governments, nongovernmental organizations, and even individuals).

Integrated safeguards

With the introduction of new safeguards measures under the AP, it was clear that some acquisition paths were covered by both traditional safeguards and the new measures. This presented the opportunity to rationalize the safeguards effort, particularly routine inspection efforts, to achieve maximum effectiveness and efficiency within available safeguards resources. The concept of ensuring the optimum combination of safeguards measures was termed integrated safeguards.

For a state to qualify for integrated safeguards, it must have an AP in force and the IAEA must have been able to reach a conclusion (termed the "broader conclusion") on the absence of undeclared nuclear activities in that state. Thus, progress to integrated safeguards requires, in the first instance, an AP.

Addressing uncertainty

Safeguards conclusions regarding the existence or otherwise of undeclared nuclear material and activities are less definitive than conclusions for known, declared nuclear programs. The absence of evidence cannot be taken to be evidence of absence. Conclusions about the absence of undeclared activities necessarily involve qualitative judgments. Key issues affecting the IAEA's ability to reach valid conclusions include the following:

- Authority: Being able to access locations, information, and people.
- Capability: Having the necessary verification technologies and resources.
- Methodology: Ensuring effective detection strategies, analytical techniques, and evaluation processes.

The revolutionary aspect of safeguards development is that judgment has come to the fore in drawing safeguards conclusions. However, conclusions about the absence of something—undeclared activities—can never be as definitive as conclusions based on quantitative methods applied to a finite problem, such as the verification of a declared inventory. For the new safeguards conclusions to be credible, a number of conditions must be satisfied. States must understand the process for looking for indicators of undeclared activities and accept that this process is appropriate. They also must be satisfied the process is applied consistently and at the requisite standard. Finally, states also must believe that judgments have been exercised and conclusions drawn in a suitably disciplined way. All of this involves new approaches compared with the traditional quantitative system, including analysis of a broader range of information, and a quality assurance system to ensure appropriate standards of implementation and decision-making. Moreover, effective communication with stakeholders (that is, states) to ensure that the IAEA's processes are well understood and provide the required level of confidence is essential.

The IAEA's foundational documents are realistic in recognizing the uncertainties that safeguards may need to address. The standard of proof for safeguards noncompliance is not absolute, but allows for the uncertainties that could arise in practice. The Board of Governors may report noncompliance if the Agency has found diversion of nuclear material for nuclear weapons or for purposes unknown, or if the Agency is not able to verify that there has been no diversion of nuclear material to nuclear weapons.[7] The IAEA Statute also has a broader reporting provision, which could apply where there are grounds for concern about diversion but insufficient evidence. The Agency is required to notify the United Nations Security Council of questions that arise in connection with the Agency's activities that are within the Council's competence.[8]

Current safeguards issues

In spite of the international community's general acceptance of IAEA safeguards, a number of issues remain of concern for future discussion and debate.

Universalizing the additional protocol

The universalization of the AP should be a consequence of the commitment made by all nonnuclear-weapon states under the NPT to accept the Agency's safeguards system. States should not be able to pick and choose which measures they accept and which they do not.[9] The combination of a comprehensive safeguards agreement and an AP is the contemporary standard for NPT safeguards. As the following discussion shows, it is recognized as such in practice by a large majority of states.

The AP is an essential part of the Agency's safeguards system. The IAEA emphasizes its importance to effective safeguards:

> It is only in countries with both a comprehensive safeguards agreement and an additional protocol in force that the IAEA has sufficient information and access to provide credible assurances to the international community of both the non-diversion of nuclear material and the absence of undeclared nuclear material and activities.[10]

Currently, not all states have accepted the AP. Looking at the non-nuclear-weapon states with significant nuclear activities, of which there are 63 in total, 54 (86 percent) have an AP in force.[11] Four more (Algeria, Belarus, Iran, and Malaysia) have signed an AP but have not yet ratified it. Iran is implementing its AP provisionally and has committed to submit it for ratification by the Majles (parliament). This makes a total of 58 nonnuclear-weapon states with significant nuclear activities, or 92 percent of such states, that have concluded or at least signed an AP. Five nonnuclear-weapon states with significant nuclear activities (Argentina, Brazil, Egypt, Syria, and Venezuela) have not commenced negotiation of an AP. There are almost 50 nonnuclear-weapon states currently without (as far as known) significant nuclear activities that do not have an AP. The AP is needed to provide assurance of the absence of nuclear activities in these states.

It is particularly concerning that several of the states that have not signed an AP have taken a political position against doing so. Brazil, Egypt, and others argue that it is voluntary, and have said they will not conclude one until the nuclear-weapon states meet their NPT disarmament obligations. In taking this position, they are ignoring the fact that the NPT is not a binary agreement between the nuclear-weapon and nonnuclear-weapon states. Importantly, the NPT also establishes commitments amongst all the nonnuclear-weapon states to accept the Agency's safeguards system to assure each other that they are not seeking nuclear weapons.

These political attitudes on the AP have been allowed to damage the credibility of the Treaty on the Prohibition of Nuclear Weapons, concluded in July 2017.[12] In contradiction of successive NPT review conferences that have recognized that nuclear disarmament will require rigorous and universal safeguards, in this treaty the negotiating states failed to require this universal high safeguards standard of comprehensive safeguards and APs.[13] These states failed to recognize that the most effective safeguards are essential for the confidence needed for major nuclear-weapon reductions, and eventual elimination, to proceed.

It is misguided to see acceptance of the AP as primarily a legal issue, or even a diplomatic issue. The purpose of safeguards is to provide confidence of a state's commitment against acquiring nuclear weapons, and to ensure timely detection of diversion of nuclear material to nuclear weapons if it occurs. A state that refuses to accept the most effective form of safeguards raises concerns about the extent of its commitment to nonproliferation.

State-level approach

Surprisingly, years after the introduction of the state-level approach, some IAEA Member States have expressed concerns about the concept and the way it is applied. The concern appears to be that decisions on safeguards implementation in particular states could be biased, leading to some states being given too much attention and others not being given enough. The critics seem to be concerned about unfairness and, more seriously, the potential for vulnerabilities—namely, a failure to detect safeguards violations in a timely manner.

The IAEA Board of Governors has been extensively briefed on and has endorsed the state-level approach. INFCIRC/153 allows for state-specific characteristics to be taken into account. The approach enables safeguards resources to be prioritized for areas of greatest safeguards significance; in other words, to allow differentiation amongst states. The Board has accepted that differentiation is not discrimination, provided that similar criteria are applied to all states in an objective way.

The previous practice of applying safeguards in a uniform, facility-by-facility way was not cost efficient and is not suitable for the broader range of safeguards activities introduced by the AP. The language of the protocol—access will be on a selective basis, the IAEA is not to act mechanistically or systematically, and the IAEA is to resolve questions or inconsistencies relating to information—makes it clear that the Agency is to base its activities on judgment. There can be no objection to the IAEA acting accordingly. Rather, the problem seems to be inadequate communication of the IAEA's processes for making and reviewing judgments. This uncertainty reinforces the fact that it is essential for the IAEA to ensure that its practices are well understood and that states have confidence in the way the Agency works.

Use of national intelligence information

Some Member States have questioned the appropriateness of the IAEA receiving and acting on information from national intelligence sources. This criticism fails to recognize that an important function of IAEA safeguards is to provide a mechanism for resolving suspicions about possible undeclared nuclear activities. If a state has intelligence information giving rise to such suspicions, the state should give the information to the IAEA to evaluate and, if warranted, investigate. Clearly, the alternatives—that suspicions remain unresolved, or worse, that a concerned state takes unilateral military action—are better avoided.

The IAEA operates its own information collection and analysis activities, but its available resources are small compared with those of most states. It is in no one's interest for the IAEA to fail to detect a major safeguards violation because it did not have sufficient information, especially if a state had information that could have been helpful but chose to withhold it. For this reason, at an early stage in the program to strengthen safeguards, the Board of Governors agreed that states with information of possible safeguards significance should give that information to the Agency for investigation.

The IAEA's role in investigating possible weaponization activities

Some states have questioned the IAEA's authority in investigating potential cases of weaponization. Weaponization refers to a range of activities, in addition to the acquisition of fissile material, necessary to manufacture a nuclear weapon.[14] The manufacture of nuclear weapons obviously requires nuclear material, but many preparatory activities do not. Some of these activities are dual-use and do not necessarily indicate an intention to manufacture a nuclear weapon. Seen in isolation, such activities may be ambiguous, but may be less so in the context of the totality of information known about the state.

There is a view that, absent some nexus to nuclear material, the IAEA's authority to investigate possible nuclear-weapon-related activity is limited. This raises an obvious question: What is a sufficient nexus? Clearly, development of nuclear weapons must at some stage involve nuclear material. A state's decision to conduct certain activities could indicate an intention to misuse nuclear material. The nexus is the potential to apply the results of such activity to the use of nuclear material. The question of weaponization activities is directly relevant to the NPT's language on prevention of diversion, and to the IAEA's responsibility to provide timely warning of diversion. In any case, the presence of nuclear-weapon-related studies or research and development in a state would raise the question of whether the state has declared all nuclear materials. Consequently, the IAEA cannot afford to ignore possible weaponization activities. It is important to investigate such activities simply to be able to judge whether a state's declaration of nuclear materials and activities is complete.

Two aspects of the weaponization issue need comment. One is the protection of sensitive information, particularly with regard to the NPT's prohibition on assisting any state to develop or produce nuclear weapons. The IAEA must ensure that any sensitive information it finds is fully protected from disclosure, especially to nonnuclear-weapon states. The IAEA is well aware of its responsibilities in this regard, and it is established practice (demonstrated in the Agency's investigations of cases such as Iraq and Libya) to limit access to sensitive information to appropriately cleared staff members from nuclear-weapon states. The other aspect concerns the IAEA's detection capabilities—not to be confused with the Agency's right to investigate indications of possible weaponization activities. Some weaponization activities will be difficult to detect, a fact that affects the level of assurance the IAEA is able to provide. In most cases, the Agency will not be in a position to specifically provide credible assurance of the absence of weaponization activities, although also in most cases state evaluation should show that there is no reason to believe such activities may be present.

Future directions in safeguards

The IAEA's safeguards activity has been evolving since the Agency's inception, and new technologies and approaches doubtless will enable it to improve its nuclear security and safety efforts. A few potential future directions of safeguards are worth closer examination.

Measures needed to complement safeguards

Although the NPT charges the IAEA with establishing safeguards to preventing diversion, it is essential to appreciate that the safeguards system cannot do so by itself. It can only prevent diversion insofar as the risk of timely detection, with the consequential risk of intervention, deters diversion. Further, proliferation-sensitive technologies and materials, such as centrifuge enrichment and separated plutonium, have been able to make timely detection difficult, if not impossible. Diversion would not result in the immediate acquisition of nuclear weapons. The diverted material will take time to weaponize, and more time will be required for deployment of the weapons produced. However, the opportunity for intervention will be limited if the locations used for processing and weaponization are secret. Accordingly, the international community cannot rely on safeguards alone. Safeguards need to be complemented by other measures.

Many of these measures are beyond the scope of this discussion. They include technical measures such as proliferation-resistant technologies, and institutional measures such as export controls and multinational control of sensitive facilities. Others, including greater transparency, can be directly relevant to safeguards implementation.

Importance of greater transparency

Transparency is likely to become all the more important both as an integral part of the safeguards system and as a complement to the system. It involves a number of aspects, including transparency of the state to the IAEA, transparency of states to each other, and transparency of the IAEA itself.

As discussed earlier, conclusions about the absence of undeclared nuclear activities are less definitive and less certain than conclusions based on the verification of declarations. Similarly, there may be less confidence in a more qualitative conclusion, but confidence can be reinforced by availability of additional information supporting the conclusion. There are many potential transparency mechanisms, including wider publication by states of information on their nuclear programs; collaborative conduct of research and operational programs; broader privatization and globalization of nuclear activities, and establishment of multilateral fuel-cycle centers; and conduct of collaborative safeguards activities on a bilateral or regional basis. In particular, bilateral or regional safeguards arrangements could play a key role, complementing IAEA safeguards in circumstances where states are looking for additional confidence-building measures. Euratom and the Argentine-Brazilian Agency for Accounting and Control of Nuclear Materials are valuable precedents here.

Enhanced cooperation with and transparency toward the IAEA will be particularly important. Strengthened safeguards bring new requirements for states in terms of information, access, and cooperation. It is no longer sufficient for a state to meet only its minimum legal commitments to the IAEA, although that is always a good start. Rather, states need to cooperate with the Agency to the standard necessary to maintain the confidence of the international community. This includes showing full transparency to the IAEA, particularly where there are issues of compliance or confidence to be resolved. A particular challenge to the IAEA is developing a sufficiently rigorous method of testing transparency and drawing appropriate conclusions. The failure to cooperate may be obvious, but where the state appears to be cooperating it will be important to avoid being misled and not to draw broader conclusions than actually warranted.

Transparency is also important for the safeguards system itself. To be most effective in its confidence-building function, a verification system must have an appropriate degree of transparency. To have confidence in the conclusions reached, states must have sufficient knowledge of how the system works, including verification methods, performance standards, decision-making processes, and quality assurance. The IAEA is devoting considerable effort to these matters, though some of the concerns raised by Member States suggest that more needs to be done in this regard. One mechanism that might be looked at here is external review: just as there is an external auditor for budgetary performance, there may be a role for an external auditor for safeguards performance.

Confidentiality in safeguards

Related to the issue of transparency is the question of whether, and to what extent, information available to the safeguards system should be shared with states. A notable feature of traditional safeguards is confidentiality: the information the IAEA holds on a state is maintained within the Agency and not shared with others.[15] This blanket proscription on sharing information contrasts with newer treaty-based regimes. For example, the 1997 Chemical Weapons Convention takes a different approach, as much of the information in parties' declarations and summary data from inspections are made available to the parties at large. The 1996 Comprehensive Nuclear Test-Ban

Treaty (CTBT) takes information sharing further. Parties are given equal access to all data collected by the CTBT's International Monitoring System. Any party is able to analyze the data for itself and to seek clarification of a suspect event, including through calling for an on-site inspection.

As a result, under both the Chemical Weapons Convention and the CTBT, parties are in a position to cross-check the information available to the verification agency. Doing so can allow them to identify gaps in that information where they may be able to assist and to reach an informed assessment on how well the verification system is operating. The safeguards system might well take this direction. Obviously, there are issues to be addressed, such as maintaining confidentiality of sensitive information and avoiding warning a state of investigations in progress. But a more transparent system, where greater information is available not merely on states' nuclear activities but on the IAEA's activities, its conclusions, and the basis for these, would have major confidence-building benefits.

Information-sharing across verification regimes

Today, several treaties and associated verification regimes are operating in the area of weapons of mass destruction. Principal examples include the NPT, CTBT, the Chemical Weapons Convention, and the Missile Technology Control Regime. To some extent, these overlap, or at least share commonalities. The relationship between NPT safeguards and the CTBT is obvious. The Missile Technology Control Regime is also relevant to safeguards, as interest in nuclear-capable missiles could indicate interest in nuclear weapons. The Chemical Weapons Convention could be relevant to safeguards, as states that are interested in one form of weapons of mass destruction also tend to be interested in other forms. There are sound reasons for coordination and information-sharing among the different regimes.

Currently, information-sharing often runs into several political and legal barriers. For example, the IAEA considers that the requirement for confidentiality of safeguards information precludes it from sharing such information with the CTBT's Provisional Technical Secretariat, even where there would be a clear mutual benefit in terms of verification effectiveness. IAEA Member States should consider modifying the proscription on sharing safeguards information to enable information-sharing with other treaty verification agencies on a confidential basis where doing so would contribute to better verification outcomes.

Greater use of monitoring technologies

For much of its life, the IAEA safeguards system has been based on regular inspections of declared materials and facilities. With the development of newer technologies, including video, radiation measurement, and other instrumentation and data transmission, unattended monitoring has assumed greater importance, and yet it is limited to declared facilities. Depending on the development of suitable technologies, in the future some form of long-range, wide-area monitoring may well play a key role in detecting proscribed activities at undeclared locations.

A current example of this approach is the CTBT's International Monitoring System. This system deploys a number of verification technologies looking for indicators that a proscribed activity (for instance, a nuclear explosion) has occurred. International Monitoring System data will show if there has been a proscribed activity and should help identify its location, enabling investigation through an on-site inspection. Extensive experience of wide-area environmental monitoring was gained in Iraq after the 1991 Gulf War, when air and water sampling were deployed to detect any indicators of undeclared chemical or nuclear activities. Subsequent studies into the IAEA's possible use of wide-area environmental monitoring have concluded that the technologies are not yet sufficiently developed to be cost-effective for safeguards. The AP anticipates the use of wide-area environmental sampling, but this will require the Board of Governors' approval.[16]

Another promising technology for safeguards application is antineutrino detection. This is being considered for monitoring the operation of declared reactors, but it may also be usable for long-range detection of clandestine reactors. Other possible areas for study for long range detection include satellite, airborne, and land-based spectroscopy; infrared and panchromatic spectrometry; and detection of acoustic and other electromagnetic emanations.

The development of safeguards monitoring of declared facilities has enabled reductions in safeguards inspection effort, and can be expected to lead to further improvements. Cost-effective technologies for long-range monitoring would significantly strengthen the IAEA's capabilities to detect undeclared nuclear activities.

Need to change political attitudes

As has been outlined here, the technical aspects of safeguards have evolved significantly. Political attitudes, however, have not kept pace. For instance, a handful of states have continued to argue that the AP is "voluntary"—an argument that was allowed to damage the Treaty on the Prohibition of Nuclear Weapons. A similar attitude lies behind arguments about the IAEA's right of access to military bases. Such arguments indicate an adversarial approach to safeguards, which sees safeguards as an imposition on national sovereignty. As long as this attitude prevails, safeguards will not realize their full confidence-building potential. Where a state is being difficult about accepting safeguards, other states will become concerned. Is the recalcitrant state trying to keep the option of pursuing nuclear weapons in the future—or does it currently have something to hide?

Safeguards do involve obligations, but it is more helpful to think of safeguards in terms of commitment. Commitments imply positive support, willingness, shared values, and a more constructive approach. A process is needed to promote an international dialogue on the issues discussed here, to reach a shared vision for safeguards as a collaborative system that serves the fundamental interests of all states.

Conclusion

The IAEA safeguards system is a unique model of treaty compliance verification, providing a rigorous process for identifying noncompliance. The system has risen to meet the challenges of changing circumstances and conditions. It has gone from basic inspector observations to the development of nuclear accountancy and associated sampling and analysis to greater use of instrumentation and unattended monitoring to today's focus on information collection and analysis. As the challenges have become more complex, safeguards have become more qualitative, moving from the apparent certainty of verifying declared inventories to an approach based more on expert judgment. They have been able to take into account a broader range of information, where outcomes are less absolute.

The fact that safeguards are becoming more qualitative, or at least that they involve a substantial qualitative element, does not mean that safeguards judgments will become less technical and more political. On the contrary, the IAEA's value to the international community is its ability to report facts based on impartial technical analysis. It is essential to the Agency's credibility that safeguards reporting and decisions continue to be based on objective technical grounds. Ensuring this in a more qualitative environment requires greater clarity of thought about the safeguards mission and greater transparency in its processes.

As mentioned, political attitudes have not kept pace with technical change. This is evident in the resistance to universalizing the AP, and more recently the questioning of the state-level approach and the use of information. The prevailing attitude continues to be adversarial, seeing safeguards as a challenge to national sovereignty. Resolution of these issues and development of a truly international safeguards culture requires a process of constructive dialogue, involving not only the expert community, diplomats, and policymakers but also national leaders.[17]

Notes

1. It is a misconception to see national and international interests as being opposed; in reality, the international interest is the aggregation of national interests.
2. Quoted in Dean Acheson, *Present at the Creation: My Years in the State Department* (New York: W.W. Norton & Company, 1969), 131.
3. See IAEA document Information Circular 26 (INFCIRC/26) of 1961.

4. NPT Article III.1 (emphasis added).
5. Based on IAEA information as of September 18, 2020, available at https://www.iaea.org/sites/default/files/20/01/sg-ap-status.pdf.
6. This is contemplated in INFCIRC/153 paragraph 81(c), but this provision had been overlooked.
7. Reports are made to the United Nations Security Council and the General Assembly. See INFCIRC/153 paras. 19 and 28; Statute Article XII.C.
8. Statute Article III.B.4.
9. John Carlson, "Is the Additional Protocol 'Optional'?" Nuclear Threat Initiative, January 1, 2011, https://www.nti.org/analysis/articles/additional-protocol-optional/.
10. "Nuclear Safeguards Conclusions Presented in 2016 Safeguards Implementation Report," IAEA News Center, June 16, 2017, https://www.iaea.org/newscenter/news/nuclear-safeguards-conclusions-presented-in-2016-safeguards-implementation-report.
11. Significant nuclear activities, as defined by the IAEA, encompasses any amount of nuclear material in a facility or *location outside facilities*, or nuclear material in excess of the exemption limits in INFCIRC/153.
12. "9. Treaty on the Prohibition of Nuclear Weapons," United Nations Treaty Collection, accessed November 8, 2020, https://treaties.un.org/Pages/ViewDetails.aspx?src=TREATY&mtdsg_no=XXVI-9&chapter=26&clang=_en.
13. See the newsletter from the Verification Research, Training and Information Centre: "Nuclear Weapon Prohibition Treaty: A Safeguards Debacle," *Trust & Verify* 158 (Autumn 2018), https://www.vertic.org/media/assets/TV/TV158.pdf.
14. Weaponization activities have not been defined in IAEA safeguards documents, but some such activities have been set out in Section T of the Joint Comprehensive Plan of Action (JCPOA). The JCPOA is expressed not to establish a precedent; however, it is inevitable that the weaponization text will be seen as providing guidance in this area.
15. The basis for this is the requirement in IAEA safeguards agreements (INFCIRC/153, paragraph 5; see also IAEA Statute, Article VII.F) for the Agency to maintain confidentiality of information obtained in connection with the implementation of the agreement.
16. INFCIRC/540, Article 9.
17. The experience of the Nuclear Security Summits showed the value of engaging national leaders in what usually would be considered an esoteric subject.

10 Nuclear nonproliferation

Six lessons not yet learned*

Pierre Goldschmidt

> The only thing we learn from experience is that we don't learn from experience.
>
> George Bernard Shaw

In 2017, the International Atomic Energy Agency (IAEA) celebrated its 60th anniversary. If one had to choose the most exceptional year in the history of the IAEA safeguards regime, it would be 2003. That year saw four events that, looking back from the vantage point of over 15 years' later, represented important challenges and in some respects missed opportunities for governments seeking to prevent the spread of nuclear weapons.

On January 10, 2003, North Korea announced its withdrawal from the Nuclear Nonproliferation Treaty (NPT), a unique case to date. On February 25, IAEA inspectors discovered an Iranian pilot centrifuge enrichment facility at Natanz ready to start operation, as well as the existence of undeclared nuclear material. On March 20, U.S. forces invaded Iraq on the false pretext that the country still had a weapons-of-mass-destruction program that included nuclear weapons. On December 19, Colonel Muammar Gaddafi announced that Libya was abandoning its 20-year covert nuclear-weapon program; and as a result, the IAEA discovered the existence of a vast international network of clandestine nuclear traffic headed by Abdul Qadeer Khan of Pakistan. Incidentally, 2003 was also the year during which, after some 15 years of an Agency budget policy of zero real growth and three years of painful negotiations, the IAEA Board of Governors agreed to increase the regular budget of the Department of Safeguards by 22 percent (in real terms) over a period of four years.

Still, the international community failed to take bold steps similar to what it had done a dozen years earlier. At that time, following the 1991 Gulf War, the world discovered that Iraq had developed a clandestine nuclear-weapon program over an extended period of time in parallel to its declared peaceful nuclear activities. Iraq had developed this program, even though it was a party to the NPT and had a Comprehensive Safeguards Agreement in force with the IAEA since 1972.[1] Realizing that this safeguards agreement did not provide the IAEA with the necessary tools to verify the declarations of

DOI: 10.4324/9781003160205-10

nonnuclear-weapon states, in 1997 the IAEA Board of Governors approved the Model Additional Protocol to provide the tools to draw the so-called broader conclusion that there are no undeclared nuclear materials and activities in a nonnuclear-weapon state, and that its declarations are correct and complete. It is disturbing that no comparable measures were adopted after the 2003 events.

The following analysis will focus on Iran's noncompliance with its IAEA safeguards agreement, North Korea's withdrawal from the NPT, and the lessons not yet fully learned nearly two decades after these events.

The lessons from Iran

Three major lessons from the experience with Iran relate to dealing with a state found in noncompliance with its safeguards agreement.

Lesson 1: In a case of noncompliance, the IAEA must refer it to the United Nations (UN) Security Council without undue delay

In November 2002, IAEA Director General Mohamed ElBaradei said, "I believe that while differing circumstances may necessitate asymmetric responses, in the case of noncompliance with nonproliferation obligations, for the credibility of the regime, the approach in all cases should be one and the same: zero tolerance."[2] Yet by failing to declare Iran in noncompliance in the IAEA Director General's November 2003 report and in the ensuing Board of Governors resolution, the IAEA created a damaging precedent with far-reaching consequences that are still felt today.

When the Safeguards Department detects noncompliance, time is of the essence in reporting it. Any noncompliant state should know that it will be referred within a short period of time, first to the IAEA Board of Governors and then to the UN Security Council. If the state cooperates proactively with the Agency to correct the situation, it should be referred to the Security Council for "information purposes only," as was the case with Libya in March 2004. If, by contrast, the state adopts a "policy of concealment, with cooperation being limited and reactive, and information being slow in coming, changing and contradictory," as was the case in Iran, the issue should be reported without delay to the Security Council for action.[3]

On September 12, 2003, the IAEA Board adopted a consensus resolution that called on Iran to "suspend all further uranium enrichment-related activities" and to grant "unrestricted access, including environmental sampling, for the Agency to whatever locations the Agency deems necessary for the purposes of verification of the correctness and completeness of Iran's declarations."[4] The problem with such a resolution, which the Board might well adopt in a future case of noncompliance, is that it is not legally binding. The only way to make it legally binding is to have it adopted by the Security Council acting under Article 41 of the UN Charter. In the case of Iran, such a resolution was adopted for the first time only in December 2006.[5] Three crucial years had been lost, making the situation practically irreversible in the sense that a lasting suspension of any enrichment activity was no longer achievable.

Lesson 2: In case of noncompliance, the IAEA should temporarily receive expanded verification authority

Under the governing IAEA Statute, safeguards are "designed to ensure that special fissionable and other materials, services, equipment, facilities, and information ... under [Agency] supervision or control are not used in such a way as to further any military purpose."[6] To reach that objective, Article XII.A.6 provides that the Agency will have the right and responsibility "to send into the territory of the recipient State inspectors ... who shall have access at all times to all places and data and to any person who by reason of his occupation deals with materials, equipment, or facilities which are required by this Statute to be safeguarded, as necessary ... to determine whether there is compliance with the undertaking against use in furtherance of any military purpose."[7] It is now over six decades since the coming into force of this forward-looking mandate. Unfortunately, in practice, the commitments accepted by nonnuclear-weapon states under a Comprehensive Safeguards Agreement and even an Additional Protocol are much more limited, particularly as they relate to access to information, persons, locations, data, and documents.[8] Iran is well aware of those limitations.

Experience has taught us, in particular in the cases of North Korea and Iran, that when a state is found in noncompliance with its safeguards agreements (or in breach of its obligation to comply with its safeguards agreements, which is synonymous) and does not show full transparency and cooperation in resolving questions or inconsistencies with regard to its nuclear program (both past and present), the Agency temporarily will need expanded verification authority.[9] This expanded authority needs to go beyond that granted under a Comprehensive Safeguards Agreement and an Additional Protocol, as clearly reflected in this statement from the September 2005 IAEA report on Iran:

> Given Iran's past concealment efforts over many years, such transparency measures should extend beyond the formal requirements of the Safeguards Agreement and Additional Protocol and include access to individuals, documentation related to procurement, dual use equipment, certain military owned workshops and research and development locations. Without such transparency measures, the Agency's ability ... to verify the correctness and completeness of the statements made by Iran will be restricted.[10]

The problem is that these additional "transparency measures" have not been defined in any precise way. Also, they were not included in UN

Security Council Resolution 1737 of December 27, 2006, in which the Security Council, acting under Article 41 of the UN Charter, decided in operative paragraph 8 "that Iran shall provide such access and cooperation as the IAEA request to be able … to resolve all outstanding issues, as identified in IAEA reports."[11]

These broader access rights, conducted under "managed access" conditions, must not exclude military sites because it is likely that the military (or related actors) would be involved in nuclear activities associated with a weapon program, should one exist.[12] The IAEA Director General should report any denial of, unwarranted delays in, or limitations to access to the Board of Governors and, as appropriate, to the Security Council.

Lesson 3: The UN Security Council should adopt a generic resolution preventively dealing with cases of noncompliance

To implement what has been learned from Lesson 2, and give the IAEA the verification tools it needs in cases of noncompliance, the Security Council should adopt a generic resolution under Article 41 of the UN Charter.[13] This resolution should state, independently of any specific case, that if the IAEA finds a state to be in noncompliance with its Comprehensive Safeguards Agreement in accordance with Article XII.C of the IAEA Statute, *upon request by the Agency*, the Security Council automatically would adopt a state-specific resolution under Article 41 of the UN Charter, requiring that state to *temporarily* grant to the Agency extended access rights. These rights, defined in the Model Temporary Complementary Protocol published by the Carnegie Endowment for International Peace in April 2009, would be terminated as soon as the Agency's Secretariat and Board of Governors have drawn the "broader conclusion" that the state has no undeclared nuclear material and activities, and that its declarations to the IAEA are correct and complete.[14]

This generic resolution should also require the noncompliant state to immediately suspend all nuclear fuel-cycle-related activities as long as the IAEA has not been able to draw the "broader conclusion"; and to conclude with the Agency, within a limited period of time (for instance, within 60 days), a facility specific safeguards agreement for all its nuclear facilities. The latter requirement is necessary to close the most damaging Comprehensive Safeguards Agreement loophole (detailed in Lesson 6).

This generic resolution also should provide that if the IAEA Director General is unable to report within 60 days of the adoption of the state-specific resolution that the noncompliant state has concluded the required facility specific safeguards agreements, or that it is fully implementing other resolution requirements, then the Security Council immediately would convene to adopt a new Article 41 resolution sanctioning the noncompliant state. The level of sanctions would not be predetermined, and the permanent members of the Security Council would still have a veto right, but such actions would make the adoption of sanctions at an early stage much more likely and therefore constitute an improved deterrence.

One should bear in mind that for almost 10 years, the Security Council adopted few legally binding sanctions against Iran. The sanctions that did exist essentially targeted designated individuals and entities involved in nuclear or ballistic missile activities. These limited sanctions did not stop Iran from continuing to make progress on its nuclear program, in contravention of legally binding Security Council resolutions. At the time of the November 2003 report, Iran had no operating UF6 (uranium hexafluoride) conversion plant or operating centrifuge plant at Natanz, and the construction of the heavy-water research reactor at Arak had not yet started. By early 2006, when the IAEA finally reported Iran's noncompliance to the Security Council, the situation was very different and there was no way Iran could be compelled to return to the status of its nuclear program at the time of the IAEA November 2003 report.

This fact is reflected in the Joint Comprehensive Plan of Action (JCPOA) concluded on 14 July 2015 between Iran and the P5+1 (China, France, Germany, Russia, the United Kingdom, and the United States), which allows Iran to continue enriching uranium under a range of restrictions. (The United States withdrew from the agreement in May 2018.) The main objective of the JCPOA is to ensure that Iran is constrained and monitored for 15 years so that it cannot break out and manufacture a nuclear weapon in less than one year.[15] As long as all parties meet their obligations, this objective will be attained. Some of the constraints that Iran accepted under the JCPOA were a remarkable, largely unexpected achievement. For the U.S. negotiators of the agreement, 15 years might have seemed a long period—it represents nearly four presidential terms—but for Iran and others this is not so long a period. After all, it is now more than 15 years since the IAEA visited Natanz for the first time.

According to UN Security Council Resolution 2231 of July 20, 2015, endorsing the JCPOA, on October 18, 2025 "all of the provisions of this resolution shall be terminated, none of the previous resolutions … shall be applied, the Security Council will have concluded its consideration of the Iranian nuclear issue, and the item Nonproliferation will be removed from the list of matters of which the Council is seized."[16] By that time, if the agreement succeeds, Iran will no longer be obliged to limit its number of installed centrifuges to 5,060, but for another 5 years its stockpile of enriched uranium must remain limited to 300 kilograms enriched to no more than 3.67 percent uranium 235 (U-235).

There is little doubt that around 2030, if not before, Iran will be a nuclear threshold state; that is, a state capable of manufacturing more than one nuclear weapon in a period of a few months and having the necessary delivery means. With that in mind, while the JCPOA negotiation was underway, in March 2014 I recommended privately to high-ranking officials at the U.S. Department of State that two important provisions be included. The first was a requirement that Iran place each of its nuclear facilities under an IAEA facility specific safeguards agreement. The second was the requirement for Iran to ratify the Comprehensive Nuclear Test Ban Treaty, as requested in June 2010 under Security Council Resolution 1929. Unfortunately, neither provision was included in the JCPOA.

It is hard to understand on what basis Iran could have objected to these two crucial requirements, since Supreme Leader Ayatollah Ali Khamenei had issued a fatwa stating that the production, stockpiling, and use of nuclear weapons is forbidden under Islam, and the JCPOA's preamble states that "Iran reaffirms that under no circumstances will Iran ever seek, develop or acquire any nuclear weapons."[17] Since France, Germany, Russia, and the United Kingdom have ratified the Comprehensive Nuclear Test Ban Treaty, it is most likely that the United States did not push for the inclusion of that important requirement in the JCPOA because it has not ratified the treaty itself.

The lessons from North Korea

There are three further lessons to be drawn from the safeguards experience in North Korea.

Lesson 4: In case a nation withdraws from the NPT, the UN Security Council must act promptly and decisively to condemn the action and impose sanctions

Shortly after North Korea submitted its initial report to the IAEA under its safeguards agreement in May 1992, inconsistencies emerged between its initial declaration and the Agency's findings, centering on a mismatch between declared plutonium production and solutions containing nuclear waste. On April 1, 1993, the IAEA Board of Governors declared that North Korea was in noncompliance with its safeguards agreement and promptly reported the case to the UN Security Council. In the meantime, on March 12, 1993, North Korea notified its intention to withdraw from the NPT. On May 11, the Security Council adopted Resolution 825, calling upon North Korea to reconsider its withdrawal.[18] Since then, the IAEA has repeatedly declared North Korea in noncompliance with its safeguards agreement.

The Agreed Framework concluded between the United States and North Korea in October 1994 resulted in the latter suspending its withdrawal and agreeing to freeze the operation of a number of sensitive facilities. Unfortunately, because of the imprecise formulation of the Agreed Framework, North Korea subsequently did not agree to some of the verification measures requested by the Agency, such as the taking of samples and nondestructive analysis measurements. The North Koreans also did not submit accounting reports to the Agency for the facilities covered by the freeze. On October 16, 2002, the George W. Bush administration stated that in a meeting earlier that month, a North Korean official, confronted with a U.S. assessment, admitted the existence of a clandestine uranium-enrichment program. That was the starting point of a crisis that led to North Korea's announcement on January 10, 2003, that it would proceed with its withdrawal from the NPT.

Over the 13 years after North Korea was first reported for noncompliance to the Security Council, the latter failed to adopt a single resolution condemning North Korea, even during the three-and-a-half years that followed North Korea's withdrawal from the NPT in 2003. Not until North Korea tested a nuclear weapon on October 9, 2006, did the Security Council adopt for the first time (on October 14) the legally binding Chapter VII Resolution 1718, imposing an embargo on arms and luxury goods, an assets freeze, and a travel ban for persons designated as involved in the North Korea's nuclear program. Further, it imposed a ban on a range of imports and exports and prohibited Pyongyang from conducting nuclear tests or launching ballistic missiles.[19] Yet even these sanctions were much too mild and came much too late to dissuade North Korea from continuing with its nuclear program. Since then, North Korea has tested nuclear weapons in 2009, 2013, twice in 2016, and most recently in September 2017, and has launched numerous and increasingly more capable ballistic missiles.

The main factor leading to this dramatic situation is that, for all those years, China consistently opposed effective Security Council sanctions against North Korea. Beijing's stated justification was its concern that harsh sanctions could precipitate the collapse of the regime, potentially driving hundreds of thousands of North Korean refugees into China and increasing the likelihood of Korean reunification under the leadership of the democratic South. China would then have, on its northeast, a border with a state friendly to the United States and home to more than 25,000 U.S. troops. Although China's concerns are legitimate, the consequence of its unconstructive and ineffective attitude is that today North Korea has an arsenal of nuclear weapons, which it is unlikely to abandon in any circumstance in the foreseeable future.

In any case, it is critical for the Security Council to adopt new measures to minimize the risk that other states could follow North Korea's example. Indeed, one should not forget that in May 2006, the Iranian parliament threatened in a letter to UN Secretary General Kofi Annan to force the government to withdraw from the NPT if the United States and its allies continued pressuring Tehran to suspend uranium enrichment.[20] Key Iranian officials would later make similar threats.

Lesson 5: The Security Council needs to deter withdrawal from the NPT by making the use of the veto right less likely

As exemplified by the cases of Iran and North Korea, one of the greatest difficulties in deterring states from violating their nonproliferation undertakings and from ignoring legally binding Security Council resolutions is their hope that, for geopolitical or economic reasons, at least one of the five veto-wielding members of the Security Council will oppose the adoption of effective sanctions. As a step toward strengthening the nonproliferation regime, the Security Council should adopt a generic and legally binding resolution deciding that if a state notifies its withdrawal from the NPT (an undisputed right under Article X.1), such notification constitutes a threat to international peace and security as defined under Article 39 of the UN Charter.[21] This generic resolution should make sure that, under these circumstances, the Security Council would meet immediately with a view to decide, under Article 41 of the UN Charter, which measures would apply as soon as the withdrawal becomes effective.

This generic resolution should include a statement by the five permanent members of the Security Council that they consider the withdrawal from the NPT to be such a major threat to international peace and security that, in such a case, they do not intend to exercise their veto right against any state-specific resolution sanctioning the withdrawing state if they are the only permanent member to do so. Because this declaration of intention is not legally binding, that generic resolution would not deprive the five permanent members of the Security Council of their veto right on any state-specific resolution. What it would achieve is to ensure that the Security Council consider the matter without delay and increase the risk of immediate sanctions for the withdrawing state. Getting there will not be easy, but as Cardinal de Richelieu once said, politics is the art of making possible what is necessary.

Lesson 6: All nuclear fuel-cycle facilities should be subject to irreversible IAEA safeguards

One of the main outstanding safeguards loopholes that deserves prompt attention is the absence of a requirement for IAEA safeguards to irreversibly remain in force should a state leave the NPT. If one day Iran or any other NPT nonnuclear-weapon state decides to withdraw from the treaty, its Comprehensive Safeguards Agreement with the IAEA would automatically lapse under the terms of that agreement. As a result, a state may withdraw from the NPT and use previously safeguarded nuclear materials and facilities to produce nuclear weapons without violating international treaties. NPT members should therefore strengthen safeguards rules and practices by creating a legal requirement to maintain safeguards, even if a state exercises its right to withdraw from the NPT.

Over the past 15 years, states and organizations have submitted proposals designed to close this significant loophole. For example, Luxembourg submitted a working paper on behalf of the European Union to the 2005 NPT Review Conference recommending that states "[a]ffirm as a matter of principle that all nuclear materials, equipment, technologies and facilities, developed for peaceful purposes, of a State Party to the Treaty on the Non-Proliferation of Nuclear Weapons remain, in case of a withdrawal from the Treaty, restricted to peaceful uses only and as a consequence have to remain subject to safeguards."[22] Germany and France made similar proposals in 2004. The UN Security Council attempted to address this issue in 2009, passing Resolution 1887, which urges states to "[r]equire as a condition of nuclear exports that the recipient State agree that, in the event that it should terminate its IAEA safeguards agreement, safeguards shall continue with respect to any nuclear material and equipment provided prior to such termination, as well as any special nuclear material produced through the use of such material or equipment."[23] However, this resolution does not extend to domestically produced nuclear material, equipment, and facilities. Moreover, because it was not adopted under Chapter VII of the UN Charter, it is not legally binding.

None of these proposals have created an effective legal barrier to a state's utilization of previously safeguarded facilities and materials for military purposes after its withdrawal from the NPT. It seems unrealistic to expect, as the Nuclear Suppliers Group (NSG) does, that a country deciding to leave the NPT and expel IAEA inspectors would thereafter agree to enter into a facility specific safeguards agreement with the IAEA, return previously delivered material and equipment to the supplier state, or accept inspectors from the exporting state to conduct verification work that IAEA inspectors are no longer allowed to do. As I recommended in March 2015, it would be much more effective to require states to conclude a facility specific safeguards agreement with the IAEA before any materials or technology are transferred, rather than as a bilateral and limited fallback obligation after a state has withdrawn from the NPT, as foreseen by the NSG.[24] Indeed, in contrast to comprehensive safeguards agreements, facility specific safeguards agreements (known as Information Circular 66 [INFCIRC/66]-type agreements) do not lapse if the state withdraws from the NPT.

NSG members should formally agree to interpret their "effective safeguards in perpetuity" export criterion as requiring the recipient state to have an INFCIRC/66-type safeguards agreement in force with the IAEA before enrichment- or reprocessing-related equipment, technology, or expertise is transferred.[25] NSG nonnuclear-weapon states should lead by example and place all their enrichment and reprocessing facilities under facility specific safeguards agreements with the IAEA. For nonnuclear-weapon states, INFCIRC/66-type safeguards agreements concluded with the IAEA are and would continue to be subsumed under existing comprehensive safeguards agreements. They would become operational only if the latter were terminated.

This approach does not create a new safeguards standard, as the Model Additional Protocol did in 1997. Instead, it involves the simple adoption of an older type of safeguards. Therefore, it should face fewer political obstacles, would impose no operational financial burden on the state or the IAEA, and would require only a little extra paperwork initially. By virtue of the current roster of NSG members, if this approach could be achieved, nearly all nonnuclear-weapon states that are parties to the NPT and currently operate enrichment and reprocessing facilities would have endorsed this new mechanism. The only exception would be Iran.

Nuclear-weapon states also should lead by example when it comes to their own facilities. Currently, nuclear-weapon states have a voluntary offer agreement with the IAEA, under which they determine which facilities they will make available for safeguards. The nuclear-weapon states provide the IAEA with a list of these "eligible" facilities. To demonstrate commitment to the principle of irreversible safeguards, each nuclear-weapon state should agree to place any enrichment or reprocessing facility mentioned on its list under INFCIRC/66-type safeguards agreements. In such a case, enrichment facilities in China, France, the United Kingdom, and the United States, as well as reprocessing plants in France and the United Kingdom, would be subject to irreversible IAEA safeguards. With negotiations on a fissile material cutoff treaty stalled, this arrangement would provide an alternate means of achieving a first step toward a similar goal and may enable the nuclear-weapon states to demonstrate some concrete progress in this area.

What now?

Whether we like it or not, an increasing number of nonnuclear-weapon states likely will acquire the necessary scientific, technical, and industrial capability to manufacture nuclear weapons and their means of delivery, thereby becoming nuclear threshold states. Indeed, as a September 12, 2008, IAEA report on Libya stated:

> In the course of its investigation into Libya's nuclear weapons programme, the Agency was drawn to an observation of a more generalized nature. Much of the sensitive information coming from the network existed in electronic form, enabling easier use and dissemination. This includes information that relates to uranium centrifuge enrichment and, more disturbing, information that relates to nuclear weapon design.[26]

It is therefore crucial to adopt without delay the measures necessary to deter nuclear threshold states from going one step further—namely, manufacturing nuclear weapons (most likely under maximum secrecy, since it would be a clear violation of Article II of the NPT) and then withdrawing from the NPT.

In the words of Nicholas Miller and Vipin Narang, from an August 2017 assessment of the situation:

> Nonproliferation efforts relying primarily on export controls and efforts to limit technology may buy time but are clearly insufficient against a motivated proliferator. Policies that depend on hoping for the regime to fail or fall are misguided in a world where impoverished dictators can indigenously master nuclear technology.

> To be successful against isolated countries like North Korea, nonproliferation policies must either address the proliferator's underlying motives—in other words, their sense of insecurity—or they must enlist a strong multilateral coalition that enforces sanctions vigorously, with few exploitable cracks. This is a tall order, but North Korea shows that the stakes are rarely higher.[27]

In his 2009 Prague speech, President Barack Obama said, "We need more resources and authority to strengthen international inspections. We need real and immediate consequences for countries caught breaking the rules or trying to leave the treaty without cause."[28] To this end, Security Council members should discuss and agree on legally binding generic procedures for responding to both noncompliance and NPT withdrawal. Because the Security Council would not know which states might be involved in the future, such discussions should be easier and less acrimonious than they would be during the heat of a crisis. An agreement on a set of standard responses to be applied evenhandedly to any state found in noncompliance, regardless of its allies, would significantly enhance the credibility of the nonproliferation regime.

If adopted, the concrete measures recommended in this chapter would make a real difference in protecting against nuclear proliferation. Yet all countries, most of all the five permanent members of the Security Council, will need to acknowledge that these measures should be adopted now in order to mitigate the consequences of the next potential proliferation crisis. Protecting against that dangerous prospect is in everyone's best security interest: an ounce of prevention is worth a pound of cure.

Notes

* A slightly shorter version of this chapter was published in the March 2018 edition of *Arms Control Today*; see Pierre Goldschmidt, "Nuclear Nonproliferation: Six Lessons Not Yet Learned," *Arms Control Today* 48, no. 2 (March 2018), https://www.armscontrol.org/act/2018-03/features/nuclear-nonproliferation-six-lessons-not-yet-learned

1. Under a Comprehensive Safeguards Agreement (Information Circular 153 [INFCIRC/153] Corrected), the International Atomic Energy Agency (IAEA) has the right and obligation to ensure that safeguards are applied on all nuclear material in the territory, jurisdiction, or control of the state for the exclusive purpose of verifying that such material is not diverted to nuclear weapons or other nuclear explosive devices.
2. Mohamed ElBaradei, "Reinforcing the World's Regime Against Nuclear Weapons," IAEA News Center, November 14, 2002, https://www.iaea.org/newscenter/news/reinforcing-world%C2%B4s-regime-against-nuclear-weapons.
3. IAEA Board of Governors, "Implementation of the NPT Safeguards Agreement in the Islamic Republic of Iran," GOV/2003/75, November 10, 2003, https://www.iaea.org/sites/default/files/gov2003-75.pdf.
4. IAEA Board of Governors, "Implementation of the NPT Safeguards Agreement in the Islamic Republic of Iran: Resolution Adopted by the Board on 12 September 2003," GOV/2003/69, September 12, 2003, https://www.iaea.org/sites/default/files/gov2003-69.pdf.

5. UN Security Council Resolution 1737, S/RES/1737 (December 27, 2006), http://www.un.org/ga/search/view_doc.asp?symbol=S/RES/1737%282006%29. It was only after finding Iran in possession of a document on the production of uranium metal hemispheres (a process related to the fabrication of nuclear weapon components) and after Iran resumed enrichment activities in January 2006, that the IAEA Board of Governors adopted a resolution (GOV/2006/14) on February 4, 2006, deciding to report the Iranian file to the Security Council. See IAEA Board of Governors, "Implementation of the NPT Safeguards Agreement in the Islamic Republic of Iran," GOV/2006/14, February 4, 2006, http://www.securitycouncilreport.org/atf/cf/%7B65BFCF9B-6D27-4E9C-8CD3-CF6E4FF96FF9%7D/Disarm%20GOV200839.pdf.
6. The Statute of the IAEA, Article III.5, https://www.iaea.org/about/statute#a1-3.
7. The Statute of the IAEA, Article XII.A.6, https://www.iaea.org/about/statute#a1-7.
8. For a detailed analysis of these Additional Protocol limitations and the way they should be temporarily corrected when a state found to be in noncompliance is not fully and proactively cooperating with the IAEA, see Pierre Goldschmidt, "IAEA Safeguards: Dealing Preventively With Non-compliance," Carnegie Endowment for International Peace, July 12, 2008, http://www.carnegieendowment.org/files/Goldschmidt_Dealing_Preventively_7-12-08.pdf.
9. Pierre Goldschmidt, "Concrete Steps to Improve the Nonproliferation Regime," Carnegie Papers No. 100, Carnegie Endowment for International Peace, April 2009, 29–41, http://carnegieendowment.org/files/improve_nonpro_regime.pdf.
10. IAEA Board of Governors, "Implementation of the NPT Safeguards Agreement in the Islamic Republic of Iran: Report by the Director General," GOV/2005/67, September 2, 2005, para. 50, https://www.iaea.org/sites/default/files/gov2005-67.pdf.
11. UN Security Council Resolution 1737, S/RES/1737 (December 27, 2006).
12. "The IAEA's existing authorities should be interpreted to give the Agency the responsibility to inspect for indicators of nuclear weaponization activities." IAEA Board of Governors and IAEA General Conference, "Report of the Commission of Eminent Persons on the Future of the Agency: Note by the Director General," GOV/2008/22-GC(52)/INF/4, May 23, 2008 (containing an annex titled "Reinforcing the Global Nuclear Order for Peace and Prosperity: The Role of the IAEA to 2020 and Beyond," 19), https://www.belfercenter.org/sites/default/files/files/publication/gov2008-22gc52inf-4.pdf.
13. Other generic resolutions are UN Security Council Resolution 1373 concerning acts of international terrorism and Resolution 1540 concerning the acquisition of nuclear, chemical, or biological weapons and their means of delivery by non-state actors.
14. Goldschmidt, "Concrete Steps to Improve the Nonproliferation Regime."
15. The JCPOA includes transparency measures extending beyond 15 years, such as a long-term IAEA presence in Iran, IAEA monitoring of uranium ore concentrate produced by Iran from all uranium ore concentration plants for 25 years, and containment and surveillance of centrifuge rotors and bellows for 20 years.
16. UN Security Council Resolution 2231, S/RES/2231 (July 15, 2015), http://www.un.org/ga/search/view_doc.asp?symbol=S/RES/2231%282015%29.
17. Joint Comprehensive Plan of Action, Vienna, 14 July 2015, Preamble and general Provisions, para. iii at https://www.documentcloud.org/documents/2165573-271540447-iran-nuclear-deal-text.html.
18. UN Security Council Resolution 825, S/RES/825 (May 11, 2003), http://www.un.org/ga/search/view_doc.asp?symbol=S/RES/825%282003%29.

19. UN Security Council Resolution 1718, S/RES/1718 (October 14, 2006), http://www.un.org/ga/search/view_doc.asp?symbol=S/RES/1718%282006%29.
20. See "Iran Threat to Quit Atomic Treaty," BBC News, May 7, 2006, http://news.bbc.co.uk/2/hi/middle_east/4981940.stm. Earlier that year, the President of Iran also threatened withdrawal. See Nazila Fathi, "Bracing for Penalties, Iran Threatens to Withdraw from Nuclear Treaty," *New York Times*, February 12, 2006 at https://www.nytimes.com/2006/02/12/world/middleeast/bracing-for-penalties-iran-threatens-to-withdraw-from.html.
21. UN Security Council Resolution 1540, S/RES/1540 (2004). In this resolution of April 2004, the UN Security Council is "Affirming that proliferation of nuclear, chemical and biological weapons, as well as their means of delivery, constitutes a threat to international peace and security." It has reaffirmed that statement many times thereafter, but has never "decided" that this is the case under an operative paragraph of a legally binding Chapter VII resolution.
22. "Withdrawal from the Treaty on the Non-Proliferation of Nuclear Weapons" (Working paper submitted by Luxembourg on behalf of the European Union), NPT/CONF.2005/WP.32, May 10, 2005, https://documents-dds-ny.un.org/doc/UNDOC/GEN/N05/339/76/PDF/N0533976.pdf.
23. UN Security Council Resolution 1887, S/RES/1887 (September 24, 2009), https://www.un.org/ga/search/view_doc.asp?symbol=S/RES/1887(2009).
24. Pierre Goldschmidt, "Securing Irreversible IAEA Safeguards to Close the Next NPT Loophole," *Arms Control Today*, March 2015, https://www.armscontrol.org/ACT/2015_03/Features/Securing-Irreversible-IAEA-Safeguards-to-Close-the-Next-NPT-Loophole.
25. Nuclear Suppliers Group (NSG), "Guidelines for Nuclear Transfers," NSG Part 1, June 2013, para. 6(a)(iv) http://www.nuclearsuppliersgroup.org/images/Files/Updated_control_lists/Prague_2013/NSG_Part_1_Rev.12_clean.pdf.
26. IAEA Board of Governors, "Implementation of the NPT Safeguards Agreement in the Socialist People's Libyan Arab Jamahiriya," GOV/2008/39, September 12, 2008, para. 38, https://isis-online.org/uploads/isis.../IAEA_Libya_Report_12September2008.pdf.
27. Nicholas Miller and Vipin Narang, "How North Korea Shocked the Nuclear Experts," *Politico*, August 26, 2017, http://www.politico.com/magazine/story/2017/08/26/north-korea-nuclear-tests-shock-experts-215533.
28. "Remarks by President Barack Obama in Prague as Delivered," Office of the Press Secretary, The White House, April 5, 2009, https://obamawhitehouse.archives.gov/the-press-office/remarks-president-barack-obama-prague-delivered.

11 The IAEA and peaceful nuclear uses

Mark Hibbs

The International Atomic Energy Agency's (IAEA's) program of work is an expression of its Statute and of its Member States' comportment. The Agency's Statute provides the legal foundation from which most IAEA activities follow and upon which the Agency's authority ultimately rests. After 60 years it likely will not change, but the political will of the states will continue to evolve. The Secretariat, responsible for managing the Agency, is free to undertake actions on its behalf; it most frequently succeeds when Member States conclude that the Secretariat's behavior and intentions conform to their own interests and the Statute. If not, conflicts may arise in which the Member States most often, but not always, will prevail.

In coming decades, the activities the IAEA undertakes will be influenced by Member States' balance of power in the Agency's policy bodies, the Board of Governors and the General Conference; the future role states foresee for nuclear energy; and how Member States support, empower, and fund initiatives and actions by the Secretariat, especially in its two most important fields, nuclear verification and development assistance. The absence of controversy surrounding most of what the IAEA does, and the long trajectories associated with nuclear infrastructure investments may assure that the IAEA's profile by mid-century will change only marginally. But, as was the case during the past half-century, significant or dramatic nuclear safety and proliferation events, and Member States' expectations for the future of commercial nuclear power generation, may provide the IAEA with new responsibilities, activities, and priorities.

The IAEA's statutory mission to advance the peaceful uses of nuclear energy was born of diplomacy in the shadow of a deepening arms race between the United States and the Soviet Union. World concern about the threat of nuclear annihilation, and the prospect that atomic powers would lose their nuclear monopoly, prompted the United States, followed by the Soviet Union and other governments, to pursue an international organization tasked to help bring to fruition and then share peaceful nuclear benefits. In December 1953, U.S. president Dwight Eisenhower proposed the creation of "an international atomic energy Agency … under the aegis of the United Nations … to serve the peaceful pursuits of mankind."[1] During the mid-1950s, U.S. and Soviet

DOI: 10.4324/9781003160205-11

diplomats, focused above all on their bipolar rivalry, considered whether they should take up Eisenhower's initiative. Some U.S. officials objected, believing that a world where sensitive nuclear technology and materials were shared among states would be a world where these goods would not likely remain under the control of the established nuclear powers.[2] In the final analysis, the United States decided to lead the way toward creation of an IAEA. Not doing so "would have an unfavorable effect on world opinion," one U.S. State Department official noted in an internal 1954 memo. "[T]he U.S. badly needs to demonstrate its interest in helping the world realize the benefits of the peaceful use of nuclear energy [and to] counterbalance fears that we are set on a course of unloosing atomic and thermonuclear weapons."[3]

When the IAEA was established in July 1957, its Statute reflected the expectation of negotiating governments that the Agency's activities would be at once regulatory, promotional, and normative. Over the 60 years of the IAEA's history to date, most of the IAEA's activities have followed from the Statute, but not all the statutory authority provided for in 1957 has been exercised in practice by the Agency. The IAEA later added other activities and aspirations that were only vaguely expressed in the Statute or, in the case of nuclear security, not mentioned at all.

The IAEA's peaceful use mandate

The first sentence of the IAEA's Statute in Article II spells out that the main objective of the Agency is "to accelerate and enlarge the contribution of atomic energy to peace, health, and prosperity throughout the world." "Atomic energy" is in the Statute positively correlated with "peace," "health," and "prosperity." The second sentence of Article II distinguishes between nuclear activities that are peaceful and those that are nonpeaceful and sets forth that the IAEA "shall ensure ... that assistance provided by it or at its request or under supervision or control is not used in such a way as to further any military purpose."[4]

This language strongly reflected the thinking referenced above concerning the utility of the IAEA in a world polarized by nuclear-armed adversaries: first, in asserting that the peaceful application of nuclear energy would significantly benefit mankind; and second, in setting forth that the dawning "atomic age" born from World War II would imperil international security unless initiatives were undertaken to limit the spread of nuclear technology to peaceful uses. The IAEA's Statute expressed the first of these two broadly shared understandings. The second understanding provided the basis for the Treaty on the Nonproliferation of Nuclear Weapons (NPT), which was negotiated several years after the IAEA came into existence and which entered into force in 1972.

Yet on one important point, the IAEA did not function as the authors of the Statute had allowed for and may have intended—that is, to serve as a global reservoir for peaceful-use nuclear materials. Eisenhower had proposed that Member States would donate to the IAEA nuclear materials from their stockpiles and that these materials would be used by the IAEA and shared with other countries for peaceful uses. By allocating nuclear materials "to serve the peaceful pursuits of mankind," the Agency would thereby also help "begin to diminish the potential destructive power of the world's atomic stockpiles."[5] It did not turn out that way. In proposing that the IAEA serve as a nuclear material "bank," U.S. officials aimed to alleviate the fears in the rest of the world of nuclear armageddon, but they also correctly perceived that "it would be difficult for the Soviets to match" an amount of nuclear material that the United States would be prepared to donate.[6] At that time, the United States had a bigger nuclear material stockpile than the Soviet Union. Without agreement on stockpile donations, the IAEA was endowed with a peaceful-use mission, but in practice the Agency did not fulfill Eisenhower's intended nuclear arms control rationale.

Article III of the Statute invested the IAEA with the authority to "encourage and assist research on, and development and practical application of, atomic energy for peaceful uses throughout the world" and to "perform any operation or service useful in research on, or development or practical application of, atomic energy for peaceful purposes."[7] These words pointed the way toward myriad future IAEA activities in many fields. Fifteen years later, in 1972, entry into force of the NPT lifted further the IAEA's aspirations to advance the peaceful uses of nuclear energy. The NPT's Article IV stated that parties enjoy an "inalienable right ... to develop research, production and use of nuclear energy for peaceful purposes without discrimination" and, moreover, that "all the Parties to the Treaty undertake to facilitate, and have the right to participate in, the fullest possible exchange of equipment, materials and scientific and technological information for the peaceful uses of nuclear energy." Article IV also established the principle that NPT parties "shall also co-operate ... to the further development of the applications of nuclear energy for peaceful purposes especially in the territories of non-nuclear-weapon States Party to the Treaty, with due consideration for the needs of the developing areas of the world." The NPT thus explicitly exceeded Eisenhower's intention that in creating the IAEA, the United States and other advanced nuclear countries would voluntarily share their nuclear know-how and materials with nonendowed states. The NPT instead established the notion among many Member States that advanced, and especially nuclear-weapon possessor states, are obligated to share their nuclear technology with the vast majority of countries that have made legally binding commitments not to possess nuclear weapons.

Equity and technical cooperation

Eisenhower in 1953 had singled out nuclear power as a leading peaceful-use field for future IAEA activities, reflecting the aspiration that in the coming atomic age countries that did not have the means to generate electricity would be eligible to power their economic development by splitting atoms. During the next half-century, successive severe accidents at three nuclear power stations led to more modest prospects for developing countries mustering the financial and human resources necessary for safe and reliable generation of nuclear electricity.

Instead, during the 1970s and 1980s, the IAEA's growing membership roll from the ranks of developing countries, many of which were former colonies of Western powers, increasingly viewed the IAEA's Technical Cooperation Program as its most important platform for advancing their infrastructure development. This program focused on the use of nuclear material in non-power areas where the benefits of application of nuclear science could be reaped with comparatively less investment and time and where needs were often acute, especially in agriculture, healthcare, disease prevention, applied nuclear research, isotope production, water management, and environmental protection. The IAEA's activities in these and other development-related areas expanded rapidly. After having trained about 20,000 scientists and technicians in Member States over three decades beginning in the 1960s, increasingly since the mid-1990s the Technical Cooperation Program has focused on projects that address specific challenges and problems on the ground in recipient countries.[8]

On a separate track, following the NPT's entry into force, a number of mostly Western advanced nuclear countries led by the United States, joined during the Cold War by the Soviet Union, increasingly focused their attention at the IAEA on nuclear proliferation. The interests of Member States appeared to bifurcate along the fault lines of technical cooperation and safeguards. The NPT's "grand bargain" was at the fulcrum of this development, as it underscored that advanced nuclear states bore the responsibility to engage in disarmament and to share peaceful-use technology with non-nuclear-weapon states in return for their commitment not to possess nuclear arms. The NPT thus added weight to arguments of developing countries that their interests at the IAEA should be served as the highest priority.

The challenge of protecting the equity interest of less-endowed countries with regard to more advanced nuclear states was apparent even before the IAEA was founded. It appeared during the negotiations over the Statute, including on over how power would be shared between the IAEA's two future policymaking bodies, which would become the Board of Governors and the General Conference. Article IV C.9 of the Statute says that the IAEA "is based on the principle of the sovereign equality of all its members, in order to ensure to all of them the right and benefits resulting from membership."[9] At the same time, Article III B.3 makes clear that the IAEA should "allocate its resources ... bearing in mind the special needs of the under-developed areas of the world."[10]

Equity dilemmas came to the fore in Member States' decision-making about how the IAEA should organize and finance the Technical Cooperation Program. At the outset, the United Nations Development Programme

(UNDP) contributed nearly half of the IAEA's technical assistance program, and the IAEA acted as an executing agency for the UNDP in this regard. Eventually, the IAEA set up a Technical Cooperation Fund independent of both the regular IAEA budget and the UNDP to finance assistance to Member States related to the objective stated in Article II of the Statute. In doing this, the IAEA argued that Member States' specific nuclear technology development needs would be best managed independently of the UNDP. According to participants, if the UNDP were to remain significantly involved in IAEA projects, economic sectors in developing countries more visible and powerful than nuclear science would secure for themselves most of the technical assistance funding. Thus in this case, as on some other occasions, the Secretariat asserted that the IAEA should be considered apart from other United Nations (UN) organizations because of its unique "nuclear" portfolio.[11]

The Technical Cooperation Fund therefore was set up as an autonomous mechanism, but this arrangement did not wholly mitigate equity concerns. During the 1980s, the share of all IAEA Member States receiving technical assistance funding increased from 20 percent of the total to close to 100 percent, including some advanced nuclear countries. Least-developed members at meetings of the Board of Governors and the General Conference urged the IAEA to refocus the Technical Cooperation Program in their direction, documenting their objections with official data that showed that most technical cooperation assistance had flowed to states that are already moderately developed. On the other side of the ledger, advanced nuclear countries have at times expressed the view that Technical Cooperation Fund appropriations are not sufficiently vetted to ensure that selected projects are cost-efficient and truly valuable from a development policy standpoint.

The abovementioned trend toward polarization of IAEA Member State interests, pitting advanced nuclear countries focused on nuclear proliferation against developing countries that view the IAEA as a source of development assistance, also was framed in equity terms. Developing states—the overwhelming majority of which are both parties to the NPT and IAEA members—routinely assert that the NPT rendered obligatory what under the IAEA Statute was an implied aspiration that advanced nuclear countries share their nuclear technology. However, because the IAEA is legally obligated to verify NPT states' peaceful-use commitments under NPT Article III, over time the Agency's verification obligations steadily increased as the amount of nuclear material used for peaceful uses in the world expanded. In parallel, advanced, mostly Western states raised additional concerns about nuclear proliferation, prompted by revelations from the 1991 Gulf War, terrorist attacks in the United States in 2001, and alarming nuclear black-market exports to Libya, Iran, and North Korea. Friction between advanced nuclear states and developing countries also spiked over concerns of advanced nuclear states that some IAEA technical assistance projects might lead to nuclear-weapon proliferation in recipient countries.

In practice the two camps agreed on a long-standing operational compromise. David Fischer, a former IAEA external affairs official, explained in 1988 what had come about: "To make growth of the safeguards budget more acceptable to the [developing countries], the richer countries have been willing to support an annual increase in the target for TCF [technical cooperation funds] as well as to separate the safeguards budget from the remainder of the regular budget and to freeze the contributions of poorer Member States to the cost of safeguards at the level that existed before the NPT entered into force in 1970s."[12] Accordingly, from 1970 until the onset of zero-growth IAEA budgets in 1994, the annual safeguards budget increased from US$1.2 million to about US$100 million. During the same period, technical cooperation funding was raised from about US$5 million to about US$50 million. Currently, the numbers are €135 million for safeguards and €90 million for technical cooperation funding.[13] As in past decades, IAEA Member State representatives from both developing countries and advanced nuclear states today commonly take for granted that an informal trade-off between the two blocs will govern their appropriation of funding of technical cooperation and verification activities.

Nuclear power activities

When the IAEA was being created in the 1950s, visionaries in advanced nuclear countries expected that the Agency's most important future activity in support of the spread of peaceful nuclear uses would be "especially that of providing abundant electrical energy in power-starved areas of the world."[14] This followed from then-current unrealistic ambitions for the near-term future of nuclear power. In fact, over the next 60 years the risks of nuclear power—largely unanticipated at the time the IAEA's Statute was under negotiation—compelled the IAEA to devote a large share of its nuclear-power-related resources and activities to nuclear safety. The IAEA's engagement in this area was pushed forward by severe nuclear power accidents in the United States in 1979, the Soviet Union in 1986, and Japan in 2011.

The mandate for many of the IAEA's nuclear safety initiatives was provided by Article III A.6 of the Statute, calling on the Agency "to establish or adopt ... standards of safety for protection of health and minimization of danger to life and property."[15] In principle, the IAEA's effective authority over nuclear safety matters could have been far greater on the basis of the preceding paragraph, Article III A.5. This paragraph states that the Agency may "apply safeguards, at the request of the parties to any bilateral or multilateral arrangement, or at the request of a State, to *any of that State's activities in the field of atomic energy*."[16] At the time of the IAEA's genesis, this broad understanding of "safeguards" reflected a common assumption that, in addition to accounting for nuclear material, the Agency would also inspect nuclear power reactors and other installations to verify their compliance with IAEA safety standards. But unlike IAEA safeguards on nuclear material, which followed from legally binding arrangements including the NPT, no equivalent commitments arose in the area of nuclear safety—a fact that impeded the establishment of a global IAEA nuclear safety oversight role.

Nonetheless, the IAEA Secretariat has sought at times to enlarge its authority at the expense of Member States' sovereign autonomy in nuclear safety matters. In 1960, the Secretariat aimed to make its nuclear safety standards legally binding, but Member States on the Board of Governors would not agree. Thereafter, the Secretariat aimed to opportunistically capitalize on the severe accidents that occurred to extend its influence and the scope of its activities. In this way, the Secretariat was instrumental in helping to establish a global regime for nuclear safety, even if the Agency had little legal authority in it. The IAEA was perhaps most effective in influencing events after the accident at Chernobyl, because the sheer magnitude of that event deprived the Soviet Union of political leverage to oppose IAEA initiatives in the Board of Governors and the General Conference. The potential for resistance by Member States to major changes was, on balance, greater after the accidents in Japan and the United States because these events were comparatively less traumatic. After the accident at Fukushima Dai-ichi, the IAEA Secretariat aimed to secure a formal commitment in principle by Member States to host IAEA-led peer reviews. Powerful countries, including China, India, and the United States, brushed off this effort, but not before the Secretariat took other procedural actions that permitted individual Member States to singlehandedly block transparency measures.[17]

More successfully, the IAEA Secretariat undertook indirect approaches to reinforce its authority in both nuclear safety and nuclear security matters. In particular, the Agency has supported the creation of international conventions to universalize acceptance and implementation of its standards, following from Statute Article III A.6. After the Chernobyl accident, the IAEA embraced negotiations prompted by Germany and other states to create a Convention on Nuclear Safety (CNS) that entered into force in 1996, with the IAEA Director General as its depositary. The convention is a legally binding instrument designed to require all countries that operate nuclear power plants to commit to specific principles of nuclear safety. The IAEA's safety standards, following from Article of III A.6 of the Statute, became an important element of this mechanism.

But as had been the case since the IAEA's inception, the parties of the CNS, all of them members of the IAEA, did not agree that IAEA safety standards should be legally obligatory. As the IAEA summarized after the CNS entered into force: "Some governments wanted to have the CNS include a provision that would have adopted IAEA safety standards as international law obligations. However most states were not willing to give principles developed as voluntary guidelines a binding legal effect."[18] In drafting the CNS, negotiators reached a compromise nonbinding solution in Paragraph (viii) of the preamble: "[T]his Convention entails a commitment to the application of fundamental safety principles for nuclear installations rather than of detailed safety standards. . . . [T]here are international formulated safety guidelines which are updated from time to time and so can provide guidance on a contemporary means of achieving a high level of safety."[19] In the view of the IAEA, this approach implies that "IAEA safety standards have been imported indirectly into the CNS as an efficient way of demonstrating how a party has complied with its obligations."[20]

The limitations of the CNS process were illuminated by the Fukushima Dai-ichi accident. In the view of many CNS parties, the accident revealed that Japan had violated the convention, regardless of its prior formal statements testifying that Tokyo was in compliance. Shortly after the accident, Switzerland and Russia proposed making IAEA safety standards compulsory under the CNS, but that was not acceptable to the majority of the parties.[21] At the end of a negotiation, in 2015, CNS parties agreed to bless that lack of consensus by arranging a compromise that did not alter existing legal obligations or commitments of Member States: "National requirements and regulations for [preventing and mitigating accidents] throughout the lifetime of nuclear power plants are to take into account the relevant IAEA Safety Standards and, as appropriate, other good practices as identified inter alia in the Review Meetings of the CNS."[22]

Although the scope of the IAEA's multilateral nuclear verification activities has expanded with the support of Member States during the past 60 years, IAEA Member States have resisted multilateralization of nuclear safety oversight. The abovementioned effort in the CNS to establish binding global safety standards after Fukushima Dai-ichi specifically concerned debate over power reactor design criteria, which flared up at the IAEA and elsewhere beginning after the Chernobyl accident. To some states, this conflict appeared to be driven less by nuclear safety concerns and more by competitive instincts of national champion nuclear industries of Member States, especially France, Canada, the United States, and Russia. Some states also argued that if a global minimal standard based on IAEA consensus rules were set in stone, standards might be permanently weaker than standards applied in individual Member States. If a global standard is made legally binding, including by all CNS parties, it may thereafter prove politically challenging to subsequently improve it. Critics of obligatory standardization also argue that empowering a multilateral body such as the IAEA with regulatory functions might also blur the understanding, spelled out in the IAEA's Fundamental Nuclear Safety Principles, that the state having jurisdiction is responsible for nuclear safety oversight.

Global civil society at large appears to have absorbed the international media's facile characterization of the IAEA's nuclear safeguards activities as fulfilling a "watchdog" function. However, the absence of a clear verification or regulatory role in the IAEA's nuclear safety profile may have encouraged criticism in some quarters that the IAEA is not a neutral party, but rather is shackled by its peaceful-use promotional mandate expressed in Article II of the Statute. Representatives from Member States on occasion acknowledge that over the past six decades, the IAEA, like its members, was caught up in a global zeitgeist that encouraged naive expectations for the future of atomic power. In retrospect, U.S. officials, increasingly preoccupied with the specter of nuclear proliferation, concede that the Atoms for Peace initiative encouraged advanced nuclear countries and their industries to export too many research reactors and too much fissile material worldwide, including to destinations that were unprepared to assure that good governance would prevail.[23]

But the experience of Chernobyl suggested that there were deeper questions. According to science communication scholar Olga Kuchinskaya, "Chernobyl strengthened the IAEA's role in establishing nuclear safety standards, but it challenged the Agency's mission to advance the use of nuclear power."[24] Efforts to reach a consensus about the extent of the damage caused by the accident quickly threatened to run aground on mistrust of the nuclear science "establishment," especially in communities and regions exposed to radioactive fallout. This fanned controversy over conclusions reported by governments and expert bodies. Critics charged that these conclusions were intended above all to allay fears and rebuild public trust, if necessary at the expense of scientific objectivity, and in the interest of promoting a long-term recovery in affected areas by shifting the emphasis in managing the aftermath of the accident from radiation risks to economic recovery. This approach was favored by Belarus, Ukraine, and Russia—the IAEA Member States that had suffered most.[25] To clear the air of doubt, in 2003 the IAEA initiated a review by UN agencies of the health and environmental effects of the Chernobyl accident. In 2006, this Chernobyl Forum reiterated previous conclusions by some of the same bodies that, beyond findings of about 4,000 cases of mostly nonfatal thyroid cancer, "no clearly demonstrated increase in the incidence of solid cancers or leukemia due to radiation in the most affected populations" was found. Instead, the IAEA and its collaborators testified to an "increase in psychological problems" among those affected by the accident.[26]

These results did not satisfy critics. Some dissenting scientists implied that the IAEA, in the spirit of its Article II aim to advance peaceful uses of nuclear energy, was biased on behalf of Member States and commercial interests to deny or play down the true extent of health risks caused by the accident's radiation releases. Yet in the general public consciousness, critics' specific objections to the work of the Chernobyl Forum, concerned with the scientific method employed by official experts and agencies, largely were relegated to debate over radiation science arcana. Objections therefore did not steamroll into a politically effective challenge to the IAEA's credibility.

Outside of the nuclear safety realm, the IAEA has participated in the development of nuclear power technology throughout its history. It did this by relying on funding and expertise provided by its Member States, most significantly through personnel contributions, including cost-free experts. The IAEA's nuclear power technology work never became truly controversial in part because for two decades after the 1979 accident at the Three Mile Island nuclear power plant in the United States, fewer Member States concluded that they could afford the expense and risks associated with nuclear power. This trend appeared to be reversing in the 1990s, when Member States and their industries began to predict that a nuclear power "renaissance" would occur within a decade. Economic growth and electricity demand were robust in many developing countries, and many governments were concerned about energy security and ultimately appeared to assume that the political risk related to nuclear safety was receding. During this period, the IAEA established a program to assist Member States that were expressly considering the possible future deployment of nuclear fission energy to generate electricity. The IAEA published survey data from Member States bearing witness to, in the term most often used by IAEA staffers, "rising expectations" for the future of nuclear power. On the eve of the Fukushima accident in Japan in 2011, the number of Member States participating in nuclear-power-related projects in the Technical Cooperation Program had increased from 13 in 2007–2008 to 35 in 2009–2011. Sixty-five countries without nuclear power had informed the IAEA that they were considering deploying nuclear power reactors in the future.[27]

To accommodate this greater interest, the IAEA included in its Technical Cooperation Program activities for nuclear infrastructure development. Some detractors of nuclear power have asserted that IAEA guidance in step with the Article II mandate to advance the peaceful use of nuclear energy would lead to foolhardy decision-making by less-endowed "nuclear newcomers." In fact, expertise provided by the IAEA, and assisted by experienced personnel from advanced Member States, has alerted developing countries to the risks and (above all) the massive commitment needed over at least a century to establish a safe, economic, and sustainable nuclear power program.

In 2006, the IAEA convened a four-day conference to provide information to Member States newly interested in nuclear power about the Agency's stepwise "milestones" approach for establishing a national nuclear power infrastructure. Advanced nuclear countries provided expertise on a cost-free basis. On the eve of the event, the leader of a delegation from an eastern African state told the author that his government intended to build and operate an initial nuclear power plant in less than 15 years. After the meeting concluded, he imparted that the information made available by experts concerning the requirements for technology, human resources, legal oversight, and industry capacity building had led him to instead project that his country might obtain nuclear power after a quarter-century or more of preparation—hardly an indication that the IAEA was overpromoting nuclear power.

Since the Fukushima accident, the number of countries reporting an interest in nuclear power has dropped by about half to 32.[28] Two additional considerations now inform the IAEA's continued assistance in this area. First, Fukushima underscored the fact that many of the Member States that had been considering nuclear power were likely unprepared and perhaps unaware of the risk associated with a severe accident at a nuclear power plant. The accident occurred at an installation operated in a state with extremely high levels of wealth, political organization, infrastructure, technology, and great nuclear power experience. Second, today, nearly a decade after the accident in Japan, nuclear industries in China and Russia have concluded agreements with over two dozen states, most of them developing countries in Asia and Africa, to develop peaceful-use nuclear industries including setting up future nuclear installations. Member States no doubt will encourage the IAEA to help ensure that participating states minimize and best manage risk.

Conclusions and outlook

For 60 years, virtually all of the IAEA's activities have followed from its statutory mission to advance the peaceful use of nuclear energy. In each main program of work—nuclear verification, nuclear safety, nuclear energy applications, technical cooperation, and nuclear security—what the Agency does is shaped and circumscribed by the IAEA's specific formal mandates and the political will of its Member States. The IAEA safeguards nuclear materials under legal obligations, binding states and the Agency that at once constrain and empower the IAEA Secretariat. Political will is comparatively more important in nuclear safety, where the IAEA's authority is less explicit. Absence of a specific mandate for nuclear security means that what Member States decide is paramount in this field, where the IAEA has more recently become active.

Dramatic nuclear verification and nuclear safety events have been critical in forming political will to support and enlarge the IAEA's sphere of activities. In response to these flashpoints, the interactions between the Secretariat and Member States often made the difference between success and failure of important initiatives. In the aftermath of systematic deception by Iraq and North Korea, during the 1990s the Secretariat succeeded in increasing its legal safeguards authority in large part because it cooperated closely with Member States in securing the approval of the Board of Governors for the Additional Protocol in 1997. Thereafter, the Secretariat retreated, defensively asserting that matters of safeguards implementation (as distinct from policymaking) were not the proper concern of the policy bodies. In this response, the Secretariat failed to effectively communicate to Member States how safeguards were evolving in theory and practice. This led to a revolt in the Board in 2012 and then to a remedial effort by the Secretariat (still ongoing) to restore confidence. As noted above, three severe nuclear power plant accidents permitted the IAEA Secretariat to enlarge its activities in the nuclear safety area, albeit without challenging the ultimate authority of the Member States.

By comparison, the IAEA's technical cooperation activities have a far lower public and political profile, yet an overwhelming majority of Member States see them as essential and most fully expressing the IAEA's statutory mandate, ensuring that Member States will receive continuous political and financial support. Developing countries refer to the Statute in negotiations over financing and appropriations to compel advanced nuclear states to increase financial support for the Technical Cooperation Funding and donate know-how to IAEA-sponsored projects. During his ten-year tenure beginning in 2009, Director General Yukiya Amano considerably raised the profile of the Technical Cooperation Program and the Agency's development mission, in effect highlighting the Agency's legitimacy through its fulfillment of its statutory peaceful-use mandate. In adopting this posture, the IAEA Secretariat attempted to close a breach that had started to open in the 1980s between advanced nuclear states increasingly occupied by nuclear verification concerns and the large majority of states for which the IAEA means technical development assistance.

It can be expected that fluid case-by-case interactions between Member States and the Secretariat will continue to determine the outcome of future deliberations over the IAEA's authority and activities. Additional topical challenges and potential opportunities on the horizon also may alter the IAEA's "peaceful use" profile in decades to come.

Funding and appropriations

For a quarter-century, the Member States have programmatically pursued annual zero-growth budgets. If this policy continues indefinitely, it will further intensify pressure on the IAEA to secure sufficient resources to support its activities. Moreover, it will exacerbate long-standing conflict between advanced nuclear states and developing countries, putting at risk their four-decade understanding that increases in safeguards funding must be balanced by Technical Cooperation Funding outlays. Since the early 2010s, consultants and civil society organizations have urged the IAEA to identify new funding sources and find ways to encourage developing countries to support a greater IAEA commitment to safeguards and nuclear security.[29]

Loss of nuclear power commitment and nuclear knowledge

For 60 years, the IAEA's activities in nuclear power technology have been supported by a comparatively small group of advanced nuclear Member States, mostly in North America and Europe and including Japan and South Korea. States in this group may be less willing or able to provide funding, experts, and political engagement if they no longer consider nuclear energy to be a national strategic priority. The Technical Cooperation Program also relies upon inputs from advanced nuclear countries, including on development of nuclear power infrastructure. This work will be more effective if industry and governments in advanced nuclear states shed more knowledge about institutional history, nuclear technology, the nuclear fuel cycle, and project management for nuclear installations. Separately, restrictive internal personnel policies deter the Agency from attracting and recruiting specialists needed to do its work, particularly in the area of verification where the ongoing evolution of safeguards increasingly will require personnel to make complex judgments that may pose great risk to the IAEA's credibility.

Atoms for Peace: A second wave?

In the years to come, the Western states that largely guided the IAEA's development and were instrumental in establishing norms for international nuclear commerce, nuclear safety, and nuclear nonproliferation, may be eclipsed by other states, most significantly Russia and China, including in IAEA policymaking bodies. This turn of events will be more likely should these rising states attain global nuclear commercial dominance through strategically driven business practices. Hand-in-hand with the establishment of the IAEA, the United States in the 1950s launched its Atoms for Peace program. It transferred a wealth of technology, equipment, and nuclear materials to many countries, but it did so in the interest of maintaining U.S. global leadership and reducing Soviet influence.[30] In recent years, China and Russia have launched initiatives that in some ways resemble the U.S. Atoms for Peace program. Less certain is whether Beijing and Moscow will seek significant changes in the global regimes for nuclear safety, nuclear security, liability, export controls, and nonproliferation and will support future efforts to strengthen multilateral nuclear governance, including at the IAEA. The battleground will be in the Agency's decision-making organs, the General Conference, and the Board of Governors, and conflict will extend into the future staffing of the Secretariat. Should Russia, China, or both claim the lead in further development of nuclear energy for peaceful use, other nuclear vendor states, on behalf of their industries, may be inclined to not challenge actions by China or Russia that depart from established norms, including at the IAEA. This especially would be the case if nuclear power industry firms and their governments conclude that they would lose influence and business that rely on having unimpeded commercial relationships with Chinese or Russian entities. Alternatively, the IAEA may become one of several theaters of greater conflict among the world's nuclear vendor states for supremacy and influence concerning technical standards, nonproliferation norms, and intellectual property.

What is "peaceful use"?

The NPT and the IAEA Statute have served as the basis for many states, especially developing countries, to assert their "inalienable right" to peaceful nuclear technology. At the same time, significant proliferation events have underscored that sensitive nuclear technologies, in particular for enriching uranium and separating and processing plutonium, can have both peaceful and nonpeaceful uses, and that peaceful rationales can serve as a cover for nonpeaceful applications. After Iran for many years systematically deceived the Agency concerning its deployment of sensitive nuclear technology, the conclusion in 2015 of the Joint Comprehensive Plan of Action (JCPOA) opened the possibility that NPT parties might seek to define what and when specific nuclear activities may be considered "peaceful." The JCPOA, for which the IAEA is the nuclear verification agency, underscored the ambiguous nature of sensitive nuclear activities by including a nonbinding commitment by Iran to provide a specific peaceful-use justification for future new and expanded sensitive activities, and by enlarging the scope of IAEA verification and monitoring. If, in the future, the NPT parties were to articulate a clearer definition of what constitutes a "peaceful nuclear activity," global understandings about how states and industries should manage sensitive technologies and materials could be strengthened. Greater clarity also would be welcome for advanced nuclear states that are aiming to develop industrial-scale advanced nuclear power generation systems, including fast reactors with complex nuclear fuel cycles. Such systems might be available by the middle of the century.

A higher IAEA development profile?

In September 2015, the UN General Assembly passed a nonbinding resolution committing all its members to implement 17 Sustainable Development Goals toward the fulfillment of specific development targets for 2030, the so-called Agenda 2030. Beginning in 2015, UN members have been tasked to "localize" these goals by setting up and providing funding for specific development projects. The IAEA's work may help fulfill a number of Sustainable Development Goals addressing poverty, hunger, health, education, global warming, water, energy, and the environment. Goal Seven aims to "assure access to affordable, reliable, sustainable, and modern energy for all." Specific UN targets for this goal endorse renewables, energy efficiency, and "cleaner fossil-fuel technology," but not nuclear power.[31] That implies that IAEA assistance provided to attain this goal must rest on the decision-making of individual Member States concerning their future energy source choices. More generally, the Sustainable Development Goals present the IAEA with an opportunity to explain to Member States how its comparatively little-known nuclear research and technical cooperation fieldwork contribute to Member States' broader, longer-term development agendas, beyond the limited audience of Member State "nuclear" professionals the IAEA engages with at the project level. This broader IAEA engagement would be consistent with the in-country bottom-up implementation approach foreseen for the Agenda 2030 goals. Funding opportunities for IAEA technical cooperation work may arise through the IAEA's engagement of a wider audience in Member States and also through the participation of the entire UN membership, including developed countries and their national official development assistance programs.

Notes

1. "Atoms for Peace Speech [December 8, 1953]", International Atomic Energy Agency (IAEA), https://www.iaea.org/about/history/atoms-for-peace-speech.
2. U.S. Department of State, International Atomic Energy Agency Conference, History of IAEA Negotiations, October 2, 1956, Confidential; declassified at National Security Archive, George Washington University (NSA GWU), https://assets.documentcloud.org/documents/4116345/Document-01-U-S-Department-of-State.pdf.
3. U.S. Department of State memorandum, David Wainhouse to Gerard C. Smith, "NSC Study Concerning Whether and Where to Proceed with the President's December 8 Proposal," May 17, 1954, Top Secret; declassified at NSA GWU, https://assets.documentcloud.org/documents/4116346/Document-02-David-Wainhouse-to-Gerard-C-Smith.pdf.
4. Statute of the IAEA, Article II, https://www.iaea.org/about/statute#a1-2.
5. U.S. Department of State, History of IAEA Negotiations, October 2, 1956.
6. John Krige, "Atoms for Peace, Scientific Internationalism, and Scientific Intelligence," *Osiris* 21, no. 1 (2006), 164.
7. Statute of the IAEA, Article III, A.1, https://www.iaea.org/about/statute#a1-3.
8. David Fischer, *History of the International Atomic Energy Agency: The First Forty Years* (Vienna: IAEA, 1997), 336.
9. Statute of the IAEA, Article IV, C.9, https://www.iaea.org/about/statute#a1-4.
10. Statute of the IAEA, Article III, B.3, https://www.iaea.org/about/statute#a1-3.
11. Fischer, *History of the International Atomic Energy* Agency, 329.
12. Ibid., 330.
13. "Budget," IAEA, n,d., https://www.iaea.org/about/overview/budget.
14. U.S. Department of State, History of IAEA Negotiations, October 2, 1956.
15. Statute of the IAEA, Article III, A.6, https://www.iaea.org/about/statute#a1-3.
16. Author's italics.
17. IAEA Secretariat official, private communication, Vienna, June 2011
18. "IAEA Regulatory Control of Nuclear Power Plants"; Legislative and Regulatory Framework; Convention on Nuclear Safety, available at https://www.iaea.org/ns/tutorials/regcontrol/legis/legis1213.htm.
19. International Atomic Energy Agency, Information Circular INFCIRC/449 "Convention on Nuclear Safety," July 5, 1994
20. IAEA Regulatory Control of Nuclear Power Plants.
21. Marie Maitre, "G8 Leaders Want Tougher Nuclear Safety Rule," Reuters, 26 May, 2011 https://www.reuters.com/article/us-g8-nuclear/g8-leaders-want-tougher-nuclear-safety-rule-idUSTRE74P38I20110526.
22. "Diplomatic Conference to Consider a Proposal to Amend the Convention on Nuclear Safety," CNS/DC/2015/2/Rev.1, IAEA, February 9, 2015 https://www.iaea.org/sites/default/files/cns_viennadeclaration090215.pdf.

23. Christopher A. Ford, U.S. Special Representative for Nuclear Nonproliferation, U.S. Department of State, "The Promise and Responsibility of Peaceful Uses of Nuclear Energy," (remarks to the 19th Annual United Nations Conference on Disarmament Issues, August 27, 2007), Department of State (archived page), https://2001-2009.state.gov/t/isn/rls/rm/92721.htm.
24. Olga Kuchinskaya, *The Politics of Invisibility: Public Knowledge About Radiation Health Effects After Chernobyl* (Cambridge, MA: Massachusetts Institute of Technology, 2014), 117.
25. Kuchinskaya, *The Politics of Invisibility*, 129.
26. "Chernobyl's Legacy: Health, Environmental and Socio-Economic Impacts and Recommendations to the Governments of Belarus, Russian Federation, and Ukraine," 2nd rev. ed. (Vienna: IAEA, 2003–2005), 7, https://www.iaea.org/sites/default/files/chernobyl.pdf.
27. "International Status and Prospects of Nuclear Power," GOV/INF/2010/12-GC(54)/INF/5, IAEA, September 2, 2010, 21–22, https://www.legacy.iaea.org/About/Policy/GC/GC54/GC54InfDocuments/English/gc54inf-5_en.pdf.
28. "International Status and Prospects for Nuclear Power 2017," GOV/INF/2017/12-GC(61)/INF/8, IAEA, July 28, 2017, 7, https://www-legacy.iaea.org/About/Policy/GC/GC61/GC61InfDocuments/English/gc61inf-8_en.pdf.
29. For example, see Andrew K. Semmel et al., "Strengthening the IAEA: Technical Cooperation and Nuclear Security," Partnership for a Secure America, June 2016, https://www.psaonline.org/wp-content/uploads/2016/07/Strengthening-the-IAEA.pdf; and Audrey Williams, "Beyond Boundaries; The Role of the IAEA in Balancing Security and Development Priorities in the 21st Century," Stimson, November, 2014, https://www.stimson.org/sites/default/files/file-attachments/role-iaea-balancing-security-and-development-priorities-21st-century.pdf.
30. Peter R. Lavoy, "The Enduring Effects of Atoms for Peace," Arms Control Association, 1 December 2003 https://www.armscontrol.org/act/2003_12/Lavoy
31. "Goal 7 Targets," United Nations Development Programme, n.d., www.undp.org/content/undp/en/home/sustainable-development-goals/goal-7-affordable-and-clean-energy/targets.html.

12 Promoting the peaceful uses of nuclear energy

Nobuyasu Abe

For the International Atomic Energy Agency (IAEA), the peaceful uses of nuclear energy include not only electrical power generation, but also its application for medical, agricultural, and industrial purposes. This chapter focuses on the narrow use of nuclear energy for power generation. This does not mean the peaceful use of nuclear energy other than power generation is negligible. In Japan, for example, the economic size of the nonpower applications of nuclear energy is now almost equivalent to that of power generation.[1]

The IAEA was established following President Dwight D. Eisenhower's "Atoms for Peace" speech in 1953. This notable beginning of the IAEA is covered in David Fischer's history of the Agency.[2] Eisenhower and the United States started with the idea of providing nuclear material (enriched uranium) and other nuclear technologies and services to countries that joined the IAEA to promote the peaceful use of atomic energy through the Agency. Yet this original idea was not realized at first. Eventually, the role of providing material and technology for nuclear energy use was more or less undertaken by the national governments and private industries. Moreover, it took quite a long time, almost 60 years, to come up with a nuclear fuel bank, which was started in Kazakhstan. A number of noteworthy developments took place during that particular interval.

Initially, the focus of the IAEA was to promote the use of nuclear energy for power generation. Later the focus shifted to include other purposes, such as agricultural, industrial, and healthcare uses. As the late Director General Yukiya Amano of the IAEA stated in his keynote address at a Conference on the International Atomic Energy Agency at 60—which was held at the Woodrow Wilson International Center for Scholars in Washington, DC, on November 6–7, 2017—the role of the IAEA in promoting the use of atomic energy for power generation has always been intended to help those countries that are interested in it.[3] Nevertheless, a number of IAEA Member States today have come out against the use of nuclear energy for power generation—including the government of the IAEA's host country, Austria.

According to Fischer's history, the initial period of the IAEA was a golden age of nuclear energy. The period from the 1960s to the 1970s was

DOI: 10.4324/9781003160205-12

deeply affected by such events as the 1956 Suez Crisis and the 1973 oil crisis; when the world faced oil supply disruptions, and countries tried to make up for the fuel shortages and to increase their energy diversity by promoting the use of nuclear energy. The golden age soon came to an end. The following chart created by Carbon Brief, a London-based nongovernmental organization (NGO), shows how the number of nuclear power reactors has increased or decreased around the world (Figure 12.1). A sharp increase of reactors around the world up until the mid-1980s is visible, but afterward the number more or less flattened.

The number of reactors under construction, shown by the darkest bars, demonstrates capacity additions and sometimes drops in capacity. It is a matter of interpretation, but around the time of the Three Mile Island accident in 1979, there was a clear drop in new construction. Since the Chernobyl disaster in 1986, there has been an even more notable decline in new construction. Likewise, the Fukushima disaster of 2011 also caused a sharp decline, in no small part because many reactors in Japan had to stop operating. Before the Fukushima accident, Japan had 54 power reactors in operational status with total generating capacity of 48.8 gigawatts. As of 2020, there are only nine power reactors in operation with a total generating capacity of 913 megawatts. Since 2011, Japanese power companies have decided to retire 21 reactors, 6 at Fukushima Daiichi station and 15 approaching legal retirement age of 40 years from the beginning of their operation. This latter decision was made in view of the significant additional cost required to meet the new stringent safety regulations introduced after the Fukushima accident. Out of the remaining 33 reactors, 10 are still under safety examination and 8 have not yet submitted requests for permission to operate, even though it has been more than 9 years since the Fukushima accident. Fifteen reactors have passed safety examination, but six are still waiting for local consent for operation.[4]

The history of nuclear energy also provides an interesting observation. Over the history of the IAEA, on a number of occasions optimistic projections suggested that nuclear power reactor construction would rise quickly. Every time, according to Fischer, the rosy picture proved to be untrue. There were slowdowns. According to the latest projections for energy, electricity, and nuclear power trends of the IAEA, global nuclear electrical generating capacity is expected to increase by 82 percent to 715 gigawatts through 2050, almost doubling the capacity. However, this is the high scenario. The low scenario provides for a fall of 7 percent to 363 gigawatts, indicating that it is difficult to know what the future will hold.

A number of factors will affect the future of nuclear power generation. The IAEA report mentions competition with "the low price of natural gas and the impact of subsidized variable renewable energy sources." It also mentions "heightened safety requirements" that raises the construction and the maintenance costs. The report lays out that "about two-thirds of nuclear power reactors have been in operation for over 30 years, highlighting the

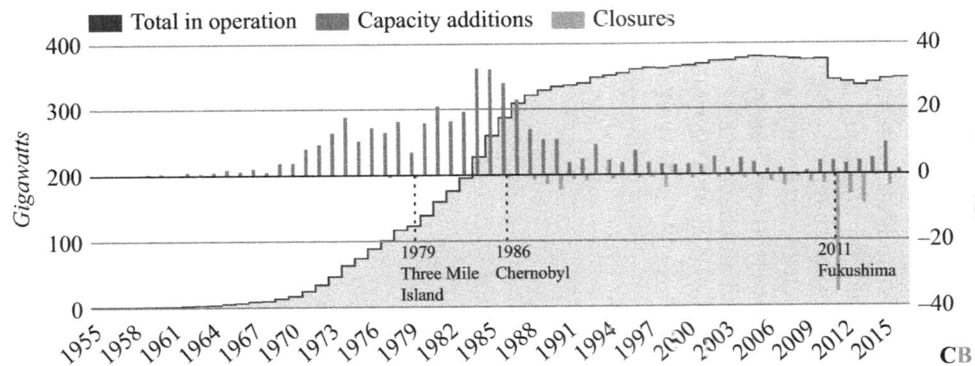

Figure 12.1 Global nuclear power generating capacity, 1955–2016

Note: Total global nuclear power generating capacity in operation between 1955 and 2016 (shaded area, left axis). Annual additions (dark bars, right axis) and the capacity of reactors going offline or being shut down (light bars, right axis).

Source: International Atomic Energy Agency (IAEA) Power Reactor Information System (PRIS) database and Carbon Brief analysis. Chart by Carbon Brief.

need for significant new nuclear capacity to offset retirements." It is not yet clear what will happen with regard to the replacement of the large number of reactors scheduled to be retired starting in 2030, particularly in North America and Europe. An increasing number of reactors are now subject to ageing management programs and other arrangements implemented to promote long-term operation.

As seen in Figure 12.1, and as noted above, major slowdowns tend to occur every time a big accident happens. These slowdowns, perhaps, also have occurred because of the concerns about proliferation and more recently about nuclear terrorism. Those concerns have increased the safety, nonproliferation, and counterterrorism requirements for nuclear facilities, which put burdens on new construction and consequently have slowed it down or stopped it altogether. Another chart, also by Carbon Brief, shows actual increase or decrease of nuclear electricity generation in absolute terms (Figure 12.2). It indicates how electricity generated by nuclear energy continued to increase, then flattened and declined.

The share of nuclear power generation as a percentage of world power generation has been slowly declining after it peaked at close to 20 percent around 1996. The fast-growing economies of China and India have resulted

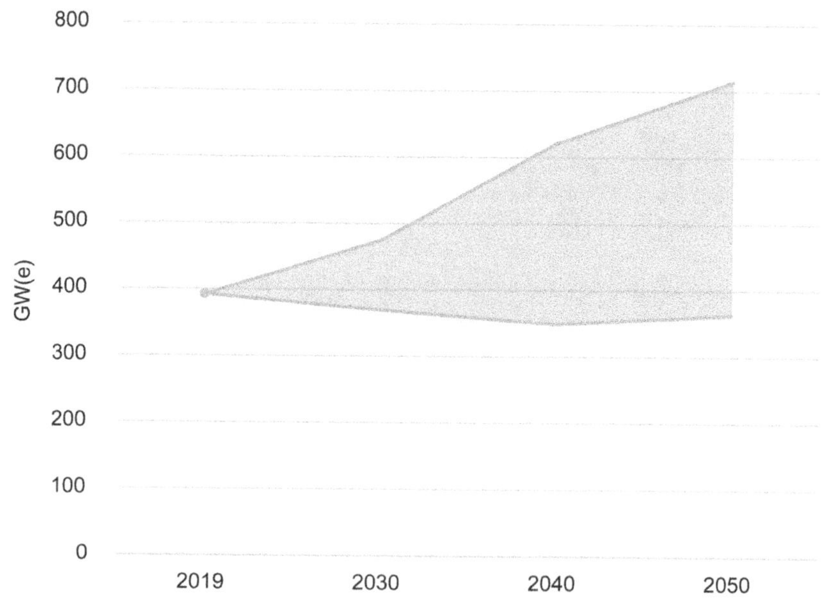

Figure 12.2 World nuclear electrical generating capacity projection

Note: In gigawatts.

Source: IAEA, *Energy, Electricity and Nuclear Power Estimates for the Period up to 2050,* 2020. https://www.iaea.org/publications/14786/energy-electricity-and-nuclear-power-estimates-for-the-period-up-to-2050.

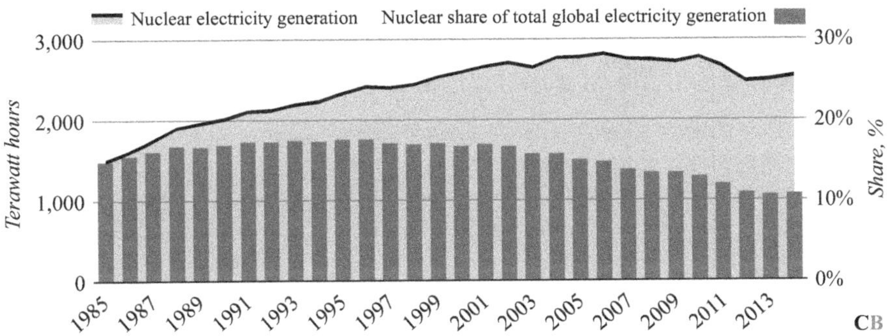

Figure 12.3 Global nuclear electricity generation, 1955–2016

Note: Global nuclear electricity generation (shaded area, left axis) and nuclear share of total world power generation (dark bars, right axis).

Source: BP Statistical Review of World Energy 2015 and Carbon Brief analysis. Chart by Carbon Brief.

in greater electricity generation more by burning coal and other fossil fuels than rapidly introducing nuclear power. Nuclear power is being introduced, but not fast enough to catch up with these countries' economic growth and power consumption requirements.

So what will be the future of nuclear power use? Some different trends seem to be taking place concurrently (Figure 12.4). One group includes the wealthy, advanced industrial democracies, which are facing increasing difficulty promoting the use of nuclear energy and even moving away from nuclear power generation in some instances. Among these latter states are Austria, Germany, Sweden (to a lesser extent), and Switzerland. The United States and Japan may be placed in that group, albeit with some question marks. The United Kingdom and France are in a gray zone.

The second group is composed of rising countries, including nonmarket giant economies such as China and Russia, or relative newcomers such as India. South Korea is another relative newcomer but with some question marks as well. President Moon Jae-in declared that South Korea will move out of nuclear power generation.[5]

In Figure 12.4, the horizontal axis shows the degree of freedom based on the assessment of political freedom and civil liberties in each country, scaled from 0 to 100 percentage points. This ranking is conducted yearly by the Freedom House NGO in Washington, D.C. Sweden scored 100 percent. Then, on the vertical axis, the eagerness with which countries are pushing nuclear energy, or are trying to move out of nuclear power generation, is represented. (This is the author's subjective judgment based on available information.) This assessment presents an interesting curve. From the top left, there are China, Russia, Pakistan, and India; as the extent of democratic freedom rises, there is a sharp decline. Canada, the Czech Republic, France,

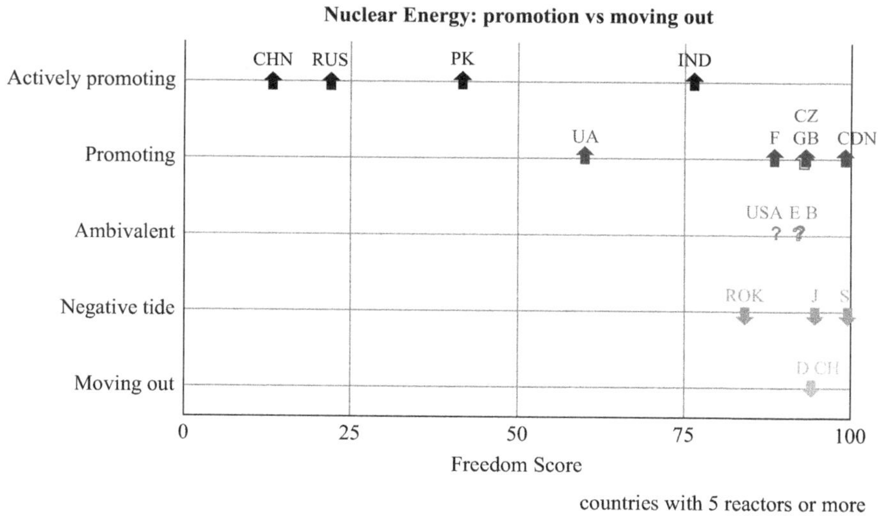

Figure 12.4 Nuclear energy promotion

Note: Countries with 5 nuclear power reactors are shown with Switzerland (CH) added for reference purpose.
Promotion vs. moving out: grading done by chart creator Nobuyasu Abe.
Country name abbreviation: based on ISO country codes.

Source: Freedom Score: based on "Global Freedom Scores" by Freedom House 2020 (https://freedomhouse.org/countries/freedom-world/scores).

and the United Kingdom are still promoting nuclear energy to some extent, but Belgium, Spain, and the United States are in a more dubious category. South Korea has declared it will go out of the nuclear business. Japan is still struggling with the issue of how to maintain nuclear power generation after the Fukushima disaster. Sweden may have decided against nuclear power generation, but opinions appear to be shifting back in favor of it. Germany and Switzerland have decided to move away from nuclear energy. As one can see, the future of nuclear energy use is unclear at present. It will depend on a number of factors.

The first major factor is climate change. There is the Paris Agreement. One major country, the United States, had declared that it would withdraw from it, although that decision has been reversed. The future of nuclear power use depends, for one thing, on the extent to which people around the world become serious about preventing global warming. To reduce carbon emissions drastically, the world may have to use nuclear energy. A second and somewhat related factor is carbon-free natural renewable energy sources. Different countries have made different efforts to try to introduce these clean energy sources. Here, one may also have to find out how the technology advances. The sun shines only in the daytime, the wind blows only at certain times depending on the weather. To use natural renewable energy on a great scale, the intermittency of those energy supplies has to be overcome. If an inexpensive way to store energy in large volumes can be found, then renewable energy use may be drastically increased. People will definitely prefer to use natural energy rather than nuclear energy under those circumstances.

Nuclear energy carries the risk of a serious accident. This view has become more prevalent among the people who have been traumatized by the events at Fukushima. The third issue, therefore, is who will be responsible for the proverbial fallout of such accidents. This is a key issue in Japan. The operator of the Fukushima reactors, the Tokyo Electric Power Company, has to compensate for the damages of the recent disaster. Payments for compensation and the cleanup operations are said to have reached more than $200 billion.[6] Any power company that may try to continue nuclear power generation faces a major business risk. Some countries have laws that place ultimate responsibility for nuclear accidents on the government. With that kind of liability, power companies and governments alike may hesitate to go into nuclear power business.

A final key factor to consider is nuclear waste disposal. Nuclear power generation produces spent nuclear fuel, but only very few countries, such as Finland and Sweden, have found places to dispose of their spent nuclear fuel. Other countries—the United States, Japan, France, Switzerland, South Korea, and Taiwan among them—are struggling to find places for the permanent disposition of spent nuclear materials. In Japan, former Prime Minister Junichiro Koizumi and Tokyo governor Yuriko Koike campaigned on this issue during a general election in the past decade, advocating that Japan should get out of nuclear power generation because Japan does not have a permanent repository.[7] By making that argument in an election campaign, they have shown the extent to which nuclear waste disposal is a vital deciding factor.

Given these uncertainties and doubts about nuclear energy, some sort of measures will have to be introduced to maintain nuclear power generation in open, democratic, advanced industrial countries. They may be such incentives as subsidies, a carbon tax, price guarantees, investment guarantees, and favorable damage compensation arrangements. Countries will have to take some of these steps to continue nuclear power generation. Such a situation is occurring in the United States, and it may also happen in other countries. The United Kingdom, for example, has introduced price guarantees.[8] Others are discussing a carbon tax, subsidies, or investment guarantees.[9] Some of these measures may have to be introduced, but any such measures should have the least amount of distortions or interference with markets as possible. A carbon tax, in that sense, is a better approach because it applies equally to the different energy sources and is the least corruptible. Alternatively, subsidies are the most corruptible means of policy implementation and are not to be recommended. In the United States, recently, Baker, Schultz, and Paulson proposed introduction of a form of carbon tax, calling it "a conservative climate solution" based on free-market principles.[10] Unfortunately, so far such a proposal has not gained momentum in the United States.

Notes

1. According to a study by the Japan Nuclear Energy Agency, in 2007—four years before the Fukushima accident—energy use represented 54 percent while nonenergy use represented 46 percent.
2. David Fischer, *The History of the IAEA: The First Forty Years* (Vienna: IAEA, 1997).
3. The speech can be found in the appendix to this volume.
4. "Nihon no genshiryoku hatsudenjo MAPPU" [Nuclear power plant map of Japan], Nippon.com, March 6 2020, https://www.nippon.com/ja/features/h00238/.
5. Christine Kim, "South Korea's President Says Will Continue Phasing Out Nuclear Power," *Reuters*, October 21, 2017, https://www.reuters.com/article/us-southkorea-nuclear-moon/south-koreas-president-says-will-continue-phasing-out-nuclear-power-idUSKBN1CR04U.
6. Mayumi Negishi, "Japan Raises Estimate for 2011 Nuclear Accident to $200 Billion," *Wall Street Journal*, December 9, 2016, https://www.wsj.com/articles/japan-raises-estimate-for-2011-nuclear-accident-to-200-billion-1481270326.
7. See, for instance, Philip Brasor, "Get Koizumi: Nuclear Village Goes on Offensive," *Japan Times*, October 26, 2013, https://www.japantimes.co.jp/news/2013/10/26/national/media-national/get-koizumi-nuclear-village-goes-on-offensive/.
8. See, for instance, "Nuclear Power in the United Kingdom," World Nuclear Organization, n.d., http://www.world-nuclear.org/information-library/country-profiles/countries-t-z/united-kingdom.aspx.
9. See, for instance, Nuclear Energy Agency, *Carbon Pricing, Power Markets and the Competitiveness of Nuclear Power*, NEA No. 6982 (Paris: Organisation for Economic Co-operation and Development, 2011).
10. James A. Baker III et al., *The Conservative Case for Carbon Dividends: How a New Climate Strategy Can Strengthen Our Economy, Reduce Regulation, Help Working-Class Americans and Promote National Security* (Washington, DC: Climate Leadership Council, February 2017), https://www.clcouncil.org/media/2017/03/The-Conservative-Case-for-Carbon-Dividends.pdf.

13 Atoms for Peace

Bringing nuclear fusion closer to reality

Bernard Bigot

The "Atoms for Peace" mission of the International Atomic Energy Agency (IAEA) has proven itself since its creation 60 years ago to be integral to the future of human civilization, in three compelling ways. First, it enables remarkable direct globally coordinated scientific and technological peaceful contributions to society that have had and will continue to have significant positive impacts. Second, it seeks to prevent the application of any science and technology advancements toward any further proliferation of nuclear weapons. Finally, and most importantly, it provides both a framework and the incentives for all parties to work collaboratively for mutual benefit.

Over its history, Atoms for Peace has become both a philosophy and a practical approach, finding its expression in bilateral, regional, and global agreements, the most well-known being the 1970 Treaty on the Non-proliferation of Nuclear Weapons (NPT). The significance of the NPT—the central strength that led to its global implementation—lies in the deal it struck between countries that were more advanced or less advanced in nuclear technology at that time. The five recognized nuclear-weapon states—China, France, the Soviet Union (now the Russian Federation), the United Kingdom, and the United States—agreed to provide their peaceful nuclear science and technology expertise to the nonweapon states party to the NPT, and further agreed to the longer-term objective of working, over time, toward global disarmament. In return, the non-weapon state parties agreed not to pursue the development of nuclear weapons.

These mutual incentives are widely known; but what is frequently under-appreciated is the immense positive impact that this treaty—and similar bilateral and regional agreements made in the same spirit—have had on modern culture and lifestyles globally. The Atoms for Peace initiative arose at a critical juncture in human history. Rival superpowers had developed the unprecedented potential to annihilate each other, but instead we have averted a third global conflict. Scientifically advanced countries were on a pathway to restrict access to their knowledge and technology, but instead we have had the global spread of nuclear applications for peaceful societal benefit.

DOI: 10.4324/9781003160205-13

The nuclear news of the past few decades often has focused exclusively on negative headlines: threats to nuclear safeguards, clandestine nuclear programs, new countries seeking nuclear weapons, and conflicts arising from these situations. What this view misses is the extraordinary societal value derived from shared peaceful nuclear technology: the global health advantages from the spread of nuclear medicine; the advent of more nutritious, higher yield crops through plant breeding using seed irradiation; more informed management of underground freshwater aquifers using isotope hydrology; the heightened effectiveness of industrial fabrication using radiography; and the clean, carbon-free electricity provided by safely operated nuclear energy facilities.

Throughout my career, particularly during my two terms as the head of the French Alternative Energy and Atomic Energy Commission (CEA; Commissariat à l'énergie atomique et aux énergies alternatives), and before that as France's high commissioner for atomic energy, I have been fortunate to observe first-hand these and other positive impacts of the IAEA and the Atoms for Peace mission on both a national and international scale. Standards of safety have been enhanced globally through information-sharing networks. The development of radioactive waste strategies has begun to provide solutions to this long-term public concern. Collaborative nuclear security efforts have hardened facilities and reduced the number of locations using highly enriched uranium in research reactors. Strengthened nuclear safeguards inspection measures have been applied. Finally, new humanitarian applications of nuclear science have improved lifestyles and led to partnerships that transcend borders.

At its best, the scientific community stands out for this feature: the scientist as a societal ambassador for peace. Scientific curiosity transcends borders: across generations, across sectors, across national and political boundaries. The advancement of scientific knowledge has always involved current researchers or innovators building on the discoveries of those who preceded them. Human scientific knowledge is a growing body of work, each generation surpassing the one before. And the translation of scientific discovery to technological innovation is almost inherently a collaborative multisector—and often a multinational—activity. In this sense, Atoms for Peace has enabled some of the most intelligent minds of the past 60 years to become more than the sum of their parts, by working together toward shared objectives.

Nowhere, across the broad spectrum of nuclear technologies, has this been more apparent than in the research and development (R&D) effort to control and harness nuclear (hydrogen) fusion for commercial energy generation. In particular, the global effort to develop a commercially feasible magnetic confinement fusion facility has been an enterprise aligned with all the best elements of Atoms for Peace: remarkable scientific and technological achievement for human benefit, minimization of weapons proliferation concerns, and unprecedented global collaboration.

The birth of fusion collaboration

Sixty years ago, when the IAEA was born in July 1957, magnetic confinement fusion was also in its early infancy. In 1950, Oleg Lavrentyev, a self-taught 23-year-old Soviet soldier stationed on Sakhalin Island, had come up with the novel concept of confining a fusion plasma in a toroidal or doughnut-shaped device: an idea that Soviet physicist Andrei Sakharov and his colleague Igor Tamm further elaborated to create a device known as the tokamak. In 1951 in the United States, astrophysicist Lyman Spitzer had separately developed the stellarator, a similar circular magnetic confinement fusion device, but Spitzer's design had a far more complex architecture of twisted coils to confine and stabilize the plasma. Both of these models for magnetic confinement fusion originated in the middle of the Cold War. It would have been no surprise if each model were to have continued to develop independently, each inventor sharing his or her breakthroughs only with other scientists of like nationality or allies. This isolated "stovepiping" would have followed the pattern that had occurred only a few years earlier for fission energy R&D. But instead, a different narrative was to be written for fusion energy, shaped by a few seminal decisions and events.

In 1956, Soviet Premier Nikita Khrushchev headed a Soviet delegation to the United Kingdom. Among other interactions, this delegation included a stunning lecture by physicist Igor Kurchatov, entitled "The possibility of producing thermonuclear reactions in a gaseous discharge," which unveiled how far the Russians had come with their fusion R&D. Much of Kurchatov's information would have been considered classified at the time; the deliberate candor and openness displayed—concerning both the progress made and the challenges facing Russian fusion science—would become the first step in the global declassification of peaceful fusion energy research.

Soon afterward, in 1958, the Russians completed the first tokamak, T-1. In that same year, in September, the United Nations held its Second International Conference on the Peaceful Uses of Atomic Energy. Early signals emerged that other governments were also willing for their scientists to collaborate in the field of fusion. Actors on both sides of the political divide—Lev Artsimovitch, Edward Teller, Lyman Spitzer, and others—were able to meet in person and exchange notes on their research.

Ten years later, in 1968, an even more remarkable event occurred. Once again, the Russians presented a paper on their experimental results, this time coming from operation of their T-3 tokamak, in which they reported achieving temperatures in excess of 1keV (equivalent to 10 million degrees C). On this occasion, they invited their British counterparts, with their advanced diagnostic instruments, to come to Moscow to verify these results independently. The British agreed and stayed for more than a year. The Americans and others soon joined in.

I emphasize these events for two reasons: because of how clearly this collaboration on fusion energy research illustrates the spirit of Atoms for

Peace, and because of how uniquely this behavior may be viewed in the history of human scientific advancement. Since the earliest annals of civilization, new knowledge and new technologies customarily have been viewed in terms of how to gain an advantage—often a military advantage—for the inventor's country or tribe. Therefore, such breakthroughs have been closely guarded. The fusion narrative breaks this pattern. Not only were the remarkable Russian results verified by the British—essentially, their Cold War enemies—and the tokamak design thereby given greater credibility, but with this interaction the nature of fusion R&D as a global collaboration for mutual benefit was born.

The evolution of the stellarator

The tokamak design did not immediately gain ascendency over the stellarator. By the late 1980s, relying on the strong progress of computer-aided design, automation, and engineering, the stellarator was continuing to gain momentum in some fusion research circles. At the Max Planck Institute of Plasma Physics (IPP) in Garching, Germany, the Wendelstein 7-AS device entered into operation in 1988 and continued for 14 years of superb research results. Japan followed with its Large Helical Device, which marked its first plasma in 1998. In the United States, a small stellarator—the Helically Symmetric Experiment—was built at the University of Wisconsin at Madison in 1993. A much larger device, the National Compact Stellarator Experiment, was launched at the Princeton Plasma Physics Laboratory in 2004, although the U.S. Department of Energy would cancel it four years later.

The crowning achievement to date applying the stellarator model for fusion energy is Wendelstein 7-X, constructed of 50 superconducting magnet coils about 3.5 meters high, at a new IPP institute in Greifswald. Assembly began in April 2005, a fruitful cooperation developed at that time between IPP and CEA with my continuous support, and W7-X produced its first hydrogen plasma on February 3, 2016. It was a real moment of excitement for me to be present at the ceremony, where German Chancellor Angela Merkel pressed the button to initiate the reaction. Following a successful run of experiments over the ensuing months, W7-X was reoutfitted with an inner wall of graphite tiles and 10 divertor modules, with the goal of achieving higher plasma temperatures and longer discharges. In September 2017, W7-X was restarted and soon had achieved the best fusion triple product—a combination of the plasma's particle density, energy confinement time, and plasma temperature—of any stellarator on record.

Growth in tokamak R&D

Meanwhile, a parallel evolution of the tokamak was taking place globally. Following the 1968 Russian announcement of the T-3 tokamak breakthrough, verified by British diagnostics, multiple countries began to work on their own tokamak devices. By the late 1970s, dozens of laboratories around the world were conducting research using their own tokamaks, and many of the conditions needed for practical fusion had been achieved. The next series of machines were ready to focus on improving aspects of tokamak performance and using deuterium and tritium as the fusion fuel.

It is beyond the scope of this chapter to describe in detail the 200-plus tokamaks built around the world over the past five decades. I will limit myself to mentioning a few significant achievements and milestones:

- The Tokamak de Fontenay-aux-Roses was the first French tokamak, located just outside Paris in a CEA research center. During the mid-1970s, it set a number of records as the world's highest-performing fusion device.
- The ASDEX tokamak began operation in Munich in 1980. Two years later, in 1982, Fritz Wagner there discovered the more stable high-confinement mode (or H-mode) of plasma control. The ASDEX Upgrade, which uses an all-tungsten first wall, has been operational since 1991.
- TFTR, the Tokamak Fusion Test Reactor at Princeton Plasma Physics Laboratory in the United States, was the first magnetic fusion device to use a 50/50 mix of deuterium-tritium fuel in its fusion experiments. It began operation in 1982 and continued through 1997, setting a number of performance records, including a plasma temperature of 510 million degrees C in 1995.
- The JT-60 tokamak, which began operation in 1985 in Naka, Japan, is noted for having achieved the highest fusion triple product using deuterium fuel in 1998. JT-60SA, an upgrade using superconducting coils, is currently under construction under the framework of the "Broader Approach"—a large and exemplary 2006 European-Japanese cooperation stimulated by the ITER Agreement—and is scheduled for First Plasma in 2020.
- The DIII-D tokamak, operated by General Atomics in San Diego since the late 1980s, enhanced plasma performance using a D-shaped, non-circular cross-section. DIII-D is a strong example of international collaboration, with more than 600 users from more than 100 institutions.
- Tore Supra, an early superconductor tokamak at the Cadarache research complex in France, operated from 1988 to 2010. It holds the world record (set in 2003) for the longest duration tokamak plasma operations at 6 minutes and 30 seconds. Following an upgrade to add tungsten walls, a tungsten divertor, and other features, the newly renamed WEST began operation successfully in 2016.
- Alcator C-Mod, at the Massachusetts Institute of Technology in Boston, was noted for advances made in exploring high-magnetic-field operation (up to 8 Tesla). Operating from 1991 to 2016, it retains the world record for volume-averaged plasma pressure.

- EAST, the Experimental Advanced Superconducting tokamak in Hefei, China, began operation in 2006, the first tokamak to use superconducting poloidal and toroidal field magnets. Among other achievements, it has been sustaining successively longer plasma pulses. In 2017, EAST sustained H-mode operation for more than 100 seconds at 50 million degrees C.
- KSTAR, a superconducting tokamak in Daejeon, South Korea, achieved first plasma in mid-2010. It has also been sustaining progressively longer duration high-temperature plasmas each year since that time (72 seconds in 2017).
- JET, the Joint European Torus, is the largest operating tokamak to date, located at the Culham Centre for Fusion Energy in Oxfordshire in the United Kingdom. JET holds the current record for fusion power production of 16 megawatts (MW) in 1997, using deuterium-tritium fuel and plasma heating input of 24 MW.

The broad range and variety of these fusion energy research achievements illustrates the global nature of fusion energy research and the complementary way in which each country and research center has built on the discoveries of the others. But for the tokamak to be commercially feasible, size is a major factor (along with the plasma density and the strength of the magnetic field). To demonstrate the commercial feasibility of fusion energy, fusion scientists required an industrial-scale machine, capable of creating and controlling a "burning plasma": that is, a plasma that would be largely self-heated (more than 80 percent) by the fusion reaction itself. This would also entail a "Q" well above break-even (Q being the ratio of fusion power output to the thermal energy used as input to heat the plasma). It was this need—for a massively scaled-up experimental platform, with the associated cost and engineering complexity—that would provide the rationale and basis for the cooperative international effort that came to be International Thermonuclear Experimental Reactor (ITER).

Envisioning the ITER project: The challenges of collaborating on a first-of-its-kind facility

Once again, it would be the Soviet Union that would take the lead, this time in collaboration with the United States. At the historic Geneva Summit of 1985, between Soviet Secretary-General Mikhail Gorbachev and U.S. President Ronald Reagan, the two leaders, meeting for the first time, were like-minded in their desire to limit the size of their respective countries' nuclear-weapon arsenals. Behind the scenes, Russian academician Evgeny Velikhov, the leader of his country's fusion R&D program, had been working on a peaceful nuclear collaboration proposal: urging his U.S. counterpart Michael Roberts of the Department of Energy and others to move forward with a bilateral agreement on an international fusion energy project.

The proposal succeeded: Reagan and Gorbachev signed a joint summit statement in November 1985 agreeing to the fusion collaboration "for the benefit of all mankind," and offered to any country to join their best efforts in a large cooperative program.[1] Within a short time, Japan and Europe had joined the effort, and a Quadripartite Initiative Committee had been formed under the auspices of the IAEA to plan the overall stages of design, construction, and operation of the International Thermonuclear Experimental Reactor—or ITER, as it has been known since that time. By 1988, the four parties had approved the Conceptual Design Activities, and by 1990 the first preliminary designs had been completed.

A difficulty arose at the next stage, however, regarding how to proceed with the more detailed engineering design activities. The working assumption was that the central design team would be sited at a single location, but each of the four parties wanted to be the host. After considerable discussion, a compromise was reached: three working sites were established in Garching, Naka and San Diego, with the formal seat of the ITER Council located in Moscow.

This challenge would continue to be an issue for the ITER project—a natural outcome for each country involved to view itself as a leader for the global fusion enterprise. Uniquely, ITER had become the converging next step in the fusion energy road map of each member. Each member therefore wanted to gain the greatest scientific insights and technological expertise possible from its role in the project. In the history of Atoms for Peace, the challenges of multilateral cooperation were well understood. Many collaborative nuclear projects had been successfully undertaken, including technology R&D. However, to collaboratively design, construct, and operate a first-of-its-kind industrial-scale nuclear facility was to enter uncharted territory.

A second challenge was how to ensure the sustained political will of the government decision-makers providing the ongoing financial support for such a long-term project. In July 1998, when the parties met to celebrate the completion of the engineering design activities and the final design report was approved, the governing ITER Council asked the project director to work on a design option that would cost 50 percent less. A three-year extension of the engineering design agreement was approved, to focus on this and site-specific issues. In October 1998, however, the United States withdrew from the project, considering the extension decision to be unsuitable.

Despite this setback, the project moved forward toward the siting stage. In May 2001, ITER Canada announced that it would launch a bid to host the ITER facility in Clarington, Ontario. One year later, Japan launched a bid to host the facility at Rokkasho, and Europe proposed two sites: Cadarache in France, and Vandellos in Spain. By January 2003, the United States had rejoined the project, and China and Korea joined that year as well, bringing the total to seven parties. Negotiations began in earnest on how the project would be organized and staffed, how information and intellectual property rights would be shared, and how members could contribute to procurement of ITER technology—each of the elements that would determine the value received by each member.

In November 2003, Europe narrowed its proposals from two to one, selecting Cadarache. One month later, Canada withdrew its offer and withdrew from the project. Following another round of negotiations and technical evaluations of the remaining European and Japanese proposals, Cadarache was selected as the ITER construction site in June 2005 during a specific ministerial meeting in Moscow, with Japan designated for additional supplementary fusion research facilities and activities under the "Broader Approach." In December of that year, India became an ITER member, bringing the total ITER membership back to seven.

With this mix of competition and collaboration as background, it should be no surprise that the ITER Agreement, signed one year later at the Élysée Palace in Paris, would settle on a complex multinational procurement arrangement. As part of the deal in becoming the host member, Europe agreed to fund 5/11ths (45 percent) of the project, with each of the other six members contributing 1/11th (9 percent). But in keeping with the desire of each member to acquire as much expertise as possible, and to prepare their most technologically advanced industrial companies for the expected fusion development after ITER's success, the ITER Agreement affirmed that most of the financial contribution of each member (roughly 90 percent) would be made in-kind, in the form of components. For a machine design that would be exceptionally complex, this procurement arrangement would make ITER manufacturing, construction, assembly, and installation even more complex.

In one sense, the engineering of the ITER machine already had been largely validated in past tokamaks. Multiple sets of superconducting electromagnets—the cylindrical central solenoid, the circular poloidal field magnets, the D-shaped toroidal field magnets, and smaller correction coils—would create a large invisible magnetic cage to accelerate and confine the charged particles of the 150-million-degree-C plasma away from the metal walls of the toroidal vacuum vessel. By design, only the uncharged neutrons would escape the plasma to convert their immense kinetic energy into heat. These behaviors had been demonstrated in smaller machines, as had most of the cryogenics, vacuum systems, robotics, and power electronics in the ITER design.

What would set ITER apart is the combination of scale and precision required. Each of ITER's main magnets weighs several hundred tons. Some have dimensions as large as 24 meters. Yet the intense magnetic fields they are to generate must be cross-woven so intricately that charged hydrogen nuclei, sized at roughly 10^{-15} meters, cannot escape. Components so large they could be fabricated in shipyards therefore would need to be positioned with the delicacy of a watchmaker. As the subsequent manufacturing and construction activities have proven, these extreme design requirements would drive a host of technology innovations and engineering "firsts," from fabrication techniques to new materials, instrumentation, tools, and components. They are required by ITER's mission, to demonstrate the feasibility of fusion energy on a commercial scale and to create for the first time on Earth the conditions necessary for a "burning plasma": in brief, to create a star on earth.

For these reasons, it was clear that each ITER member would want to be involved as much as possible in gaining the knowledge and technology breakthroughs associated with each aspect of the machine and its support systems. It was also clear that ITER would be arguably the most complex physical experiment to ever take shape in the long history of Atoms for Peace.

ITER: On the way to new energy

The ITER Agreement required a unique multinational structure, with the ITER Organization (IO) as owner and coordinator of the whole ITER program as well as nuclear operator, and seven Domestic Agencies (DAs) each in charge of procuring that member's share of the ITER components. This approach has many desirable elements, both for the sharing of costs and for the joint creation and acquisition of intellectual property. It lowers the financial and other risks for any one member, it pools the best fusion expertise and experience globally, and the many spin-off technologies that emerge are applicable to other industries and open significant opportunities for multinational trade.

However, this multinational ITER structure, as formulated and implemented, also had an inherent vulnerability: it could cause each entity to focus on the production of their specific components or design elements rather than on the facility as a whole. At the outset, the project lacked institutional elements critical to the design and construction of a complex first-of-its-kind facility, such as project management orientation and tools; a systems engineering emphasis (project integration); and the type of expertise in quality control, human resources, procurement, and contracts that would be suited to the project. Predictable disconnects occurred at the points of integration between the IO and DAs, and even between IO departments.

A highly critical U.S.-led 2013 management assessment identified deficiencies in the project. The sharing of work among many parties, coupled with the lack of a strong central integration approach, had led to significant inefficiencies. The detailed design had been assumed to be near-complete at the start, which was not the case after thorough analysis of safety requirements, constructability, and operability. The complexity of a first-of-its-kind full-scale fusion reactor, built to nuclear construction standards, had not been fully taken into account. The interfaces between parties in design and assembly activities (such as the vacuum vessel sectors manufactured in part by Korea and in part by the European Union) were particularly challenging. Many such aspects of the project had not been fully considered in initial schedule or resource estimates.

In late 2014, when I was approached by several ITER members to take over as the new ITER Director-General, I viewed the offer with some reluctance, understanding the time needed to overcome the immense challenges involved, and the fact I was on the verge of retiring from my French career at 65 years old. Yet I also believed wholeheartedly in the value that the ITER mission represented for the global community: to establish, once and for all, the feasibility of fusion as a reliable source of clean, massive, reliable, safe, and virtually unlimited energy.

After careful consideration, and the sincere and deep feeling that I could not decline to help the project to move forward, if needed, I agreed to run for the position with the other candidates who responded to the call for application. I presented the ITER members with an action plan that would be necessary to put the project on track for success. Acceptance of the plan by all members and their commitment to support it was my condition for accepting the position—and all agreed. The plan was designed to accomplish several specific objectives: effective, efficient centralized decision-making; profound integration of the work of the IO with that of the DAs; a comprehensive technological understanding of all aspects of the ITER machine; finalization of design of ITER's critical path components; an updated, challenging, but reliable schedule developed with all the stakeholders including the suppliers; and above all, a project culture capable of reliably delivering on our commitments while maintaining the highest levels of safety and quality.

These project reforms were put into place when I started my tenure in March 2015. Looking back, more than five years later, I am pleased to see that ITER has since remained on track for success according to the agreed schedule and cost. According to multiple external reviews that have considered the performance of the ITER project since 2015, we have established the needed robust project culture and committed to continuous improvement, with strong, effective processes for international project management, systems engineering, and risk management. Most significantly, we have continued to deliver on our construction and manufacturing commitments, in accordance with the expected ITER Council milestones, working within agreed cost constraints. We have achieved this performance as a fully integrated ITER team of seven members representing 35 countries.

As of July 2020, the ITER project had reached two significant milestones: the readiness to begin Machine Assembly Phase, and the completion of 70 percent of the total construction work scope through First Plasma. This is no small achievement. "Total construction work scope," as used in ITER's project performance metrics, is a start-to-finish term. It includes design, component manufacturing, building construction, shipping and delivery, assembly, and installation. Globally, these indicators show that the ITER project is progressing steadily. This has not happened easily. A project of this complexity is full of risks, and our schedule to First Plasma in December 2025 is set with no "float" or contingency. Effective risk management is a daily discipline at ITER. We are now continuing to progress at a monthly pace of 0.6–0.7 percent. With more than 50 months until the end of 2024, when we plan to start overall facility commissioning, we are on track to complete the remaining 30 percent, provided that all ITER members maintain their in-kind and in-cash commitments.

ITER's success so far has demanded extraordinary commitment from the ITER members, high-performance project management, and near-perfect integration of our work. Our design has taken advantage of the best expertise of every member's scientific and industrial base. No country, not even the most advanced, could have done this alone. We are all learning from each other, for the world's mutual benefit.

Looking ahead, we know that we will need the continuing commitment and support of every member to maintain the successful performance of the past three years. By choosing to build this machine in an integrated way, we have made our success interdependent. The ITER project is built on this condition: if our partnerships perform well, each partner contributes its expertise, we all learn from each other, the interfaces are well managed, the project succeeds, and everyone wins. However, a shortfall in the commitment of any member, if it impacts the delivery of that member's components or the capacity of the ITER Organization to meet the machine assembly and installation schedule, will have a cascading effect in delays and costs to all other members. It is therefore vital that each member approaches the ITER project with a sense of pride, ownership, and responsibility.

At the ITER Organization, we are committed to ensuring the delivery of the ITER machine on time and the full achievement of the associated scientific and technological benefits, as the launching pad for the eventual commercial deployment of fusion-generated electricity. We are committed to delivering the project in a manner that lives up to the trust placed in us by all ITER members. We are committed to making ITER the model for international collaboration on complex science and technology challenges. And we are committed to making ITER a sound investment for all our partners and for the world. In short, we are fully committed to "Atoms for Peace."

The vision of fusion energy

Fusion energy is desirable because of its near-perfect characteristics. Fusion releases no carbon or other greenhouse gases. The fusion reaction, while difficult to create, is inherently safe; unlike nuclear fission, there is no possibility of a Three Mile Island-, Chernobyl-, or Fukushima-style nuclear meltdown. Nor does a fusion reactor produce any high-activity, long-lived radioactive waste. And magnetic confinement fusion, as envisioned in the stellarator or tokamak reactor models, offers minimal vulnerability in terms of nuclear-weapon proliferation.

Best of all, fusion fuel is abundant. Deuterium is easily extracted from seawater, and lithium, used in the tokamak to breed tritium as the second element of the fuel mix, is similarly plentiful. This translates to millions of years of fuel supply for consumption of a global population of more than 8 billion inhabitants of Earth. With this fuel accessible to every region and country, it is not difficult to foresee a transformed geopolitical landscape, an energy-rich global community no longer scarred by conflicts over access to petroleum resources.

In no way does this mean a rejection of other forms of energy generation. Throughout my career, I have long been a vocal advocate of nuclear fission, and my country, France, has benefited from many decades of safe, clean nuclear energy generation from its 58 nuclear power plants. I also have been an outspoken advocate of renewable energy: solar, wind, and hydroelectric power generation, among other technologies. We have to be open-minded and consider any option that can be part of a sustainable energy mix. But it is clear that nuclear fusion holds advantages over any of these energy sources, as a baseload source of electricity generation. We owe it to ourselves, and to future generations, to demonstrate the potential of fusion energy as a transformational legacy for centuries to come.

As with all aspects of the Atoms for Peace mission, the stakes are high for humankind. I am confident that—with some of the most talented scientists, engineers, managers, and entrepreneurs in the world, provide they all work together—ITER will meet the challenge.

Note

1. Joint Soviet-United States Statement on the Summit Meeting in Geneva, November 21, 1985, at https://www.reaganlibrary.gov/research/speeches/112185a.

14 Nuclear safety and security after Fukushima

The role of the IAEA and the prospects for global governance

Joseph F. Pilat[*]

Introduction

Before the 2011 Fukushima nuclear accident, the prospect of global nuclear expansion—in the view of some, a "nuclear renaissance"—appeared to be defining the future nuclear landscape as a result of increasing energy demand, growing concerns over energy security and climate change, and other emerging issues. It was believed that the prospects for dramatic growth in nuclear power would depend not only on economic competitiveness but also on safety, security, and proliferation resistance. Whatever long-term impact that Fukushima may have on global interest in nuclear power, the pre-accident rationale for nuclear power remains, and at present it still appears that nuclear power will expand, although at a slower rate and less widely than might have been the case before the accident. All of these issues affecting the prospects for nuclear power remain; however, Fukushima renewed concerns about safety and underscored concerns about security.

Prior to Fukushima, the safety of current nuclear power reactors appeared to have been well demonstrated, and the prospects for future improvements were seen as significant. Although the impact of the 1979 Three Mile Island incident and, more importantly, the 1986 Chernobyl accident had been diminishing in public perceptions, Fukushima changed this and has once again put safety at the fore. Fukushima also exacerbated security concerns, which had been growing since the terrorist attacks on the United States on September 11, 2001. The infrastructure failures in Japan are directly relevant to both security and safety, and the accident highlighted the vulnerabilities of spent fuel storage and the potential effects of a terrorist attack.

Since the accident, the attention of nuclear policymakers has focused more on safety issues, including risk assessments, the adequacy of peer reviews, emergency preparedness, and the competence and independence of national regulatory bodies. However, nuclear security has also risen in importance as a consequence. A growing international consensus has

DOI: 10.4324/9781003160205-14

formed on the need for enhanced nuclear safety and security, and concerns about the potential impact of failure of these objectives on the industry have been on the rise.

After Fukushima: The need for a global response

If these concerns are to be addressed effectively, and nuclear power is to be sustainable in the future, there will need to be a global response. However, it is by no means certain that nuclear policymakers will be able to marshal sufficient global attention and resources for these critical ends.

The framework for global nuclear governance is a patchwork, with widely differing rights and obligations and significant gaps. The international nuclear nonproliferation regime, centered on the Treaty on the Non-proliferation of Nuclear Weapons (NPT) and the International Atomic Energy Agency (IAEA), is increasingly being challenged by non-compliance and other problems. The nonproliferation regime has some residual impact on nuclear security, and there have been efforts to extend its provisions to this arena, notably in 2004 through United Nations (UN) Security Council Resolution 1540, which sought to prevent states from providing support to nonstate actors that attempt to acquire weapons of mass destruction. Despite this initiative, there is nothing comparable to the nonproliferation regime in the nuclear security or safety realms. Several relevant industrial groups, including the World Association of Nuclear Operators (WANO) and the World Institute for Nuclear Security (WINS), work to promote best practices on the use of nuclear materials, but no one entity has the ability to set and enforce nuclear safety and security regulations.

Although global institution building and good nuclear governance should be objectives, they are longer-term goals at best and unlikely to be accepted any time soon. Other, more limited efforts are being pursued in the near term. In the nuclear safety and security arenas, agreements and arrangements have been reached, and best practices, standards, and norms are developing and capabilities are growing in the IAEA and elsewhere. Regional institutions and other forums can also promote cooperation on safety, security, and safeguards. Further, it is both possible and desirable to better integrate safety and security with safeguards, though such an outcome may be difficult to realize. A near- to medium-term approach should build on current efforts, including those initiated or expanded after Fukushima, and strengthen them by expanding the role of the IAEA, building on and expanding ongoing proliferation resistance and physical protection activities, and furthering enabling technology research and development (R&D) programs. The role of the IAEA will be central to the continuing global response to Fukushima, especially as its missions in these areas expand.

Expanding the role of the IAEA

To prevent future nuclear disasters, it will be important to strengthen, pursue universal adherence to, and improve implementation of all nuclear safety and security protocols, as well as safeguards arrangements, agreements, and instruments. However, it is increasingly being argued that a global response to the challenges of integrating safety, security, and safeguards in the post-Fukushima environment should begin with the IAEA. Although there are opponents of expanding the IAEA's role, the Agency has a mandate to promote nuclear power and administer safeguards, along with explicit and growing roles in nuclear safety and security. An effective, strengthened international safeguards system, with a strong focus on verification and searching for undeclared nuclear materials and activities, is essential to provide confidence that shared nuclear technologies and expertise, as well as nuclear materials themselves, are not being diverted to nuclear-weapon programs. The state-level approach being championed by the IAEA is especially important and should offer a level of unprecedented transparency and openness that could have impacts well beyond the safeguards themselves.

Even as the IAEA is strengthening its safeguards, it also is being requested to expand its role in the safety and security arenas. The IAEA has had a long-standing role in safety and security, which has been evolving in response to global challenges. The accident at Chernobyl led to an expansion of the IAEA's role and capabilities in safety. Despite the Agency's initial difficulties in dealing with Fukushima, it was able to play a positive role there as well. As a consequence, many if not all Member States have called for a further expansion in the safety area.

The adoption of the Action Plan on Nuclear Safety in 2011 was a promising step. The plan was designed to strengthen the global framework for nuclear safety. It defined a program of work to enhance safety in a dozen areas:

1 Safety assessment of nuclear power plants.
2 IAEA peer reviews.
3 Emergency preparedness and response.
4 National regulatory bodies.
5 Operating organizations.
6 IAEA safety standards.
7 The international legal framework.
8 Member States planning to embark on a nuclear power program.
9 Capacity building.
10 Protection of people and the environment from ionizing radiation.
11 Communication and information dissemination.
12 Research and development.[1]

The work under the action plan—including efforts to enhance safety standards and peer reviews, as well as capacity building in Member States—has been completed. Many elements have become part of the Agency's safety mission. Among other safety activities, the IAEA also has a role in peer reviewing reports submitted by parties under the Convention for Nuclear Safety, which commits parties to maintain a high-level of safety on land-based nuclear power plants.[2]

As for security, the increasing concerns about radiological and nuclear terrorism following the terrorist attacks on the United States of September 11, 2001, led to an ongoing effort to address the nuclear terrorism threat through the IAEA. In March 2002, the IAEA Board of Governors approved a program to strengthen nuclear and radiological material security worldwide. This program provides technical advice, legislative and regulatory assistance, training, equipment upgrades, and peer reviews. In addition to working with states, the IAEA coordinates with other UN agencies and bodies and has helped to create or strengthen old legal instruments. One of the most notable of these projects was the successful IAEA-led effort to amend the Convention on the Physical Protection of Nuclear Material, which extends the scope of the Convention to cover the physical protection of nuclear material used for peaceful purposes in domestic use, storage, and transport, and the protection of peaceful nuclear facilities against sabotage. Following the end of the Nuclear Security Summits initiated by President Barack Obama, the IAEA has become a central player in its efforts to continue to promote global cooperation on nuclear security.

There are good reasons why the IAEA should be expanding its role in these areas. There is a growing advocacy for it to do so, as seen in statements by key states at the IAEA General Conference, the UN General Assembly, and other post-Fukushima nuclear forums. However, there are challenges to pursuing these growing roles, and some institutional risks associated with its greater involvement in safety and security, where national responsibilities remain central. There also will be concerns about the IAEA's ability to obtain the necessary resources and to pursue these new missions without undermining its traditional nonproliferation mission, especially since it is being requested to expand its role in arms control and disarmament.[3] In all, as the IAEA moves ahead on safety and security issues, it will need to ensure that it has the capabilities, resources, and Member State support that will allow it to succeed.

Building on efforts to improve nuclear safety, security, and safeguards

Steps to expand and strengthen IAEA programs in nuclear safety and security are necessary but insufficient. These steps must be integrated with the other initiatives to address new and emerging proliferation and terrorism risks through threat reduction, detection, and interdiction. Key proposals and efforts that have been set in motion over the past 30 years include Cooperative Threat Reduction programs, the Proliferation Security Initiative, the Global Initiative to Combat Nuclear Terrorism, UN Security Council Resolution 1540, the

Convention on the Suppression of Nuclear Terrorism, and the amendments to the Convention on the Physical Protection of Nuclear Material. Several other ideas are being considered, or rather reconsidered, today to address proliferation and terrorism risks, including proliferation resistance. This multipronged effort will need to continue if nuclear proliferation and terrorism risks are to be contained. Current work on proliferation resistance may offer an attractive path to integrating safety, security, and safeguards.[4]

Although proliferation resistance has often been oversold and has had limited results to date, reactors and other facilities designed to minimize proliferation risks coupled with effective safeguards and other nonproliferation measures could prove useful for both state and nonstate threats. The novel approach involves technologies and facility designs that embody cost-effective means to safeguard material or, where possible, refit old facilities and technologies to make them more "safeguardable." The objective of safeguardability, or "safeguards-by-design," is to improve the application of safeguards. Examples of such improvements include reducing or eliminating diversion or misuse pathways, or increasing the prospects for detection along pathways by facilitating verification. Innovative verification technologies and approaches are likely to involve greater physical access as well as increased process and operating information.

Safeguards-by-design should be complemented by a specific "security-by-design" effort. Some discussions have envisioned such an integrated approach. It appears that fuel cycle design, facility layouts, and protective measures can reduce or eliminate the feasibility of certain theft scenarios and make thefts extremely unlikely. Such design measures could include steps to track and locate nuclear material accurately and cheaply throughout the cycle; to eliminate scenarios that are costly to address with external measures, such as additional guns, gates, and guards; to make a facility inaccessible to outsiders (and to unauthorized access by insiders); and to increase the role of "passive" security features (e.g., material matrices that are self-protecting). Safety-by-design has been to date more of a priority for industry and academia. It has not yet been integrated with safeguards and security, but it could be a useful adjunct to ongoing efforts to realize safeguards and security design objectives.

In the post-Fukushima environment, there may be incentives for integrating safety with safeguards and security. However, in addition to optimizing synergies, addressing tensions between the three objectives will be necessary. Moreover, the levels of international authority, norms, and standards, as well as the manner in which industry best practices are pursued, differ significantly. With the IAEA's role, reinforced by treaty obligations, safeguards have the most well-developed international mechanism for promoting verification and compliance. As safety and security have historically been seen as domestic responsibilities, equivalent international regimes do not exist. Nonetheless, significant efforts have been made to develop and promote international standards and best practices in each area. The Agency has taken a leadership role in both safety and security, as has the nuclear industry with, for example, WANO and WINS. Best practices are easier to promote in the area of safety, as there is greater consensus around methods of assessing performance and fewer sensitivities are involved.

A technology program for improving nuclear governance

In the post-Fukushima environment, good nuclear governance will be needed to address the challenges of enhanced safety, security, and safeguards. To ensure that these objectives are balanced, that the IAEA has sufficient capabilities to carry out its safeguards mission, and to ensure that decisions on expanding roles and missions are wisely deliberated and made, the UN, the IAEA, and key nuclear states will have to provide statesmanship. However, in order for the IAEA and the international community to be able to address the challenges they confront now and in the future, certain technical issues will have to be addressed.

The IAEA's capabilities to meet current safeguard requirements will require continuous improvement in order to enhance efficiencies; better address current, nonoptimized requirements; and be positioned to deal with future proliferation challenges. Addressing these and other challenges, both anticipated and unanticipated, will require a defense-in-depth approach that includes:

- State-of-the-art instrumentation and methodologies for materials measurement, accounting, and tracking, including sensor platform integration;
- Enhanced containment and surveillance, including portal and area radiation monitoring, and measures to ensure that there are no materials or radiation signals where they should not be;
- Integration of access denial and transparency elements of physical protection and safeguards; and
- Integration of traditional process monitoring with nontraditional indicators, such as detection of radiation signals at suspicious locations or questionable movement of equipment and people.

To support such an approach, it will be necessary to develop a flexible, adaptive technology base for advanced safeguards as well as a new generation of inspectors and analysts. The IAEA safeguards infrastructure also will have to be modernized. A technology R&D program should investigate next-generation technologies to determine the best near-term detection, measurement, and forensic technologies, along with analytic tools and methods for development. It should also explore issues relevant to safety and security, including the following:

- Integrated facility design to enable advanced safeguards, physical security, and safety measures, (e.g., safeguards-, security-, and safety-by-design) and to optimize proliferation resistance throughout operational life cycles.

- Intrinsic transparency in facility operations in support of all objectives.
- A more robust integration of physical protection and safeguards, and an effort to bring safety into the equation.
- Thorough systems analysis to evaluate design trade-offs between facility operations, safety, security, and safeguards effectiveness and cost, as well as to assess the effectiveness of an integrated system as a whole.

These areas could become a focus for the Agency's technical cooperation, which would strengthen implementation.

Conclusion

The long-term impact of the Fukushima Dai-ichi accident remains uncertain, but the rationale for nuclear power that existed before the disaster has not changed. Many states regard nuclear power as a component of the energy mix, primarily because of security and climate change concerns.

If it is to be sustainable, nuclear energy will have to address safety, security, and proliferation risks, ensuring they are all minimized. There are ongoing activities on safety, security, and safeguards, but greater regional and global cooperation will be required. It will be important to continue to strengthen the nonproliferation regime, and work to build up norms and standards in safety and security, with a view to building institutions and promoting good nuclear governance in these arenas. Ultimately, states will have to understand that all of these issues cannot be addressed as purely national concerns and take the necessary steps to work together. Harmonization to build on synergies and reduce tensions among these obstacles is difficult but essential, and technology can play a role.

However attractive these concepts, the feasibility, costs, operational impacts, and other possible effects of such approaches have not yet been demonstrated and will need to be analyzed further. If the issues identified above, and any others that may come to the fore, can be addressed in design in an optimal fashion without undue construction and operational costs, they can be successful. They could in principle strengthen all three objectives—safety, security, and safeguards—by building on common systems and protocols, while minimizing any tensions, for example, between safety and security.

Notes

* The views expressed are the author's own and not those of the Los Alamos National Laboratory, the National Nuclear Security Administration, the Department of Energy or any other agency.

1. See "IAEA Action Plan on Nuclear Safety," IAEA, https://www.iaea.org/topics/nuclear-safety-action-plan.
2. See "Convention on Nuclear Safety," IAEA, https://www.iaea.org/topics/nuclear-safety-conventions/convention-nuclear-safety.

3. The IAEA's role in arms control and disarmament was central to its founding (envisioned in the Atoms for Peace speech that set out the idea of the IAEA and embodied in the IAEA Statute) and has been intermittently pursued in recent decades, but it has not been at the forefront of thinking about the IAEA's future. The Fissile Material Cutoff Treaty and interest in disarmament could change this situation. The IAEA will need to have adequate resources if it is to expand its arms control and disarmament role. It also will have to overcome the impact of potential compliance disputes on its credibility and effectiveness, the possible inadvertent spread of classified or proliferation-sensitive information, and other issues.
4. Although there has been some controversy and continued debate over the meaning of *proliferation resistance*, the IAEA has developed a widely accepted definition that addresses the technological elements (dating back to the Acheson-Lilienthal report) and looks explicitly at institutional elements: "Proliferation resistance is that characteristic of the nuclear energy system that impedes the diversion or undeclared production of nuclear materials, or misuse of technology, by the host state in order to acquire nuclear weapons or other nuclear explosive devices." *Intrinsic proliferation resistant features*, according to the IAEA, "are those features that result from the technical design of nuclear energy systems, including those that facilitate the implementation of the extrinsic measures." As for *extrinsic measures*, the IAEA's definition states: "Extrinsic proliferation resistance features are those features that result from the decisions and undertakings of states related to nuclear energy system." See also Joseph F. Pilat and Kory W. Budlong Sylvester, "Safeguards-, Safety- and Security-by-Design after Fukushima" (paper presented at the ESARDA Symposium on Safeguards and Nuclear Non-Proliferation, Bruges, Belgium, May 28–30, 2013).

15 How nuclear security arrived at the IAEA

Piet de Klerk

The person who looks for "nuclear security," or even for "security" by itself, in the statute of the International Atomic Energy Agency (IAEA) ends up only with references to … the *Security* Council. The word "secure" comes up several times in the text with different meanings: to *secure* the greatest benefit, or to *secure* necessary financing, but never in combination with "nuclear."[1] In David Fisher's book about the Agency's first 40 years, the term "nuclear security" never appears.[2] Indeed, for decades the combination of the words "nuclear" and "security" had a completely different meaning than it has today, at least for most professionals. For example, one might look at a declassified U.S. Central Intelligence Agency report from 1984, which discusses trends in South Africa's Nuclear Security Policies and Programs. The report examines South Africa's security policies at the time in relation to the production of highly enriched uranium (HEU) and its nuclear test capability; however, it does not discuss the security of nuclear materials.[3] When one combines the words "nuclear" and "security" with "international," matters even become fuzzier, because most people who hear about "international nuclear security" will think of the international security situation in the world as related to nuclear weapons.

"Nuclear security" still might not be a concept that is immediately clear to most people in English. In most other languages, the situation is worse. In many languages, it is difficult to distinguish "nuclear security" from "nuclear safety." In Dutch, for instance, the words for safety and security rest on the same word: *veilig*. *Veiligheid* has come to mean safety and *beveiliging* security, but this is not a distinction that most people make in daily life. In German, the situation is not very different: the distinction between *Sicherheit* and *Sicherung* is not intuitively clear to most people.

Since the early 2000s, the term "nuclear security" has become to mean protecting nuclear (and radioactive) material against theft and other malicious acts.[4] This chapter will examine the ways in which this concept has developed over four phases, and the important role that the IAEA has played in all of them.

DOI: 10.4324/9781003160205-15

The slow road to nuclear security

During the first decade after World War II, nuclear activities were mostly wrapped in secrecy.[5] As long as only a select group of scientists was working with weapons-grade nuclear material, kept on military sites, one did not have to take many measures to prevent nuclear material from falling into the wrong hands. Indeed, nuclear security was not a high priority.

In many ways, the situation changed after the presentation of Eisenhower's "Atoms for Peace" plan, announced at the United Nations (UN) General Assembly in December 1953. It led to a concrete proposal for the establishment of the IAEA the year after, negotiations about its statute in 1955 and 1956, and large scientific Atoms for Peace conferences in Geneva from 1955 to 1958.[6] At these conferences, much technology was shared—technology that from today's perspective would be regarded as proliferation-sensitive. Reprocessing is a good example. It is true that the transfer of nuclear material and technology was accompanied by "safeguards"—first national American safeguards, and later IAEA safeguards—but such safeguards essentially were a system of accountancy, a bookkeeping system that checked whether the nuclear material was where it was supposed to be. The physical protection of nuclear material was not an important concern.

Phase 1

In 1972, Robert Leachman and Philip Althof edited a book called *Preventing Nuclear Theft*.[7] In 1973, John McPhee wrote three long articles in the *New Yorker*, mainly about bomb designer Ted Taylor, who had grown concerned about how easy it was to steal or to divert nuclear material.[8] There were many places in different parts of the United States where nuclear material was processed or used, and often that material was transported on flatbed trucks through the country. "The trucks carried ten 'birdcages' at a time," McPhee wrote. "Each birdcage weighed about four hundred pounds, and held a ten-liter flask of plutonium nitrate. A hijacker taking such a truck would have enough plutonium for four or five bombs." In an eerie scene, McPhee and Taylor take the elevator to the 40th floor of the World Trade Center in New York and discuss, not bothered by anyone, the incineration of the building. In Taylor's words: "It's so simple that I just don't want to describe it. I will tell you this: just to make a crude bomb with an unpredictable yield—but with a better than even chance of knocking this building down—all that is needed is about a dozen kilos of plutonium-oxide powder, high explosives … and a few things that anyone could buy in a hardware store."[9]

Also influential was the book *Nuclear Theft: Risks and Safeguards*, which Taylor wrote in 1974 with Mason Willrich.[10] Taylor and Willrich are concerned about "the possibility of nuclear violence using fissionable material that might be stolen from the US power industry," given the large increase in nuclear power around the world and a spike in terrorist attacks in the early 1970s.[11] The authors develop their theme that nuclear weapons are relatively easy to make, assuming the requisite materials—a few kilograms of plutonium, HEU, or uranium-233—are available. They conclude that there are no effective safeguards against nuclear theft, that there are no specific requirements for the physical protection of less than 2 kilograms of plutonium in the United States, that there are ineffective requirements for communication between vehicles during transport, and that there are no requirements for physical protection of nuclear-weapon material exported out of the United States.[12] One of the incidents that increased their concern was the possible theft of a considerable amount of HEU from a private nuclear facility in Apollo, Pennsylvania, in 1965. The amount was in excess of 100 kilograms of over 90 percent enriched uranium.[13] The question whether the HEU ended up in scrap or whether it was stolen has never been fully clarified.[14]

The awareness that more needed to be done to protect nuclear material, in particular direct-use material, manifested itself in different ways. First it led to improved accountability in the United States. Second, it led to U.S. proposals in the international arena. The stage was the UN General Assembly in New York, the date was September 23, 1974, and the U.S. representative was Henry Kissinger. Nonproliferation was a major part of his speech, not surprising given the recent Indian peaceful nuclear explosion (in the phrase of the day) on May 18, 1974. Having discussed the start of the Strategic Arms Limitation Talks (SALT) negotiations, Kissinger's first proposal was to strengthen IAEA safeguards and "to establish practical controls on the transfer of nuclear materials."[15] This would lead to a U.S. aide-mémoire the month after and to meetings of a small group of states in London in 1975, a group that became known informally as the London Club, and more formally as the Nuclear Suppliers Group (NSG). One of the guidelines of the NSG pertains to the physical protection of nuclear material. Kissinger's second proposal was to draft an international convention for enhancing physical security against theft or diversion of nuclear material. "Such a convention", he said, "should set forth specific standards and techniques for protecting materials while in use, storage, and transfer."[16] That U.S. proposal in 1974 was endorsed by the 1975 NPT Review Conference and led to negotiations in Vienna in the years thereafter.

During the Carter administration, concerns about nonproliferation and the lack of physical protection took center stage. It became U.S. policy to reduce the enrichment levels of exported uranium for research reactors and to ban reprocessing of spent fuel, so that no pure plutonium would be generated. In the first phase, therefore, *nuclear theft* and *physical protection of nuclear material* were the central concepts.

Phase 2

The second phase starts with the dissolution of the Soviet Union in 1991, and the fear that the security of Soviet nuclear material would dissolve and that unemployed Soviet nuclear scientists would set up shop in third countries. Indeed, in many places in the former Soviet Union in the 1990s, physical security left much to be desired. The ball started to roll in Kazakhstan, when the director of the Ulba Metallurgical Plant outside Ust-Kamenogorsk, a former navy submarine commander, approached Andrew Weber of the U.S. Embassy in Almaty about selling HEU to the United States.[17] Half a year later, after the topic had been discussed with President Nuristan Nazarbayev in Washington, American experts visited the plant where the uranium—90 percent enriched fuel for *Alfa*-class submarines—was stored, protected only by what Weber described as a "Civil War padlock." Ultimately, in November 1994, in a covert operation known as Project Sapphire, the United States cooperated with the Kazakh government to fly the 600 kilograms of weapons-grade uranium from the Ulba plant to the United States, as part of the Cooperative Threat Reduction Program.

All the same, weapons-grade nuclear material, mostly in small quantities, made it to the black market. Under the Nunn-Lugar and Cooperative Threat Reduction Programs, some bilateral measures were agreed upon, including the "From Megatons to Megawatts" program in which HEU was downblended for use in nuclear power reactors. The best term to describe concerns in this second phase is *illicit trafficking of nuclear (and radioactive) materials*. It also is worth noting that "nuclear material security" as a term was first used during the Nuclear Safety and Security Summit in 1996 in Moscow.

This is not to say that concerns about nuclear terrorism were absent in this period. During the 1990s, fear of terrorist attacks revived in many parts of the world. In Europe, there were delayed rumblings of Red Army Faction terrorism, as well as terrorist activity from Basque separatists and the Irish Republican Army. In Latin America, the FARC (Fuerzas Armadas Revolutionarias de Colombia; Revolutionary Armed Forces of Colombia) and the ELN (Ejercito de Liberación Nacional; National Liberation Army) were active in Colombia, as were the Tupac Amaru in Peru. On the Indian subcontinent, former Prime Minister Rajiv Gandhi was assassinated in 1991, and the Tamil Tigers carried out scores of attacks in Sri Lanka. In the Middle East and North Africa, Hamas and Hezbollah were active, as were right-wing Israelis; in Algeria, a brutal terrorist war lasted the entire decade, and Al-Gama'at al-Islamiyya was active in Egypt. On a global scale, al-Qaeda and its associates were responsible for the 1993 World Trade Center bombing in New York, the attacks on the U.S. embassies in Kenya and Tanzania in 1998, and the bombing of the USS *Cole* in Yemen. In New York, concerns about terrorism led to three conventions: the International Convention on the Suppression of Terrorist Bombings, the International Convention on the Suppression of Financing of Terrorism, and the International Convention on the Suppression of Acts of Nuclear Terrorism. The first two were adopted in 1997 and 1999, respectively; the third, a Russian proposal made in 1997, was still under consideration in 2001. The terrorist attacks of September 11, 2001, provided impetus to the negotiations with input from many Member States and the IAEA, but the talks lasted till 2005 before the convention was adopted and entered into force in 2007.

Phase 3

The third phase starts with the September 11th terrorist attacks. Even though these attacks had nothing to do with nuclear matters, they were a watershed in thinking about nuclear security for three reasons. First, they showed that (al-Qaeda) terrorists could organize complex operations. Second, it demonstrated that terrorists were prepared to become martyrs, and thus would not be deterred by lethal risks like radiation sickness. For these reasons, IAEA Director General Mohamed ElBaradei often spoke of 9/11 as a wake-up call for the nuclear community. But there is a third factor: the focus on al-Qaeda brought to light a meeting between leading Pakistani scientists and the al-Qaeda leadership. In the summer of 2001, Sultan Bashiruddin Mahmood and Chaudhry Abdul Majeed had visited Osama bin Laden and Ayman Zawahiri in their secret headquarters near Kandahar. Mahmood had played an important role in the 1972 Multan meeting, which can be considered as the start of the Pakistani nuclear-weapon program.[18] He had been in charge of enrichment before he was pushed out by Abdul Qadeer (A.Q.) Khan in July 1976 and ultimately became the head of Pakistan's Nuclear Power Division. Majeed, a chemist with a doctorate from Leuven University, had been a nuclear-fuel expert at the Pakistan Institute of Nuclear Science and Technology and had taken over as the head of the New Labs reprocessing project.[19] Both Pakistani scientists had retired before August 2001, when they traveled to Afghanistan and stayed in the al-Qaeda hideout for several days.[20] It was understandable that when U.S. intelligence officials heard about the meeting, alarm bells went off. The alarm was sounding louder, because around this time the scale of the activities of Khan's network was becoming clearer.

In October 2001, Mahmood and Majeed were arrested.[21] Mahmood's story was that he went to Afghanistan to ask for money for his not-for-profit organization Ummah Tameer-e-Nau, intending to build up a polytechnic institute in Kabul to help explore and extract Afghanistan's natural resources. But according to some of the interrogators, the al-Qaeda side had quizzed them about the manufacture of nuclear, biological, and chemical weapons.[22] Whatever the truth, the fusion of al-Qaeda with a variation of the A.Q. Khan franchise was alarming enough.

This phase, with its focus on potential *nuclear terrorism* more than on the physical protection of nuclear material, led to international measures in the G-8: the Global Partnership of 2002 and the Global Initiative to Combat Nuclear Terrorism of 2006, measures that subsequently were opened up for broader participation. Of special note in this context is also the adoption of Security Council Resolution 1540 (2004).[23] Couched in terms of preventing nonstate actors from acquiring weapons of mass destruction, it demands that all states have effective legislation and procedures in place and a proper export control system to prevent export of relevant weapons of mass destruction materials and equipment.

Phase 4

The fourth phase started with President Barack Obama's Prague speech in April 2009, in which he described a series of steps toward a world without nuclear weapons. The New START negotiations were a part of that, as were the ratification of the Comprehensive Test Ban Treaty, a fissile material cut-off treaty, a strengthened NPT, and a new framework for nuclear cooperation.[24] Last but not least on his list was the need to prevent terrorists from acquiring a nuclear weapon. This required "a new international effort to secure all vulnerable nuclear material around the world within four years" and hence a Global Summit on Nuclear Security in the United States in 2010.[25] As is well known, the Washington Summit was followed by further Summits in Seoul, The Hague, and again in Washington. Through this Nuclear Security Summit (NSS) process, nuclear security became *Chefsache* (a top priority) for the first time.[26]

In the course of the meetings, the scope of the summits was widened from nuclear materials to nuclear and radioactive materials. Not all countries possess nuclear material, but all have radioactive sources for a range of applications. Radioactive materials of course cannot be used in itself to create a nuclear explosion, but the fear of "dirty bombs" was enough to also include this broader category of materials in the summit conclusions. Taken together, the summits have strengthened the international legal nuclear security regime. The number of parties to the International Convention to Suppress Acts of Nuclear Terrorism increased by more than 50 percent in the period of the summits; just after the second Washington Summit, the Amended Convention on the Physical Protection of Nuclear Material (CPPNM) went into force. Many countries decided to send their weapons-grade nuclear material, mainly HEU, to the United States and Russia.[27] Many updated their national protection systems, decided to commit to implement IAEA Guidelines, or availed themselves of IAEA services.

The communiqués contained useful language about the international nuclear security architecture; the need to minimize stocks of weapons-grade nuclear material; and elements of transportation, trafficking, and forensics. Individual contributions of participating states were neatly captured in "house gifts" or "gift baskets": contributions to improved nuclear security made by individual countries or groups of countries, respectively. This type of contributions clearly filled a need, as most heads of state and/or government insisted on coming to the summits with a "gift." The house gifts of some of the nuclear-weapon states included information on their military nuclear material.[28] During the 2016 summit, Washington released the size of its total HEU stockpile: 586 tons of military and civilian HEU in September 2013.[29] The White House Press Office also assured the public that the United States had full measures in place to safeguard and secure military materials, including the fact that criteria and standards for military material met or exceeded the recommendations in the IAEA's revised Information Circular 225 (INFCIRC/225/Rev.5) on the physical protection of nuclear material.

In this fourth phase, the concept of *nuclear security* thus came full circle. As a concept, it evolved through times in which it was realized that nuclear security would have to be improved in relatively normal times and especially in times of great upheavals, because other states or nonstate actors might prey on such nuclear material. It was a phase with an emphasis on "return to sender". From that perspective, the NSS phase might be seen as the antithesis of the Atoms for Peace program.[30]

The four phases in the IAEA

The Agency started work on physical protection in the early 1970s as an offshoot of the development of the safeguards system. Although the IAEA had been developing its safeguards system since the late 1950s, the period around 1970 was a time of rapid change. In 1968, the NPT had been concluded and it had entered into force in March 1970. For the first time, the Agency's safeguards became based on an international, legally binding agreement. The structure and model for a Comprehensive Safeguards Agreement were worked out in the Safeguards Committee between June 1970 and March 1971.

In that period, an Agency panel ("On Safeguards Methods and Techniques with Special Reference to Inspections," Tokyo, 1969) realized that without a state's physical protection program, the containment and surveillance dimension of safeguards would not work. It advised that the Agency should develop recommendations for physical protection standards. And so it happened in typical Agency fashion: an Open-Ended Working Group meeting and a consultants' meeting in 1971, and finally an experts' panel in early 1972. The "Grey Book," the first set of recommendations on physical protection, was published in June 1972.[31] It was a coincidence that the publication appeared around the time of the 1972 Munich Olympics, which were marred by terrorist violence, but it showed the timeliness of these considerations. The early 1970s saw many terrorist acts in the Middle East, in Japan, in Europe, and in Latin America. None of these acts were linked to nuclear theft, but they no doubt had some impact on the thinking of Ted Taylor and others. Later in the decade, the Grey Book evolved into INFCIRC/225 (1975) and 225/Rev.1 (1977).[32]

After the U.S. suggestion in 1974 and the blessing of the 1975 NPT Review Conference, negotiations about a CPPNM started in Vienna in 1977 and were concluded in October 1979.[33] Many delegations argued that physical protection of nuclear material was a national responsibility, and in the end the convention only dealt with nuclear material during international transport. The role and responsibility of the Agency remained limited. It became the depositary, and its INFCIRC/225 classification of nuclear material evolved into a similar classification under the CPPNM.

In the second phase, with its emphasis on the security of nuclear material in the period after the dissolution of the Soviet Union, the IAEA's main focus was the illicit trafficking of nuclear and radioactive materials. From 1994 on, the General Conference adopted resolutions on the illicit trafficking of nuclear material, and later radioactive sources as well. An Incidents and Trafficking Database was set up in 1995.[34] Other IAEA activities in this period involved prevention, including strengthening legal provisions, training, and developing responses to trafficking cases. In 1999, an Office of Physical Protection and Material Security was established for the coordination of all program activities, which was moved in 2002 from the Department of Safeguards to the Department of Nuclear Safety and renamed the Office of Nuclear Security.[35]

In the third phase, after the September 11 attacks, IAEA resolutions were formulated in terms of "security of nuclear materials" or (since 2002) "nuclear security" for short. In September 2002, the phrase "nuclear terrorism" also appears for the first time. The Advisory Group on Nuclear Security, which the IAEA Director General set up in January 2002, defined "nuclear security" as "the prevention and detection of and response to, theft, sabotage, unauthorized access, illegal transfer or other malicious acts involving nuclear material, other radioactive substances or their associated facilities" and advised on activities in the areas of:

- Legally binding and nonbinding international instruments;
- International guidelines and recommendations acceptable to the international community;
- Related assessment services, training, equipment and technical advice; and
- Exchange of information and related services.

In March 2002, the IAEA Secretariat put forward the first post-9/11 set of activities under the title "Protection against Nuclear Terrorism: Specific Proposals."[36] It included proposals to enhance the capacity of member states to protect nuclear facilities by:

- Organizing International Physical Protection Advisory Service (IPPAS) and other missions;
- Reviewing the Design Basis Threat methodology and organizing trainings;
- Better detecting and interdicting incidents of theft and trafficking;
- Ensuring that Member States have state systems for material accountancy and control in place;

- Improving national security measures with regard to radioactive material (which led to a revised Code of Conduct for the Safety and Security of Radioactive Sources in 2004); and
- Strengthening preparedness for and response against nuclear or radiological emergencies.

The third phase also led to a renegotiation of the CPPNM. Before 2001, a group of experts meeting under the auspices of the IAEA had convened and recommended that the convention should be strengthened.[37] However, after the 9/11 attacks, that process accelerated in an open-ended group of legal and technical experts (2001–2003), with the outcome (in 2005) that the amended convention should protect nuclear material during all phases, not only during international transport.

In the fourth phase, the Agency was swept up by President Obama's initiative. In the summit process that followed, its role in this field was never in doubt. On the contrary, its "essential responsibility and central role" were highlighted in the NSS process, and the summits were an excellent platform to raise the IAEA's profile with world leaders.[38] IPPAS missions had started well before the summits—they were a result of the first Secretariat proposals in the 1990s—but the summits provided a boost for the number of requests for such missions.[39] Even though proposals of NSS participants were sometimes met with resentment in Vienna, the net result was that nuclear security became much more prominent in the Agency's program and budget. The Office for Nuclear Security became a Division and regular budget funding increased from €1.1 million per year in 2009 to €5.4 million in 2016. Extrabudgetary resources grew from €15.5 million to €18.4 million per year in the same period.[40] All in all, this resulted in a considerable broadening of the Agency's activities in this field. In an effort to create a soft landing at the end of the NSS process, a first ministerial meeting on nuclear security was held in Vienna in July 2013.[41] The summit process also stimulated Member States' adherence to IAEA guidelines. The three hosts of the summits, the United States, the Netherlands, and the Republic of Korea, introduced a gift basket in 2013 to strengthen nuclear security implementation, and many participants joined.[42] In the run up to the second Washington Summit, new signatories included China and India.

The security-safeguards interface

In recent years, not least stimulated by the NSS process, much attention has been paid to the interface of nuclear safety and nuclear security. It is an interesting area in its own right. Both sets of measures serve a common purpose in protecting the public and the environment from radiological hazards and share a common philosophy of defense in depth. But at times, a safe solution is not necessarily a secure solution, and vice versa. Both must be viewed in an integrated way.

Less attention, however, has been paid to the safeguards-security interface. The Agency's safeguards system and measures to protect and secure nuclear material are different in a number of ways, but also have a lot in common.

Once a safeguards agreement has been concluded, the IAEA has rights, even though those rights are limited in states with unsafeguarded facilities, in particular the nuclear-weapon states. Essentially, the Agency has no rights in the field of nuclear security, which is (and for the time being will remain) fully a state responsibility. Still, safeguards measures, more in the control than in the accountability dimensions, form a protective layer around nuclear material and thus make the nuclear material more secure. The application of safeguards often makes it more difficult for nonstate actors to lay their hands on nuclear material. Likewise, well-protected nuclear material can make the application of safeguards easier; for example, if Agency seals can be applied on top of existing national seals or locks. As we have seen, the application of safeguards was built on the existence of national physical protection measures. The Agency has had its experiences, often negative ones, by trying to combine physical protection (nuclear security) observations by inspectors and safeguards activities. States did not like this approach—but in my view, this is a short-sighted perspective. It is one thing to consider nuclear security as a national prerogative; it is another thing not even to consider good advice. More can be done in this area.

The outlook for the agency

In the past 25 years, the IAEA has created a growing portfolio of tasks in the field of nuclear security, but essentially nuclear security has remained a state responsibility. What more can the Agency do? Here are a few examples.

- *Legally binding and nonbinding international instruments.* With the Amended CPPNM in force since 2016, a Review Conference is scheduled for 2021. It is commendable that the Agency has already proactively assembled the states' parties to determine the consequences of the amendment's entry into force, and to see how the Member States and the Secretariat can enhance the implementation of the amended Convention. This process should continue.
- *International guidelines and recommendations acceptable to the international community.* Stimulated by the NSS process (INFCIRC/869), and generally by the increased attention for nuclear security, commitments to implement IAEA recommendations have grown.[43] The primary challenge now is to help states implement them. As the number of IAEA implementing guides and technical-guidance documents have grown over the years, there is also scope for integration and streamlining.
- *Related assessment services, training, equipment, and technical advice.* The assessment services, IPPAS in particular, have seen quite a growth

in recent years and are now broadly accepted. It is important that the Agency keep up the advisory and training work that this entails. Although it may be a bridge too far to require states to implement the advice of assessment missions, the presence of assessment missions might become the norm in the coming years. The IAEA Secretariat should play a proactive role in this regard. Implementing the conclusions of the assessment missions can be promoted by informing the Board of Governors of important issues raised in the assessments.

- *The exchange of information and related services.* Transparency about nuclear security matters was an important theme in the NSS process. States can be transparent about nuclear security matters without giving away operational information that might assist terrorists and other harmful actors. Transparency and exchange of information and experience can lead to peer pressure, and peer pressure leads to improvements.

Finally, neither the nuclear security landscape, nor the nuclear power landscape, nor the terrorist landscape is static. What one entrusts to international organizations is not static. All these variables will affect the IAEA's role in the field of nuclear security in the coming years. During the NSS process, a call was heard for a comprehensive nuclear security convention. Such a convention is not in the cards in the foreseeable future, taking into account that the summit process did not bring any progress in that direction and given the entry into force of the Amended CPPNM. But further improvements are possible, desirable, and even necessary from the broader perspective of the future safe and secure application of nuclear power. The best way forward is the further promotion of Agency security missions, striving to conduct them as universally as possible, first and foremost in countries with nuclear power and then in other states so that forms of peer pressure can be built. Such a system would start to approximate the security audits of the International Civil Aviation Organization. In February 2020, the World Institute for Nuclear Security published an interesting comparison between the security assessments of both organizations.[44] It focuses on the changes made in the International Civil Aviation Organization (ICAO) since the September 11th attacks, when ICAO Member States agreed on making security assessments mandatory. One of the suggestions of the study is that the IAEA and ICAO jointly explore opportunities for cross-cultural improvements. Such improvements might preserve the prerogatives of IAEA Member States, but it would stimulate them to do better—to strive for excellence in nuclear security.

Notes

1. The Statute of the International Atomic Energy Agency (IAEA), Article III.B.3, and Article XI.B, at https://www.iaea.org/about/statute.
2. David Fisher, *History of the International Atomic Energy Agency: The First Forty Years* (Vienna: IAEA, 1997).

3. Central Intelligence Agency, *Trends in South Africa's Nuclear Security Policies and Programs*, October 5, 1984, in "U.S. Intelligence and the South African Bomb," National Security Archive, George Washington, University (NSA GWU), document 27, https://nsarchive2.gwu.edu/NSAEBB/NSAEBB181/index.htm.
4. See the official IAEA definition later in this chapter.
5. All the same, much was published soon after the war on the Manhattan Project; for example, the Smyth Report. See Anthony Cave Brown and Charles B. MacDonald, *The Secret History of the Atomic Bomb* (New York: Delta, 1977).
6. Which was agreed upon on 23 October 1956 and entered into force 29 July 1957.
7. Robert Leachman and Philip Althof, *Preventing Nuclear Theft: Guidelines for Industry and Government* (New York: Praeger Publishers, 1972).
8. John McPhee, "The Curve of Binding Energy," *The New Yorker*, December 3, 10, and 17, 1973. These articles were published as a book; see John McPhee, *The Curve of Binding Energy* (New York: Farrar, Strauss, and Giroux, 1974).
9. Both quotes from the December 17, 1973, article, 80 resp. 94.
10. Mason Willrich and Theodore B. Taylor, *Nuclear Theft: Risks and Safeguards* (Cambridge, MA: Ballinger Publ Cie, 1974).
11. Willrich and Taylor, *Nuclear Theft*, 1. For instance, the airlines witnessed 29 Palestinian hijackings between 1969 and 1977.
12. Ibid, 167–70.
13. Ibid, 79.
14. See the NSA GWU document collection, *The NUMEC Affair: Did Highly Enriched Uranium from the U.S. Aid Israel's Nuclear Weapons Program?*, https://nsarchive.gwu.edu/briefing-book/nuclear-vault/2016-11-02/numec-affair-did-highly-enriched-uranium-us-aid-israels.
15. See *Foreign Relations of the United States, 1969–1976*, Volume E-14, Part 2, *Documents on Arms Control and Nonproliferation, 1973–1976*, eds. Kristin L. Ahlberg, Bonnie Sue Kim, and Chris Tudda (Washington, DC: Government Printing Office, 2015), Document 84.
16. Ibid.
17. David E. Hoffman, *The Dead Hand: The Untold Story of the Cold War Arms Race and Its Dangerous Legacy* (New York: Doubleday, 2009), chapter 21.
18. Feroz Hassan Khan, *Eating Grass: The Making of the Pakistani Bomb* (Stanford: Stanford University Press, 2012), 84–88. See also p. 361.
19. Hassan Khan, *Eating Grass*, 200, 361.
20. Douglas Frantz and Catherine Collins, *The Man from Pakistan: The True Story of the World's Most Dangerous Nuclear Smuggler* (New York: Twelve, 2007), 264.
21. They were released in January 2002. Feroz Hassan Khan, *Eating Grass*, 362.
22. Frantz and Collins, *The Man from Pakistan*, 271. In 1998 bin Laden had sent emissaries to contact A.Q. Khan to seek Khan's help in building a nuclear weapon.
23. UN Security Council Resolution 1540 (2004), United Nations Office for Disarmament Affairs, https://www.un.org/disarmament/wmd/sc1540/.
24. Negotiations for a new treaty on strategic nuclear weapons would start in May 2009. The New START (Strategic Arms Reduction Treaty) would be signed in April 2010 and enter into force on February 5, 2011.
25. "Remarks by President Barack Obama in Prague as Delivered," The White House, Office of the Press Secretary, April 5, 2009, https://obamawhitehouse.archives.gov/the-press-office/remarks-president-barack-obama-prague-delivered.
26. As the head sherpa for the 2014 summit in The Hague, I have been able to observe that also at this level the term *nuclear security* was not always well understood.

27. In his April 1, 2016, press conference, President Obama said that in the course of the NSS process, more than 3.8 tons of HEU and plutonium had been removed or secured, more than enough to create 150 nuclear weapons. See "Press Conference by President Obama, 4/1/2016," The White House, Office of the Press Secretary, April 1, 2016, https://obamawhitehouse.archives.gov/the-press-office/2016/04/01/press-conference-president-obama-412016.
28. Many of the paragraphs in the different NSS communiqués do not differentiate between civil and military material. Obviously, paragraphs about the IAEA implicitly only refer to civil material.
29. Versus 740 metric tons in 1996. See "Fact Sheet: Transparency in the U.S. Highly Enriched Uranium Inventory," The White House, Office of the Press Secretary, March 31, 2016, https://obamawhitehouse.archives.gov/the-press-office/2016/03/31/fact-sheet-transparency-us-highly-enriched-uranium-inventory.
30. While it is beyond dispute, that a central storage of weapon-grade materials in a nuclear-weapon state is generally more secure than more dispersed storage in other states, storage in a nuclear-weapon state is not necessarily more secure.
31. Recommendations for the Physical Protection of Nuclear Material, IAEA, June 1972. Technically, these were not IAEA recommendations, but recommendations by "a panel of experts working under IAEA sponsorship."
32. With INFCIRC/225/Rev.5 (2011) as the latest iteration.
33. Entry into force would have to wait till 1987.
34. The database now contains around 3,700 incidents, although in most cases the malicious intent cannot be determined. A relatively small portion involves HEU or plutonium, usually in small quantities. See the statistical overview in the IAEA fact sheet at https://www.iaea.org/sites/default/files/20/02/itdb-factsheet-2020.pdf.
35. IAEA, GC(43)/13, August 30, 1999, para 52.
36. IAEA, GOV/2002/10, March 2002. As the Agency's director for policy coordination, I was involved in these activities, but the work was mainly done by Anita Nilsson and other colleagues in the Nuclear Safety Department and more particularly in the Office for Nuclear Security.
37. The Informal Open-Ended Expert Meeting convened for the first time in 1999 and concluded its work in May 2001.
38. See The Hague Nuclear Security Summit Communiqué at https://www.consilium.europa.eu/media/23823/141885.pdf.
39. See IAEA, GC(40)/15, 20 August 1996. The concept was developed in 1995; IPPAS missions as an IAEA service were announced in April 1996.
40. Compare the Agency's Programme and Budget documents in GC(51)/2 and GC(59)/2. Figures are not corrected for inflation.
41. It was followed by further ministerial meetings in December 2016 and February 2020.
42. By committing to implement the guidelines in documents 13, 14, and 15 in the IAEA Nuclear Security Series. See INFCIRC/869.
43. This pertains both to the CPPNM related recommendations in INFCIRC/225/Rev.5, and the recommendations in NSS14 for radioactive material and radioactive sources, and in NSS15 for material and sources out of regulatory control.
44. See World Institute for Nuclear Security, "Security in the Civil Nuclear and Aviation Sectors – Identifying Transferable Best Practices," Vol. 1, Research Summary & Recommendations (Vienna: World Institute for Nuclear Security, February 2020).

16 The nuclear security summits and the International Atomic Energy Agency

Laura S. H. Holgate

In April 2009, U.S. President Barack Obama chose nuclear challenges as the centerpiece of his first major foreign policy address, famously referred to by the name of the city in which he gave the speech as the Prague Agenda. In this speech, he embraced a vision of a world without nuclear weapons, and proposed a four-part policy to make progress toward that vision:

- Reducing the number and importance of nuclear weapons in U.S. national security strategy;
- Bolstering the nuclear nonproliferation regime and addressing its violators;
- Securing weapons-usable nuclear materials against theft and misuse by terrorists or others; and
- Creating a new framework for global nuclear energy cooperation.[1]

A key element of President Obama's vision was the convening of a Nuclear Security Summit (NSS) of world leaders to focus high-level attention on the urgent challenge of securing all nuclear-weapon-usable materials. This initiative stood on the shoulders of several decades of efforts to address the potential for terrorists or others to gain access to highly enriched uranium (HEU) or plutonium—the necessary ingredients of nuclear weapons.

Fortunately, for now, it takes a large, expensive, and technically demanding infrastructure to create these materials, which is generally understood to be beyond the capacity of nonstate actors. But in the nuclear age, states have generated thousands of tons of HEU and plutonium for both weapon programs and civilian uses. The Atoms for Peace program pushed out research reactors fueled with HEU to universities and research centers all over the United States, and to civilian research centers in U.S. client states abroad. The Soviet Union followed suit. At one point, weapons-usable materials were located in more than 50 countries and often were not secured and accounted for with the rigor that we now know is necessary to protect them against modern, sophisticated, well-resourced terrorist groups with apocalyptic world views. Al-Qaeda religious leaders famously issued a fatwa in 2003 calling on the faithful to develop nuclear and other weapons of

DOI: 10.4324/9781003160205-16

mass destruction,[2] and several other terrorist groups have expressed nuclear ambitions. The Islamic State has mastered chemical weapons technology, proving that there is no durable taboo on terrorist use of weapons of mass destruction.

Although it is not easy for terrorists to manufacture a nuclear device, it equally is not so very difficult for terrorists to craft one that is crude but effective. This is because terrorists have different requirements from nation-states in making a nuclear explosive device. Nation-states typically are seeking small, reliable devices that can be safely handled and delivered primarily by military aircraft and missiles. By contrast, terrorist bombs are likely to be large, simple devices delivered by truck or small airplane or boat, and terrorists will not be reliably constrained by safety concerns in the assembly process or by the need to test a weapon. Design information is widely available in the public domain. The most effective way, therefore, to prevent a terrorist nuclear weapon is to prevent access to nuclear material.

Beyond the 22 countries currently in possession of the materials necessary to create an actual nuclear explosive device, more than 150 countries have thousands of radioactive sources—made of special forms of cobalt, cesium, iridium, and other elements—that are used every day in medicine, industry, agriculture, and research. Some types of sources are especially vulnerable to being used in a "dirty bomb," which would not likely kill people but which would spread panic and cost billions to clean up. Such a radiological device would be quite simple to make, given the ease of access to disused or inadequately secured radioactive sources.

Why a nuclear security summit

The first summit to highlight nuclear security was held in 1997 in Moscow among what was then called the P-8 (the G-7 countries—Canada, France, Germany, Italy, Japan, the United Kingdom, and the United States—plus Russia), at the height of the worries about "loose nukes" that might emerge from the chaos of the Soviet breakup. However, concerns about nuclear terrorism extended back to the 1970s, and initial steps were taken through the International Atomic Energy Agency (IAEA) and the negotiation under IAEA auspices of the Convention on Physical Protection of Nuclear Materials (CPPNM), covering the security of HEU and plutonium in transit between countries.

Even now, however, there are no binding international rules or inspections to verify effective nuclear security. This is because nuclear security has long been understood as an exclusively sovereign, national responsibility, and the five recognized nuclear-weapon states historically were seen as generally responsible stewards of their nuclear material. The Soviet collapse called this assumption into question with the creation of three new countries with nuclear weapons and materials on their territories: Belarus, Kazakhstan, and Ukraine. The United States and several other countries reacted with the creation of a range of cooperative programs to remove and consolidate materials, improve storage, update accounting, install equipment, train personnel, and many other efforts under the Cooperative Threat Reduction (CTR) rubric, first championed by U.S. senators Sam Nunn and Richard Lugar. The CTR program helped achieve the denuclearization of Belarus, Kazakhstan, and Ukraine, thereby assuring a single nuclear successor state: Russia.

After the 2001 terrorist attacks in the United States, these bilateral programs expanded into global efforts to remove, reduce, and protect weapons-usable material wherever it was located. These efforts were motivated by the recognition of the high degree of skill and resources displayed by the September 11th attackers, as well as by their stated intent to kill two to four million people. These were shocking differences from the more limited political terrorism of the 1970s and 1980s, and created both a sense of urgency and a wider geographic scope for these materials security programs. Four major international efforts were spawned in the aftermath. The first was the creation of the Global Partnership Against the Spread of Weapons and Materials of Mass Destruction out of the G-8, which expanded the countries and resources working on nuclear security, among other weapons-of-mass-destruction threat-reduction efforts. The second was the negotiation of an amendment to the CPPNM, completed in 2005, that expanded the treaty's application to nuclear materials in use and storage as well as transit. The third was the Bratislava Initiative, under which United States and Russia deepened and hastened their work to secure nuclear materials in Russia and third countries. Fourth, the United States and Russia worked together to launch the Global Initiative to Combat Nuclear Terrorism, through which more than 80 countries cooperate and share experiences to build their own national capacities against nuclear terrorism.

President Obama's call for a summit eight years after the September 11th terrorist attacks was intended to ramp-up these efforts, recognizing that while enormous progress had been made, it would take political will at highest levels to do some of the hard (and, in some cases, expensive) work required to eliminate materials and reduce nuclear terrorist threats. Examples include shutting down facilities, shifting away from established technologies, and cultivating enduring security capacities and cultures across a variety of government and nongovernment entities.

With these threats in mind, the NSSs had two goals. First, they were designed to energize, elevate, enhance, and empower existing international organizations and initiatives already working to address nuclear security problems. These organizations and initiatives include the United Nations (UN), which has mandated binding steps for all countries to prevent terrorist access to weapons of mass destruction; the IAEA, which generates voluntary guidance on nuclear security and provides technical advice to Member States; Interpol, which coordinates the law-enforcement aspects of nuclear smuggling, nuclear forensics, and nuclear detection; the Global

Partnership Against the Spread of Weapons and Materials of Mass Destruction, which grew from its G-8 roots to include more than 25 countries providing resources and cooperation to improve nuclear security; and the Global Initiative to Combat Nuclear Terrorism. These five groups form the core of the global nuclear security architecture.

The second goal of the NSSs expected participants to generate specific deliverables as part of their summit participation: they would have to announce real, tangible steps they would take to increase nuclear security and thwart nuclear smuggling either in their own country or in cooperation with other countries or international organizations. These commitments were called "house gifts"; later, the power of gathering similar pledges from different countries generated "gift baskets," or collective voluntary commitments to take a common set of actions. As a point of comparison, house gifts were pledges made by single countries to improve nuclear security, whereas gift baskets were pledges made by different groups of countries on specific nuclear security topics that went beyond the summit communiqués.

As with any international gathering, building the guest list was critical. Recognizing that a summit of almost 200 leaders would be too unwieldly to yield meaningful progress, a diverse set of participants was intended to be seen as representative of the global community. Organizers intended that the areas that found agreement among such a heterogenous group would be accepted by others as more legitimate than a set of pronouncements from a narrower but more like-minded group. The invitations spanned not only geography and ideology, but also a range of experiences and expectations regarding nuclear weapons and nuclear energy. The leaders of the UN, the IAEA, the European Union, and Interpol were also invited, reflecting their respective roles in setting nuclear security norms and supporting member states in implementing their nuclear security obligations. In total, 53 countries participated in the NSS.

The first NSS was held in Washington, D.C., in 2010, and marked the largest gathering of world leaders in the history of the U.S. capital. Subsequent summits were hosted in 2012 by South Korea in Seoul, in 2014 by the Netherlands in The Hague, with the final summit returning to Washington, D.C. in 2016. The summits focused narrowly on the security of nuclear (and later, radiological) material, leaving the canonical "three pillars" of the Nuclear Non-proliferation Treaty (NPT)—disarmament, nonproliferation, and peaceful uses of nuclear energy—to the forums in Geneva, New York, and elsewhere that were designed to host those increasingly bitter debates.

Summit outcomes

Each summit generated a communiqué, agreed by consensus, containing shared principles and commitments but also several caveats and constraints. The IAEA featured strongly in each communiqué, especially its central coordination role, reflecting many other IAEA documents that are negotiated in Vienna. The communiqués also called on the IAEA to support Member States' efforts around focal points such as HEU minimization, radiation source security, nuclear security guidance and training, and the Incident and Trafficking Database. The communiqués shone a spotlight on the wide range of activities by which the IAEA was supporting Member States to implement nuclear security measures. The 2010 NSS also generated a work plan with detailed steps to promote nuclear security, including a detailed chapter on the IAEA.

Over the course of the four summits, 935 commitments ("house gifts") were presented through national progress reports or leaders' statements during the summits. Many of these featured IAEA programs and activities and helped bolster the role and experience of the Agency. Notable examples included the following:

- More than 40 NSS participant countries have engaged in capacity building, whether through training, Centers of Excellence, or exercises.
- More than 30 countries have updated national laws, regulations, or structures relating to nuclear security.
- Approximately 28 countries have held or invited peer-review missions, either bilaterally or through the IAEA's International Physical Protection Advisory Service (IPPAS), and additional requests keep growing.
- Thirty-nine countries have pledged to strengthen nuclear security implementation through subscribing to the 2014 Joint Statement on Strengthening Nuclear Security Implementation (INFCIRC/869), to implement IAEA guidelines into national regulations.
- Eighteen countries have taken steps to increase the security of radioactive sources.
- Seventeen countries have been involved in removal or disposal of nuclear materials, or minimization of HEU. Today, only 22 countries, down from more than 50, have weapons-usable nuclear materials on their territory. As a result, three entire geographic regions—South America, Southeast Asia, and Central and Eastern Europe—have entirely eliminated HEU.
- Fifteen countries have carried out physical security upgrades or acquired security or detection equipment.
- A dozen countries have joined or launched new international or regional structures to support nuclear security cooperation.
- Twelve countries have indicated their financial contributions to support bilateral or international cooperation in nuclear security.
- Twenty-nine countries and the UN have committed to ensure adequate cybersecurity at industrial control and plant systems at nuclear facilities.

Moreover, 39 "gift baskets" represented pledges made by different groupings of summit participants who were taking particular actions. Topics included Centers of Excellence, radioactive source security, nuclear security smuggling, HEU minimization, insider threats, and support for the World Institute of Nuclear Security. Many of these gift baskets had strong connections to the work of the IAEA.

In addition to these national and collective pledges, a further notable accomplishment of the NSS process was that two key nuclear security treaties gained dozens of new adherents. The 2005 Amendment to the CPPNM saw a fivefold increase in ratifications between 2009 and 2016, finally reaching the 101 countries required for that amendment to enter into force. The IAEA is the depositary for this important legal instrument, and its entry into force increases several actions the Agency is required to take or support, such as receiving and making available national compilations of the laws and regulations by which states parties implement the amended convention. A similar influx occurred in the ratifications of the International Convention on Suppression of Acts of Nuclear Terrorism, which is deposited with the UN and criminalizes many specific acts related to nuclear terrorism and trafficking.

Recognizing the need for a forward vision as the summit process concluded in 2016, participants approved five action plans that were designed to infuse summit priorities into the five enduring organizations and initiatives through their respective decision-making processes. It was evident that the summits had no authority to direct actions within these organizations and initiatives, but all summit participants were members of the three official international organizations and most participated in the other two initiatives, and the action plans reflected steps summit participants would pursue through their memberships and voices in those groups. The IAEA Action Plan received by far the most attention and is the lengthiest of the five action plans, reflecting the hopes and expectations of the summit participants for a strengthened and expanded role for the Agency in supporting Member States on computer security, nuclear forensics, nuclear detection, incident response, security during transit, security culture, nuclear security guidance and training development, and other critical nuclear security activities.

These achievements represent tangible, practical steps toward protecting nuclear and other radioactive material. The summits did much to build up the global nuclear security architecture (of which the IAEA is the centerpiece), the awareness of Member States regarding their nuclear security responsibilities, and the usage of Member States of the resources the IAEA offers them in carrying out these responsibilities. The central coordinating role for the IAEA is a large and challenging job, given the enormous number of official and informal structures that make up the global nuclear security architecture. The IAEA routinely convenes information exchange meetings among many of these groupings, and member states have routinely expressed a wish that those meetings contribute to the improved impact and efficiency of the myriad nuclear security efforts. Less tangibly, the NSSs began to dilute the idea that nuclear security is the exclusive purview of sovereign states and gave traction to the notion that a country's neighbors, allies, or rivals have a legitimate stake in how effectively it implements its nuclear security responsibilities.

Postsummit challenges

All the same, the hopes and expectations of many of the NSS participants regarding prioritization of nuclear security still remain unrealized. Many of the reasons for this state of affairs have implications for how the IAEA addresses nuclear security.

The first is the challenge of divergent perceptions of the nuclear security threat. Despite the statement agreed by 53 countries in each of the communiqués—that nuclear terrorism was the greatest threat to international security—this is not a universal viewpoint. Participants likely realized that this quote from President Obama's Prague speech was the price of admission to the summit process, but there was still an underlying argument about what was actually the threat and how real it was. The United States and many other countries have consistently held that terrorists have in fact demonstrated the intent to utilize weapons of mass destruction, including nuclear weapons; that historical information about how to make nuclear weapons is available in the public domain; and that securing and reducing weapons-usable material is the best way to prevent a nuclear terrorist attack. For most Western countries these arguments are axiomatic, but they are not universal. A strong counterargument holds that nuclear weapons in the hands of the nuclear-weapon states are the biggest danger, not nuclear terrorists, and it suggests that nuclear disarmament will in fact eliminate the risk of nuclear terrorism. Whether those differential viewpoints are held sincerely or whether they are put forward as debating points, they are blocking progress on nuclear security at the IAEA and elsewhere.

Derivative of this disagreement over the nature of the nuclear threat is the disarmament issue and the rising frustration among many in the world, as reflected most recently in the nuclear ban treaty, regarding the slow pace of disarmament among those countries that have weapons. Although the summits were designed to try to avoid that debate, the topic became increasingly divisive over the four summits. Many hours and some of the toughest negotiations of the summits were devoted to describing how the nuclear security issue related to the three pillars of the NPT. Ultimately, participants were unable to improve on the language that was formally agreed in the first summit. This frustration has sometimes blocked progress in Vienna, as some IAEA Member States have tried to hold progress on nuclear security hostage to their efforts to highlight the lack of disarmament progress. The IAEA General Conference's annual nuclear security resolution has since the summits become a battleground for the disarmament issue. The statement from the 2016 IAEA nuclear security ministerial conference was most contentious not over whether to seek more resources for nuclear security or how to create new opportunities for the Agency, but rather what it would say about disarmament; as a result, it was much weaker than the 2013 ministerial statement. Fortunately, the negotiations over the ministerial statement for the 2020 conference avoided this paralyzing debate.

Third, the issue of sovereignty continues to loom large. Every summit communiqué and numerous IAEA documents on nuclear security restate that nuclear security is a national responsibility, reflecting a fear that addressing nuclear security in a collective way threatens that sovereignty. To the contrary, that essential sovereign responsibility is the basis of the state's power to enforce regulations, to create penalties for smugglers, or to control nuclear material transfers. That said, each country has a legitimate expectation to be assured about the nuclear security behavior of its neighbor or ally or enemy. The more countries do to reveal their nuclear security behavior in ways that protect sensitive information, the more confident every nation is in the nuclear security architecture. This tension continues between sovereignty on one hand and assurances on the other, with the IAEA caught in the middle. The IAEA can be the contributor to those assurances, for example, with IPPAS missions, the results of which countries may choose to publicly release. That said, the Agency is not going to be a security inspector or create verification procedures for nuclear security. There is no evidence that the Member States are interested in giving the Agency the kind of power on nuclear security that it has on safeguards. This dichotomy plays out in large and small ways in Vienna every day.

A fourth challenge is the continuation of the "exclusivity" complaint leveled by some countries that were not part of the summit process. The "diverse minilateralism" of the summit participants was intended to create connectivity to those who were not present, but it did not fully achieve this goal. Some countries were sincerely disappointed, but others saw it as an opportunity to critique the United States. Iran took it upon itself to hold a kind of "counter summit" on nuclear security for the Nonaligned Movement; this effort had limited participation and no meaningful outputs, but it bolstered their narrative that the Nuclear Security Summits were intended to undermine the formal multilateral institutions. This was precisely the opposite intent of the summits, but this critique continues even though the summits are over. Efforts to dilute this "exclusivity" residue have had limited impact. The Nuclear Security Contact Group (described in more detail below) is open to all countries that wish to contribute to nuclear security activities. Several of the abovementioned "gift baskets" were translated into IAEA Information Circulars (INFCIRCs) to allow nonsummit participants to join them. These mechanisms, however, have attracted few nonsummit participants. Though the negative impact of limiting participation was underestimated, the positive outcomes the summits achieved are difficult to imagine, especially if compared to summits conducted in the UN General Assembly.

Another battleground for nuclear security is the IAEA budget. The annual nuclear security budget grew from US$1 million to US$6 million over the past decade, but this remains a tiny fraction of the IAEA's regular budget. The Nuclear Security Fund, made up of voluntary contributions, adds resources, but they tend to be unpredictable and have many strings attached. Recent budgets have tried to avoid a pure "zero-sum" perception by allowing small increases across the IAEA budget, but the Nonaligned Movement continues to portray any increases in nuclear security funding as inimical to the growth that its members desire in the Agency's technical cooperation fund, through which the Agency supports peaceful uses of nuclear technology. This debate significantly constrains the contributions the IAEA could make on nuclear security. Related to this divided perspective is the underlying concern expressed by some Member States that advocates of nuclear security are seeking to limit access to the benefits that nuclear technology can bring to developing states. This explains the insistence of some Member States on language in IAEA documents stating that nuclear security will not hamper access to peaceful nuclear technology. Nuclear security advocates have sought to flip this statement on its head by stating that nuclear security actually enhances access to peaceful nuclear technology, with little success. A breakthrough was achieved in the 2018 Nuclear Security Resolution, where it was stated that strong nuclear security can enhance public acceptance of nuclear and radiological technologies.

An enduring political challenge is the disconnect between some capitals and their Vienna-based diplomats when it comes to bringing the summit commitments into the work of the Agency. In many countries, nuclear security expertise tends to be based in the capital, and the awareness of leaders' summit commitments has not necessarily translated to their diplomats in Vienna. Several Vienna ambassadors were part of the summit process, but it has been a challenge to maintain an awareness and a commitment to do hard political and diplomatic work in Vienna in support of the summits' outcomes, even by countries that are part of that summit process. This challenge only increases with the passage of time and the rotation of knowledgeable officials.

Finally, Russia's current behavior as a spoiler is an important factor. Russia participated in the first three summits but distanced itself from the fourth summit based ostensibly on complaints about how the summit would be run. The Kremlin's decision more likely reflected tensions over the Russian invasion of Ukraine. Russia's absence concerned several participants, but in the end it did not detract from the value of the final summit or the import of its outcomes. Currently, Russo-American tensions are playing out in the IAEA, where Russia sees a win for summit-derived proposals to be a win for the United States and therefore something to be blocked. This behavior is of a piece with Russia's efforts to diminish the authority and capability of the IAEA Secretariat across a range of issues beyond nuclear security to include safeguards, nuclear safety, and other areas where Russia appears to be trying to limit the Secretariat's independence and actions.

Lessons from the summits

Perhaps the most important lesson learned from the summits is that top-level leadership still matters. Given the "summit fatigue" that clearly drove the NSS leaders to agree that 2016 would be the last, it is unlikely there will be enthusiasm to restart the process. But somehow, leaders and their immediate advisors need to maintain focus on the commitments made during the summit process and hold their bureaucracies accountable for executing them, whether in Vienna, in New York, or in other relevant venues.

The IAEA's ability to play a leadership role in this regard is fairly limited, because it serves its Member States. It does not, by and large, make judgments about the appropriateness of Member State behavior as long as such behavior is within the state's NPT commitments, and the Agency's support offerings are provided only upon Member States' requests. That said, expanded leadership has been beneficial. Through the summit process, countries such as South Korea, Australia, Morocco, Spain, Hungary, Jordan, Norway, the Netherlands, Canada, Lithuania, and Argentina have stepped up to take on various parts of the nuclear security agenda and put time and political resources into specific projects. Other countries are needed to diversify this team regionally, especially as the United States becomes a less visible (and potentially less attractive) leader on this topic.

One project still on the table is the formal recognition of de facto HEU-free zones in South America, Central and Eastern Europe, and Southeast Asia. Initial efforts to create such zones in 2016 fell afoul of certain countries' hope to preserve the potential for HEU usage in naval propulsion or perhaps even nuclear energy. Now that the artificial division between summit participants and those who were not participating within a single region has been softened, these initiatives may be able to be rejuvenated.

The security of nuclear materials in military programs remains another area where progress is needed. Organizations with universal memberships have proven to be poor venues to make progress on this issue, both because fewer than ten countries have military nuclear material, and because nonweapon states have been unable to articulate their precise expectations. Nonetheless, countries with weapon programs can and should do more to inform nonweapon states about the nature of security applied to nuclear-weapon programs. The United States, and to a lesser degree the United Kingdom and France, provide some unilateral transparency on the security of their military materials, but more coordinated ways could be explored to provide assurances, perhaps starting with the P-3 (United States, United Kingdom, and France), then spreading to the P-5 (the P-3, China, and

Russia), then eventually involving all states with weapons. Countries can also provide such information through their reports under the UN Security Council Resolution 1540.

Maintaining momentum

The international community has no fewer than six mechanisms at its disposal to continue to strengthen the global nuclear security architecture.

1 The highest hopes for carrying forward the spirit of the summits are lodged in the **IAEA Nuclear Security Ministerials**. These quadrennial IAEA ministerial meetings provide platforms to stimulate high-level commitment to nuclear security and to convene international experts to discuss nuclear security technologies and operations. The first was held in July 2013 and the second in December 2016. The third such meeting was in 2020, with the fourth is planned for 2024. Most nuclear security advocates were disappointed with the decline in ambition and common viewpoint between the 2013 and 2016 Ministerials. Contrary to the expectation of many, the problem of using the IAEA Action Plan as inspiration for the ministerial declaration was not primarily about moving from 53 summit states to 170 Member States. In the end, it was essentially the same countries that had been most active in the summits that were arguing well-known sides of the canonical arguments about funding, military materials, and disarmament. Unfortunately, the U.S. goal of transferring the tradition of deliverables from the summits to the ministerial also went largely unfulfilled, despite extensive diplomatic engagement in the months before the meeting. It remains to be seen whether these Ministerials can become more effective tools for transferring concepts and behavior from the summits into the broader IAEA community. The 2020 Ministerial statement recovered some of the earlier ambition, and several countries included their nuclear security progress in their national statements.

2 The **Nuclear Security Contact Group** was created to maintain the valuable connections among the senior expert officials who guided the summit preparations, known as sherpas, and to offer a role to countries not included in the summits who wished to promote nuclear security. The Contact Group is the logical engine for ongoing work on the five action plans, for maintaining connections with civil society and industry communities, and for staying abreast of evolving nuclear security challenges. Leadership of the Contact Group has passed from Canada to Jordan to Hungary. However, finding the right blend of ex-sherpas, Vienna- and New York-based ambassadors, and new players to preserve and transfer knowledge will be a challenge.

3 The Strengthening Implementation joint statement, also known as Information Circular 869 (INFCIRC/869), is one of the most powerful

gift baskets to have come out of the summit process. In this statement, 36 countries pledged to incorporate the intent of the primary IAEA nuclear security guidance documents into their national regulations, essentially making these voluntary guidelines binding at the national level. This statement attracted critical new adherence at the 2016 summit from India and China, but there has been little action since then, despite repeated diplomatic pressure on key countries to make such an announcement at the 2016 Ministerial. Several other gift baskets were also turned into IAEA INFCIRCs, allowing countries not part of the summit process to participate in these pledging exercises. This continues to be a worthwhile effort, but it will need ongoing attention-raising efforts in Vienna and in capitals.

4 The two dozen or so **Centers of Excellence and Nuclear Security Support Centers** provide additional platforms for the continuation of nuclear security efforts. Whether it is certification of demonstrable competence, as called for in INFCIRC/869; or development of security technologies to keep up with new threats, such as cyber and drones; or platforms for standardized IAEA curricula for regional training or venues for engaging industry and civil society partners, these centers have enormous potential. The IAEA's coordination of these centers gives the Agency a role in elevating the value and connections among these centers.

5 The Nuclear Threat Initiative has built out the participation of nuclear industry participants in its **Global Dialogue Plus** continuation of its successful track 1.5 effort, combining government officials and civil society experts, which it began in 2012 to support the NSS process. This dialogue provides a useful platform for **nuclear industry-civil society cooperation**. The Contact Group also has that mission, but it is not yet clear how that will be implemented. Industry can do much more to contribute to nuclear security outcomes, although the Nuclear Industry Steering Group in Security, the post-summit organization created to maintain the commercial nuclear community's focus on nuclear security, appears to be dormant.

6 With the entry into force of the **Convention on Physical Protection**'s 2005 Amendment, its terms require a conference to review implementation in 2021. Some countries are already developing concepts that are nearly ready for adoption at this meeting, such as recreating a habit of deliverables and submitting national reports on the progress of implementing the Convention. As depositary, the IAEA has an important role in setting out and supporting the procedural framework for preparation for this review conference.

These six mechanisms point the way to the next great challenge of nuclear security: how to "bake it in" to the thought process and behavior of the full range of entities that have nuclear security responsibilities. By incentivizing good behavior with benefits that are attractive to the operators, which include fuel-cycle facilities, hospitals, universities, power plants, and weapons complexes, they can embrace their role alongside governments and regulators in promoting nuclear security. As long as nuclear security remains an unpredictable externality to be resisted, it will be fragile. Excellent nuclear security behavior should become part of the branding or value proposition for nuclear commerce.

Conclusion

In the four years since the final summit, and despite best intentions and specific efforts, the NSS momentum has certainly slowed.[3] The ambitions of the summits to elevate, enhance, empower, and energize existing multilateral organizations (especially the IAEA) and other initiatives that work on nuclear security have been only partially fulfilled. Nevertheless, many of the achievements of the summit process are enduring and permanent, and individual countries like Jordan, Lithuania, Hungary, Argentina, and others are continuing to prioritize nuclear security in their domestic policies and international advocacy.

Looking forward, we must collectively find the motivation for continued concrete action to enhance nuclear security. Otherwise, we are doomed to wait for a major nuclear security incident to finally take the steps that we already know must be taken.

Notes

1. "Remarks by President Barack Obama in Prague as Delivered," Office of the Press Secretary, The White House, April 5, 2009, https://obamawhitehouse.archives.gov/the-press-office/remarks-president-barack-obama-prague-delivered.
2. Nasir Bin Hamd Al-Fahd, "A Treatise on the Legal Status of Using Weapons of Mass Destruction Against Infidels," Carnegie Endowment, http://www.carnegieendowment.org/static/npp/fatwa.pdf.
3. "Progress on Global Nuclear Security Has Slowed Significantly, According to 2020 NTI Index," Nuclear Threat Initiative, n.d., https://www.ntiindex.org/news/progress-on-global-nuclear-security-has-slowed-significantly-according-to-2020-nti-index/.

17 Nuclear security advocacy following the nuclear security summits

The nuclear security contact group

Heidi Hulan

In 2016, as the Nuclear Security Summit (NSS) process was gearing up for what would clearly be its final leader-level event, its members had a problem.[1] The U.S.-led summit process, hosted between 2010 and 2016, had been extremely successful in sharpening political recognition of nuclear security as a "live" threat that transcends borders.[2] The summits, buttressed by intersessional work at the sherpa table, had also galvanized participating states to take on concrete individual commitments to reduce highly enriched uranium (HEU) and plutonium stocks, enhance physical protection at civilian nuclear facilities, counter the smuggling of nuclear and radiological materials, and otherwise address domestic vulnerabilities in the nuclear security domain. Yet as the NSS process drew to a close, there was a risk—indeed, a high probability—that without regular summits to concentrate bureaucratic minds and incentivize action after 2016, attention paid to nuclear security would dissipate and summit follow-up would flounder.

The NSS summits had identified five organizations and initiatives which together represented the locus of forward policy and programming action: the United Nations (UN), the International Atomic Energy Agency (IAEA), Interpol, the Global Initiative to Combat Nuclear Terrorism (GICNT), and the G7-led Global Partnership Against the Spread of Weapons and Materials of Mass Destruction (GP). They also had enumerated actions the group felt that each organization could take to nurture the nuclear security agenda.[3] However, the question remained: who would ensure that this work was pursued over time? After the NSS drew down, whose job would it be to get out of bed in the morning thinking about how all of the pieces were working together? And from where would the impetus come for continued progress on threat reduction at the domestic level? In other words, how would momentum be maintained to ensure that summit progress translated into concrete results within the global nuclear security architecture?

The prospect that inertia would unravel the momentum of the NSS process was real. Moreover, in order to succeed in the post-summit period, support for this agenda would need to be broadened beyond the limits of the NSS membership. Critics had been vocal about a process that was perceived as exclusionary in nature, given that NSS participation had been by

DOI: 10.4324/9781003160205-17

invitation only. There were particular concerns about Russia's absence from the final summit, given its obvious importance to this agenda.[4]

Recognizing these challenges, the United States, supported by other NSS members, introduced a joint statement on Sustaining Action to Strengthen the Global Nuclear Security Architecture (Joint Statement) at the 2016 summit. Forty NSS members signed on.

Contact group: Origins, objectives, and orientation

The sponsors of the joint statement committed themselves to actively advance the five summit Action Plans as a means of sustaining momentum on NSS commitments. The statement also created a Nuclear Security Contact Group (NSCG, or Contact Group) of senior officials to ensure coordination of effort. It was announced at the summit that Canada would serve as the inaugural Convenor of the group. Its purpose was threefold: (1) to maintain focus and energy on the coordination of action within the main pillars of the global nuclear security architecture, (2) to translate NSS commitments into real work in the relevant fora, and (3) to enlarge participation and engagement on nuclear security efforts and initiatives beyond the 52 NSS participants. Originally open to NSS participants who signed onto the joint statement, the NSCG immediately moved to expand participation to include any state that was in good standing with its nonproliferation obligations and was prepared to subscribe to the Contact Group's goals as laid out in the joint statement and subsequently circulated to all IAEA Member States as Information Circular 899 (INFCIRC/899).[5]

The baseline commitment of Contact Group members was to promote implementation of NSS outcomes and recommendations. Secondary commitments included appointing a national NSCG focal point with sufficient seniority to speak on behalf of their government; convening annually on the margins of the IAEA General Conference; promoting and assessing implementation of nuclear security commitments, including those reflected in the four NSS communiqués, the 2010 Washington Work Plan, the 2016 Action Plans, and associated joint statements; and determining any additional steps needed to support these goals.

The NSS Action Plans for the main pillars of the global nuclear security architecture were detailed and specific.[6] Yet translating this aspirational agenda into concrete results within these organizations would require both focused policy effort and diplomacy. This was particularly true in relation to the UN and the IAEA, where competing agendas had the potential to complicate or even prevent the uptake of policy objectives highlighted by the NSS process. By contrast, the GP, GICNT, and Interpol were widely viewed as self-propelling and self-incentivizing in a manner that assured forward momentum aligned with NSS outcomes.[7] The core objective of the Contact Group would be to ensure the same result for the IAEA and the UN.

The agenda

The multidimensional character of international policy advocacy presents an enormous logistical and policy challenge for all informal "friends" groups, and the Contact Group was no exception. Contact Group members realized early on that their task would be much more complex than the simple identification of next steps for a series of willing audiences. In order to ensure effective implementation of NSS Action Plans, it was evident from the group's first meeting that work would be required on several fronts.

First and foremost, coordination was needed to ensure that NSS proponents could effectively identify and take full advantage of diplomatic opportunities on the horizon, and do so in a timely manner. Obvious opportunities included the IAEA Ministerial Conferences on Nuclear Security in 2016 and 2020; the Review Conference in 2021 of the Amended Convention on the Physical Protection of Nuclear Materials (CPPNM/A); and the Nuclear Non-proliferation Treaty (NPT) cycle, particularly the 2020 NPT Review Conference. Leveraging these events in the service of deeper global commitments to nuclear security would require strategy, clear objectives, and understanding of the perspectives of those who might not be immediately drawn to this agenda.

A second core task for the Contact Group was outreach. There was a clear need to broaden beyond the 52 participants of the NSS process if the agenda was to be mainstreamed in the relevant institutions, and if accusations of exclusivity were to be overcome. States were understood to represent only part of the solution in this regard. To establish a truly effective nuclear security strategy, the Contact Group needed to obtain buy-in from key stakeholders, particularly among industry partners, whose collaboration is essential to both the identification of emerging threats and the implementation of concrete commitments. The Contact Group therefore made it a priority to engage all relevant partners, including industry and civil society, in its work.

A third, cross-cutting task for the Contact Group was to lead efforts to depoliticize the nuclear security agenda, a task that members viewed as a genuinely strategic challenge for the agenda. Over time, concerns that nuclear security would somehow act as an impediment to the spread of legitimate peaceful uses of nuclear energy and technology—for instance, that it would bleed attention and resources from technical cooperation—had spread and become an entrenched part of the nuclear security discourse. For many these arguments were genuine preoccupations, but they also had been used as a reason not to invest further in nuclear security and had constrained debate in Vienna. For many in the Contact Group, politicization of this agenda was and remains dangerous: it deflects attention from risks that manifestly require both policy and operational responses.

Beyond these three cross-cutting objectives, the Contact Group focused on several additional priorities:

- *New and emerging threats.* Given the proven adaptability of terrorist actors, threats to nuclear security are constantly evolving. Constant vigilance and horizon scanning is needed to ensure that our capacity to protect nuclear infrastructure and materials outpaces the ambitions of those who would seek to misuse them. The Contact Group aimed to create partnerships and activities that would push forward this effort.
- *Maintaining a culture of deliverables.* A hallmark of the NSS process had been concrete commitments by states to enhance the physical protection of vulnerable nuclear facilities and materials, reduce overall quantities of sensitive nuclear materials, strengthen capacities at border crossings to prevent nuclear smuggling, and generally bolster the global nuclear security architecture and its associated legal framework. Following the NSS, the Contact Group sought to ensure continued implementation of existing commitments and incentivize additional undertakings.
- *Improved resourcing.* Resourcing for nuclear security was and is a particular concern for many—not only at the national level, where too many states lack sufficient resources to develop adequate nuclear security frameworks (legal, regulatory, oversight, and training), but also at the international level. This is particularly true for the IAEA, where more than 80 percent of nuclear security activity relies on extrabudgetary contributions made by a small group of Member States. To ensure that the Agency can effectively play its central coordination role while also helping Member States meet their nuclear security needs, the Contact Group recognized that this resourcing situation would have to be placed on a more predictable and sustainable footing, without encroaching on other Agency tasks.

Beyond these areas of effort, I as chair had two ancillary priorities. First, although maintaining high-level engagement was a priority, I wanted to create a subgroup in which cross-regional strategizing could take place on the nuts and bolts of implementation, work which was not taking place elsewhere. Second, I hoped to create a mechanism by which a wider range of states would come to "own" the issue of nuclear security, as this agenda could not be made sustainable if leadership was primarily seen as the business of the United States and a handful of others.

Nuclear security contact group: Progress under Canadian chair

Although the record of the Nuclear Security Contact Group in its first two years was mixed, a significant amount was accomplished. Particularly noteworthy was the extent to which the group had been able to leverage its workplan to make leadership on nuclear security more diffuse. The vehicle for this was the Group's nine action items, each of which has a Contact Group "lead" to spearhead policy effort and diplomacy on the theme in question:

1 Coordinated diplomatic messaging across fora (Canada, United States);
2 Cooperation with industry (Germany);
3 Resources for nuclear security (Netherlands);
4 Concentrated support to the IAEA (United States);
5 Outreach and diplomacy on global nuclear security architecture (Republic of Korea);
6 Emerging nuclear security challenges (United Kingdom);
7 Regional capacity building (China);
8 International Physical Protection Advisory Service missions (United Arab Emirates); and
9 Coordination of effort in preparation for CPPNM/A 2021 Review Conference (Australia).

Taken together, this division of labor was a substantial broadening of leadership on nuclear security beyond the United States and the other NSS hosts and encouraged active participation beyond the narrow circle of early enthusiasts. Other Contact Group outcomes during this period included the following:

- *Sustainability.* During the group's first year, Convenors for the second and third years were identified, signaling that the group and its policy agenda would be sustainable in the medium term.[8]
- *Increased outreach to key stakeholders.* These stakeholders include nongovernmental organizations (e.g., the Nuclear Threat Initiative, the World Institute for Nuclear Security, the NPS Global Foundation) and industry groups (e.g., the former Nuclear Industry Steering Group on Security) that have a unique role in implementing nuclear security or identifying new and emerging threats. This work is still in its early stages, but currently there is no other sustained effort to bring governments together with expert and industry communities on nuclear security, and therefore is a genuine added value on the part of the Contact Group.
- *Sustained focus.* The NSCG met nine times in its first two years. Between 2016 and 2018, it was able to do so by piggybacking on related international meetings.[9] However, it was also convened for three more extensive standalone sessions in London (January 2017), Amman (February 2018), and at Interpol headquarters in Lyon (June 2018). This pacing allowed the group to establish a workplan covering its nine action items. The corresponding papers and other products furnished substantial food for thought and identified prime opportunities to advance nuclear security internationally—work which probably would not have been undertaken without the Group.

- *Resources.* The securing of four new positions within the IAEA's Nuclear Security Division proposed by the IAEA Secretariat in 2017 was an important development; it was not specifically an NSCG accomplishment, but it likely would not have survived the IAEA's program and budget negotiations without the sustained support of delegations of group members. Though some 80 percent of the Agency's nuclear security work will continue to be funded on an extrabudgetary basis, these regularized positions, which represent a modest €526,000 within the Agency budget, produce an outsized impact in that they help the Agency plan and deliver nuclear security programming on a more sustainable, predictable basis.
- *Expanded membership.* Since the 2016 NSS, nine new members have joined the Contact Group: Colombia, Ireland, Luxembourg, Malaysia, Philippines, Slovenia, Pakistan, Qatar, and the European Union. Five of these members (Colombia, Ireland, Luxembourg, Slovenia, and Qatar) were not original NSS participants. Some 15 others are considering joining as well, demonstrating that long after the end of the NSS process, this agenda continues to attract new adherents keen to advance nuclear security commitments.
- *Maintaining a culture of deliverables.* The NSS process was characterized by the assumption of voluntary commitments by individual states, a culture which is being upheld through the NSCG in a number of ways. Of note, some 10 "gift baskets" from the 2016 NSS have been reopened in the IAEA context as INFCIRCs, allowing a wider range of states to associate themselves with these documents and, in doing so, assume voluntary nuclear security practices that are consistent with or exceed IAEA guidelines.[10] For example, at the 2016 NSS, Canada and the United Kingdom co-led the World Institute for Nuclear Security (WINS) Certified Training Gift Basket, which committed signatories to foster greater links between WINS and the IAEA and support the professionalization of nuclear security through certified training.[11] When Canada reopened this basket as an INFCIRC in Vienna, the group was able to attract additional cosponsors (Jordan, Malaysia, and Romania at the time of publication), thereby advancing the work of the WINS Academy.[12] Others have similarly attracted new adherents, with concrete commitments being assumed in transportation security, high-activity sealed radioactive sources, countering nuclear smuggling, and nuclear/radiological terrorism preparedness.

Notwithstanding the significant progress against a number of benchmarks, forward momentum has not yet matched the ambitions of the contact group's founding members. For example, there has been progress in expanding adherence to the gift baskets, but the actual number of new signatories to each has been relatively modest. Similarly, membership in the

Contact Group has been expanded, but this expansion has been less extensive and less cross-regional than hoped for.

There also have been a number of missed opportunities since the Group's creation, notably:

- *An underwhelming 2016 IAEA Ministerial Declaration.*[13] The declaration was sidetracked by a debate over what references should be made to nuclear disarmament. In the end, it lacked an explicit acknowledgment of the need for sufficient and predictable nuclear security resources for the IAEA, and it contained language suggesting that nuclear security might be prejudicial to the spread of peaceful uses of nuclear technology. The NSCG was not able to have a meaningful impact on these negotiations because it engaged too late in the process.
- *An equally unambitious IAEA Nuclear Security Plan (NSP) for 2018–2021.*[14] This plan contained weaker language on management and resources than previous NSPs and excised important scene-setting language that would have made the case for nuclear security as an Agency priority. In these ways, the 2018–2021 NSP was a disappointment in relation to the level of ambition laid out in the leader-level NSS 2016 Communiqué and associated IAEA Action Plan, in which the clear goal was to advance nuclear security within the Agency. Had NSCG members not made continued, concerted efforts to support the Agency's original proposals on resources and the importance of nuclear security, the result would have been worse still, but the latest NSP nonetheless is something of a step backward.

These outcomes reflect the substantial difficulty that NSCG members have had in depoliticizing the nuclear security agenda, particularly in the IAEA context, and dispelling misperceptions that nuclear security impedes, rather than enables, the peaceful uses of nuclear technology. They also underscore that as an advocacy mechanism for NSS outcomes, the NSCG has yet to rise to its fullest potential. This is partly a function of the Group's structure. On this, three points are particularly noteworthy.

First, the NSS process had 52 members, of which only 40 originally joined the NSCG.[15] That means that, at the time of the 2016 NSS, 12 NSS states felt they could not commit to further advancing summit outcomes that they themselves had negotiated and agreed upon at the leader level. In this fact lies the crux of the enduring challenge to the nuclear security agenda in relevant multilateral forums: insufficient consensus among key players about the nature of the problem or the priority to be placed on it. Former U.S. sherpa and U.S. Ambassador to the IAEA Laura Holgate has argued that these disputes are grounded in the differing threat perceptions of states.[16] Others have observed that the fault lies with a lack of understanding of what constitutes nuclear security, coupled with competition over scarce and unpredictable extrabudgetary resources. Whatever the source, disagreements about the relevance of nuclear security and its importance to the Agency continue to shape this debate within relevant international institutions.

Second, the NSCG is a *contact* group, but it is not a *core* group. Core groups are typically small, characterized by a high degree of policy alignment, and a shared vision of how best to advance their interests. By contrast, the NSCG's composition is large and cross-regional, and though its members share common objectives its diverse membership reflects diverging views on both priorities and preferred solutions. This broad composition is both a strength and a weakness: On one hand there is little point to a gathering of solely like-minded countries; but on the other, there is a natural limit to how much strategizing can be done in such a group.

Third, the NSCG is, by agreement of its members, not a decision-making body.[17] But without some capacity for developing shared positions, it will be difficult for its members to lead advocacy on new and emerging issues, collaborate in support of various negotiations, or make group statements that would bring its collective weight to bear on relevant policy discussions.

NSCG: Forward priorities

There has never been a shortage of interest and dedication among Contact Group members. Before the end of its first year, the group had already asserted its sustainability by confirming a medium-term succession plan, with Jordan volunteering to follow Canada as Convenor for 2017–2018, and Hungary taking on the role in 2018–2019. But the question remains: what is needed to marshal the sincere commitment of the group's membership to maximize impact where it counts for the global nuclear security architecture? Four priorities come to mind.

A key determinant of success in the nuclear security agenda will be the effectiveness of the proponents in the domain of myth-busting and depoliticization of this debate in the multilateral space. The current tenor of debate, which pits technical assistance recipients against those seeking progress on nuclear security in a seemingly zero-sum fight, constrains support and assistance for nuclear security measures, and has created a chill that has reduced the political appetite for maturing this agenda. At the same time, few delegations deny that nuclear security is a priority. Indeed, even the most vocal opponents of norm development at the IAEA have sought the Agency's services and assistance in this domain, suggesting that as a matter of practice, nuclear security remains a priority shared well beyond the confines of the NSCG membership. Shrinking both the real and rhetorical distance between these two camps is probably the single most effective thing that advocates could do to advance this agenda in the medium term. To do so, NSCG members will need to move beyond the mutual exchange of national positions with those on the other side of the debate and tackle head-on the underlying drivers of political opposition to nuclear security. This will in turn require considerable cross-regional outreach with a view to finding ways to address the legitimate residual concerns of states, while simultaneously debunking arguments of convenience. It will also require increasingly robust nuclear security guidance from the IAEA that can shape international expectations and propel action at the state level. Finally, advocates will need to articulate much more clearly than in the past the benefits of more robust nuclear security measures and what success in this domain looks like.

Second, for the nuclear security contact group to emerge as more than the sum of its parts, enhancing coordination between NSCG members' capitals and their representatives in Vienna is vital. A lack of alignment within individual NSS/NSCG participating states has constrained the NSCG's capacity for consistent messaging and made sustained advocacy challenging. NSCG members have had frank and constructive debates on issues such as resources, but these debates have not always translated into action within the other groupings to which NSCG members belong, as they would in a more classic core group model. This is not to say that Vienna-based missions are not speaking up, including within their regional groups; however, the NSCG's presence is not felt as a bloc in IAEA discussions. This situation might be improved by the establishment of a Vienna Chapter of the NSCG, a regular forum in which ambassadors from NSCG countries are briefed on NSCG efforts and can coordinate their support of this work.

Third, more meaningful collaboration with industry will be required. The Contact Group made a good start by engaging the Nuclear Industry Steering Group on Security. While that group is regrettably no longer active, it is clear that more concrete collaboration with nuclear operators would drive practical nuclear security improvements in countries with large nuclear sectors, creating new de facto industry norms without the burden of political debate that often dominates multilateral negotiations. Additionally, drawing on the operational expertise of industry would better inform NSCG members in the effort to enhance international nuclear security guidance and regulations.

Finally, effective advocacy, if it is to flow through the Contact Group, will require more robust institutional support to the Convenor. Despite the establishment of the Contact Group, and despite the considerable personal resources that any future Convenor may put into the effort of leading this group, nuclear security is not the full-time job of any of the senior officials at the NSCG table. Fragmentation of responsibility for nuclear security was also a reality during the NSS process, but it was obscured by the increased staff support NSS participants were investing to support the NSS sherpa process and summit meetings. Without the critical advantage of a summit process to drive decision-making, other means of maintaining focus and drive beyond periodic Contact Group meetings need to be identified. One way to compensate for this reality might be the establishment of a virtual secretariat composed of full-time nuclear security staff drawn from different members of the Contact Group, tasked with providing ongoing support to the Convenor. Such a structure would provide the kind of systematic policy and advocacy support needed to drive deeper coordination between members over time, and help with capacity issues for members that do not have dedicated staff working on nuclear security issues.

Conclusion

During the NSS process, it became commonplace to note that the world could not afford to wait for a nuclear security failure on the scale of past safety failures such as Chernobyl or Fukushima to spur international action. Seen in this light, a strong nuclear security culture is an essential insurance policy for the international community. At the same time, the work of constructing and implementing a common political agenda on nuclear security in the absence of a major galvanizing event will, almost inevitably, be slow and painstaking. What is evident is that this effort needs to be shaped by the type of activities described above.

The NSCG has made a meaningful start down this path. The ongoing challenge for states is to maintain focus and capitalize on future opportunities, not least the regular cycle of IAEA Nuclear Security Ministerial Conferences, to advance an increasingly shared, fact-based understanding of nuclear security needs and priorities. In the meantime, sustained working-level efforts led by the NSCG and Vienna-based ambassadors are needed to promote collaboration, leverage diplomatic opportunities as they arise, and advance nuclear security at a practical level.

Ultimately, when it comes to delivering on the considerable nuclear security ambitions defined by leaders of NSS-participating states, the NSCG is only one part of a much larger picture. National and industry efforts in the regulatory domain, standing multilateral processes such as the CPPNM/A and its Review Conference in 2021, plurilateral initiatives such as the GICNT, and programming work between donors and recipients and the Agency and its Member States all have critical roles to play. At the same time, sustained multidimensional focus among states remains essential if the global nuclear security architecture is to be meaningfully and sustainably strengthened over time. On this front, whatever its shortcomings, the NSCG has emerged as a viable mechanism for advancing nuclear security, providing its energies can be suitably harnessed. If not, its members will need to be open to developing new vehicles for advocacy.

Notes

1. The 52 participants at the 2016 NSS in Washington, D.C. were Algeria, Argentina, Armenia, Australia, Azerbaijan, Belgium, Brazil, Canada, Chile, China, Czech Republic, Denmark, Egypt, Finland, France, Gabon, Georgia, Germany, Hungary, India, Indonesia, Israel, Italy, Japan, Jordan, Kazakhstan, Korea, Lithuania, Malaysia, Mexico, Morocco, Netherlands, New Zealand, Nigeria, Norway, Pakistan, Philippines, Poland, Romania, Saudi Arabia,

Singapore, South Africa, Spain, Sweden, Switzerland, Thailand, Turkey, Ukraine, United Arab Emirates, United Kingdom, United States, Vietnam. Four observer organizations also attended: International Criminal Police Organization (Interpol), the United Nations (UN), the International Atomic Energy Agency (IAEA), and the European Union (EU).

2. Nuclear Security Summits took place in 2010 (Washington, D.C.), 2012 (Seoul), 2014 (The Hague), and 2016 (Washington, D.C.).
3. These took the form of individually negotiated "action plans"; for more details, see the 2016 NSS website at http://www.nss2016.org/2016-action-plans/.
4. Russia participated in the first three Summits, but withdrew from the process after the 2014 Summit.
5. See "Communication Dated 24 October 2016 Received from the Permanent Mission of Canada Concerning the Statement of Principles of the Nuclear Security Contact Group" (INFCIRC/899), IAEA, November 2, 2016, https://www.iaea.org/publications/documents/infcircs/communication-dated-24-october-2016-received-from-the-permanent-mission-of-canada-concerning-the-statement-of-principles-of-the-nuclear-security-contact-group.
6. The main pillars of the global nuclear security architecture, as understood in the context of the NSS process, were the Global Initiative to Combat Nuclear Terrorism (GICNT), the G7-led Global Partnership (GP) Against the Spread of Weapons and Materials of Mass Destruction (GP), IAEA, Interpol, and the UN.
7. The NSCG does not hold any common positions beyond the agreed NSCG Statement of Principles and associated Terms of Reference. However, at various points in this chapter, I summarize my understanding of concerns, objectives, and analysis widely held by the Group's membership. This understanding is grounded in the statements made by Group members either during its formal meetings or other exchanges with me during my tenure as Convenor in 2016–2017.
8. Jordan served as the second NSCG Convenor in 2017–2018 and was succeeded by Hungary in September 2018.
9. The NSCG piggybacked on the following international meetings: (1) 60th General Conference of the IAEA, September 2016; (2) the IAEA Ministerial Conference on Nuclear Security, December 2016; (3) the NPT Preparatory Committee meeting, May 2017; (4) the 61st General Conference of the IAEA, September 2017; (5) the IAEA International Conference on Physical Protection of Nuclear Material, November 2017; and (6) the 62nd General Conference of the IAEA, September 2018.
10. Gift baskets were first introduced by the United States in preparation for the 2012 NSS and constitute an approach to multilateral negotiation aimed at forwarding progress on a particular theme or issue without the requirement of consensus. Accordingly, this allowed a smaller grouping of states wishing to take action on a specific issue or make a joint statement on a certain subject that may not enjoy consensus with all NSS participants. This was a means of going beyond the lowest common denominator reached by consensus. Information Circulars (INFCIRCs) are published by the IAEA or brought forward by its Member States "for the purpose of bringing matters of general interest to the attention of all Members of the Agency," as explained in INFCIRC/1. The NSS-relevant INFCIRCs can be found at http://www.nscontactgroup.org/iaea-info-circulars.php.
11. This gift basket was signed by Canada, Finland, Hungary, Indonesia, Kazakhstan, Mexico, the Netherlands, New Zealand, Norway, Thailand, the United Kingdom, and the United States.

12. "Communication Dated 1 December 2016 Received from the Permanent Mission of Canada Concerning Certified Training for Nuclear Security Management" (INFCIRC/901), IAEA, December 7, 2016, https://www.iaea.org/publications/documents/infcircs/communication-dated-1-december-2016-received-from-the-permanent-mission-of-canada-concerning-certified-training-for-nuclear-security-management.
13. This refers to the IAEA's triennial Nuclear Security Ministerial, which last took place in 2016. The declaration is available at https://www.iaea.org/sites/default/files/16/12/english_ministerial_declaration.pdf.
14. See *Nuclear Security Plan 2018–2021*, IAEA Doc GC(61)/24, September 14, 2017, https://www-legacy.iaea.org/About/Policy/GC/GC61/GC61Documents/English/gc61-24_en.pdf.
15. Subsequently, Malaysia and the Philippines, both NSS members, have joined the Contact Group.
16. See Holgate, Chapter 16, "The Nuclear Security Summits and the International Atomic Energy Agency," in this volume.
17. The NSCG Terms of Reference can be found at http://www.nscontactgroup.org/terms-of-reference.php.

18 The IAEA and Euratom after six decades

Maria Betti, Willem Janssens, Vincenzo V. Rondinella, and Jean-Paul Glatz

The decisions taken at an international and European level in 1957, through the creation of the International Atomic Energy Agency (IAEA) and the European Atomic Energy Community (Euratom), have guaranteed to date the peaceful use of nuclear energy while lowering the risks of nuclear proliferation and misuse of nuclear technology for nonpeaceful purposes. They also have contributed to the safe and secure operation of nuclear reactors and other facilities, including the implementation of appropriate radioprotection measures and the handling and management of nuclear waste.

Nuclear power has played and is continuing to play an important role in the energy portfolio of many countries, allowing the provision of significant amounts of sustainable, low-carbon energy. It is a source of energy envisaged in many developing countries, especially in those parts of the globe most in need of energy resources. Whereas the initial focus of the IAEA and Euratom initiatives was on fostering the use of civil nuclear energy for electricity production to bring industrial development and prosperity, today significant additional activities are undertaken to contribute to the United Nations Sustainable Development Goals. Medical applications for diagnosis and therapy with radioisotopes; industrial applications, such as providing high-temperature steam; and new aeronautical, biological, and agricultural use of nuclear technologies, including desalination to help provide clean drinking water, are receiving increasing attention. Maintaining and transmitting the necessary nuclear knowledge to new operators and to future generations are essential requirements to ensure that the same levels of confidence, safety, and safeguards are applied globally and over time.

In the past 60 years, nuclear-weapon tests and both horizontal and vertical proliferation have reminded the international community of the military potential application of peaceful nuclear technology. However, as IAEA Director General Mohamed ElBaradei stated after he and the Agency received the 2005 Nobel Peace Prize, without the courage and vision of the creators of the nonproliferation community 60 years ago, the situation today would have been much worse. History has taught us that in most cases, the drive for proliferation is inspired by political considerations rather than technological capabilities. The proof is that a number of countries,

DOI: 10.4324/9781003160205-18

all of whom clearly had the technical potential to develop nuclear weapons, decided not to pursue that direction but to focus only on civil nuclear technology. Some other countries effectively had developed nuclear weapons, but gave them up after intense political pressure. Still, today there are nine de facto nuclear-weapon states. This shows that much work has still to be done at the political level to address this situation, which is not sustainable over the long term. We should never give up striving for this ideal. This is a concept which is shared at the highest levels, as seen in President Barack Obama's 2009 Prague speech stating his vision of a long-term future without nuclear weapons.[1]

In the meantime, and over the same period, it also became clear that when a state decides to possess nuclear weapons, it can manage to go a long way without necessarily having to build up a Manhattan Project-like undertaking. The availability and exchange, often clandestine, of relevant nuclear-weapon knowledge, technologies, and related materials is relatively widespread and difficult to control or intercept. Long-standing proliferation networks, which may still be operating today, have delivered nuclear capabilities to countries that do not necessarily have a superpower status at the economic or geopolitical level. The configuration by which United Nations Security Council permanent seats are reserved for the five official nuclear-weapon states, independently from other global economic or geopolitical parameters, is another challenge for a future "stable" system—that is, moving toward a nuclear-weapon-free world.

In the nuclear safety area, major nuclear accidents have significantly shaped the subsequent enhanced international collaboration. This was the case for the Chernobyl accident, which, for example, gave rise in Europe to the creation of a unique regional early warning and information sharing system. The IAEA today uses the principle and format of this system in its Incident and Emergency Centre. In the aftermath of the Fukushima accident, the Euratom Joint Research Centre (JRC) provided essential contributions to the IAEA Comprehensive Report on Fukushima; to relevant IAEA consultancy meetings, such as on assessment and prognosis assistance during nuclear power plant emergencies; and to the IAEA technical meeting that reviewed the draft safety requirements in emergency preparedness and response.

The Nuclear Security Summits, held between 2010 and 2016, were noteworthy for both their content and the levels of international engagement. The concern about the threat of nuclear terrorism was unprecedented, triggered in particular by the September 11 terrorist attacks in the United States, and the direct engagements of heads of state was exceptional. In the enthusiasm to get buy-in for a large number of states to increase the depth of defenses to this challenge, the IAEA's role and capabilities were not always the center of attention. However, this state of affairs did not prevent the IAEA from being able to ride the wave of increased attention to nuclear security. In fact, more than a few new developments have been initiated, including the organization of the ministerial-level conferences on nuclear security in the wake of the last Nuclear Security Summit in 2016. It is still clearly stated that nuclear security is a state responsibility, but the amount of guidance documents and recommendations issued by IAEA under international consensus is both impressive and highly valuable.

In the meantime, the United States, the European Union (EU), and other funding partners have stepped up their nuclear security commitments. Further enhanced coordination between their capacity-building mechanisms and outreach activities would be desirable. In fact, many countries that are gearing up to better deal with nuclear security challenges continue to look to the IAEA as the international reference point, and thus they will feel more comfortable when bilateral capacity building with other partners is to a certain degree coordinated with IAEA support.

IAEA and EU collaboration

Ever since its conception in 1957, the IAEA has pursued a strong, intense collaboration with the EU. Whereas originally Euratom consisted only of six countries, over its continued expansion, the EU has strengthened this collaboration. Ever since its creation, Euratom assigned to the European Commission the responsibility for nuclear materials accounting and control. Post-World War II considerations, combined with external allied pressure (mainly from the United States), led to the contemporary creation of the European Supply Agency. When the Nuclear Non-proliferation Treaty (NPT) entered into force in 1970, most EU Member States signed a safeguards agreement with the IAEA at the level of the European Commission. France, a full Euratom member as of 1957 but a NPT signer (as a nuclear-weapon state) only as of 1992, represents an interesting case study of the interplay between civil use of nuclear energy, under multinational control, with a national nuclear military program.

In the fields of nuclear safety, radiation protection, emergency protection, nuclear waste management, and nuclear decommissioning—the last one being relatively new, but developing rapidly—the EU and the IAEA also collaborate intensely. One such example is the creation of the Nuclear Data Exchange Mechanism in the EU (now called ECURIE/EURDEP) directly after the Chernobyl disaster. Based on the Early Notification and Mutual Assistance Conventions, the mechanism was picked up by the IAEA as the standard tool for reporting on nuclear emergencies on a global scale. Today, the European Commission is the second most important contributor to the full portfolio of IAEA activities. Some of these activities will be described in more detail below.

Collaboration with the Department of Nuclear Safeguards

The European Commission operates a Support Programme to the IAEA Safeguards Department, which has executed close to 50 projects since it was created in 1983. It covers all relevant fields in nuclear safeguards, such as nondestructive analysis, radiochemistry, containment and surveillance, advanced verification technologies, safeguards by design, and contributions to safeguards methodologies. It represents about 25 person-years of JRC work on an annual basis as in-kind contribution and is executed in close collaboration with the support programs of the EU member states. The European Commission's Directorate-General for Energy (DG ENER) operates both high- and low-level liaison committees to coordinate the intense collaboration on nuclear safeguards inspections for European facilities, exchange best practices, share tools for inspections, and jointly develop new approaches.

European Commission support is based on the unique experiences gathered in Europe, under the Euratom umbrella, in major nuclear fuel-cycle facilities. These experiences cover procedures and processes, such as large-scale uranium enrichment facilities, fuel fabrication (including mixed oxide fuel), and spent fuel reprocessing. The Commission has 25 years of experience in operating the on-site laboratories for the major European spent fuel reprocessing facilities (La Hague and Sellafield), where up to a 1,000 samples per year are analyzed to allow Euratom to implement an integrated and near-real-time safeguards approach in these complex bulk-handling facilities. The JRC also recently developed a genuinely new approach to implement Physical Inventory Verification in large gas-centrifuge enrichment plants (in this case for George Besse II in France) based on near-real-time load cell monitoring and mass balancing. This approach allows both Euratom and IAEA inspectors to implement a new way of working, increasing both the efficiency and the effectiveness of their work on site.

For the analysis of particles, the JRC operates the hypersensitive Large Geometry Secondary Ion Mass Spectrometer to analyze swipe samples with minuscule particles that might contain uranium or plutonium. This analysis can provide hints with regard to activities that historically have been executed on certain sites and the type of materials typically used there. The JRC is also part of the IAEA Network of Analytical Laboratories for a variety of uranium and plutonium sample analyses.

Today, the EU is front-runner in the development and near-term implementation of nuclear safeguards for final disposal of spent nuclear fuel. This applies in particular to the imminent operation of the Finnish final disposal facility, closely followed by the corresponding Swedish undertaking. The challenges of safeguarding future spent fuel encapsulation plants and finding techniques to reverify spent fuel containers (e.g., Castor, Constor) in case of a lack of continuity of knowledge are among the actual safeguards problems being addressed in support of both Euratom and the IAEA.

In the past few years, five innovative technologies developed by the JRC have been accepted and validated as routine safeguards equipment. The JRC delivers both substantial training and in-field assistance for the implementation of safeguards worldwide. These European contributions are not only based on the in-house contributions from JRC and DG ENER, but also on the collaboration with EU member states which in safeguards are all grouped in the European Safeguards Research and Development Association (ESARDA). In fact, ESARDA, strongly supported by the JRC, typically is a strong sponsor and co-organizer of IAEA Safeguards Symposia, along with its international partner the Institute for Nuclear Materials Management, with which ESARDA has signed a Memorandum of Understanding.

In almost all fields described above, the JRC delivers training courses to Euratom and IAEA inspectors. With and for ESARDA, it also organizes an annual education event on nuclear safeguards and education, known as the "ESARDA course," which over the past 15 years has educated more than a 1,000 young professionals and students in these fields. The course is currently being exported to regions outside Europe in close collaboration with the IAEA.

Collaboration with the Department of Nuclear Safety and Security

In 2016, the European Commission and the IAEA concluded a delegation agreement (INSC/2016/378-378) amounting to €3.5 million.[2] The agreement defines the activities entrusted to the IAEA for the implementation of the Action Plan on Nuclear Safety and in providing assistance to Instrument for Nuclear Safety Cooperation beneficiaries for improving global nuclear and radiation safety. The European Commission also has signed several practical arrangements with the IAEA's Nuclear Security and Safety Department, and as mentioned above, maintains a close collaboration with the Incident and Emergency Centre through which EU Member States and the European Commission participate regularly in the Convention Exercises to test and improve the preparedness and response system. Another good example of collaboration and mutual synergies is the coordination of border nuclear security work (detection, response, and nuclear forensics activities), where the Commission not only coordinates its outreach with the IAEA and the United States but also contributes significantly to the development of the IAEA Nuclear Security Series, expert meetings, and hands-on training for nuclear security in dedicated JRC training facilities. The IAEA regularly sends representatives from a variety of countries to these facilities. In 2013, the IAEA and the Commission signed a Memorandum of Understanding for further cooperation, including on expert peer reviews and on strengthening emergency preparedness and response. A key tool in this context is the Storage of Thermal Reactor Safety Analysis (STRESA) Database, developed by the JRC in 2000 and since then permanently updated at the JRC.[3] The main objective of this database is to disseminate documents and experimental data from large scientific projects related to nuclear safety.

The Generation IV International Forum (GIF), where the JRC is the implementing agent of EURATOM contributions, and IAEA's International

Project on Innovative Nuclear Reactors and Fuel Cycles (INPRO) cooperate, through methodology working groups (with strong JRC participation), on developing specific assessment methodologies in the areas of economics, proliferation resistance and physical protection, and risk and safety. GIF and the IAEA hold annual interface meetings to exchange information about ongoing projects of mutual interest on six selected reactor technologies and related activities in the IAEA. The European Commission is a full member of most of the technical working groups coordinated by the IAEA.

The JRC's involvement with IAEA also includes participation in Coordinated Research Projects, expert contributions in consultancy meetings and courses, international expert meetings, technical meetings, and the organization of joint or cosponsored events. A broad range of experimental and modelling domains, from reactor and fuel safety during irradiation to severe accidents, nuclear decommissioning, and waste management, are covered in these efforts. Knowledge dissemination and training efforts are specifically considered. The JRC participated in several of these programs, including projects related to the extended interim storage and potential retrievability of spent nuclear fuel. JRC contributions included sharing experimental results from tests performed on spent fuel rods under conditions relevant for handling and transportation after extended storage in view of their final disposal.

The JRC and the IAEA are actively involved in the definition of proposals for European projects aimed at establishing common research approaches among European and international partners, and for the application of innovative techniques in the domain of nuclear decommissioning. For instance, one proposal specifically targets establishing a framework for collaboration on research and development activities. Another proposal aims at evaluating the capabilities of innovative tools (namely the 3D Building Information Model) to develop a facility wide decommissioning plan and a detailed decontamination and dismantlement plan. The European Learning Initiatives for Nuclear Decommissioning and Environmental Remediation (ELINDER) is a training program in nuclear decommissioning, organized as a set of complementary training courses to provide a common qualification. ELINDER is coordinated by the Joint Operational Coordination Centre in collaboration with several European universities and institutes. The IAEA supports the ELINDER project through its expert networks, training tools, and technical cooperation program. As an example, the ELINDER "Decommissioning Summer School," held yearly in Ispra, Italy, is a week-long course for undergraduate students in engineering, science, and technology. The course provides an overview of key issues related to nuclear decommissioning and waste management and practical illustrative case studies. It also includes visits to JRC nuclear installations at the Ispra site. These collaboration efforts are based on making available the research and development results obtained through JRC expertise, experimental infrastructure, and know-how.

Collaboration with the Department for Technical Cooperation

More recently, the European Commission has supported the IAEA significantly in the nonenergy applications of nuclear technology. These applications cover, for example, the use of selected radioisotopes for medical applications. Over 20 years, the JRC has developed a targeted cancer therapy using short-lived alpha-emitting radionuclides. It provides support directly to hospitals and universities for the application and further research and development on other treatments of these specifically suited nuclides. This targeted alpha therapy is based on the coupling of alpha particle emitting radioisotopes to selective carrier molecules, such as monoclonal antibodies or peptides. These molecules have the ability to selectively target tumor cells even if they are spread throughout the body. They recognize the targeted cancer cells through antigens that are expressed on the cell surface and can bind selectively to them. Since alpha emission has a short range in the tissue, the deposited energy is used to destroy the cancer cell and spares the surrounding healthy tissue.

Under the same umbrella is the JRC's open access scheme. This program opens JRC research facilities to international researchers who want to gain experience in basic nuclear physics experiments (e.g., cross-section measurements) or work with actinides and transuranium elements.

Current challenges

By 1970, the United States, Russia, China, France, and the United Kingdom all had nuclear weapons. However, the Indian tests and subsequent Pakistan demonstration of nuclear military capabilities put the NPT under immense pressure from an early stage. The South African, Israeli, Libyan, Iranian, and North Korean cases (among the most publicly known) further challenged the NPT. Each of these cases presents one or more unique aspects, the discussion of which would be far too exhaustive for this chapter. What these cases show, however, is that even though the NPT is essential and needs to be maintained and cared for, it is not fully comprehensive; additional complementary approaches and solutions must be sought out and implemented.

A first challenge is political instability and its impact on today's international governance. The tensions in the Middle East, the discussions around the North Atlantic Treaty Organization (NATO) and its post-Cold War posture, the fragile India-Pakistan border, and international concerns about Iran and North Korea are all factors that have nuclear-weapon concerns at the core. Owing to the highly technical nature of the nuclear-weapon domain, the key persons involved in the international discussions on these issues are often skilled engineers, physicists, or missile experts. However, these individuals are not necessarily prepared to grasp the broader political and geostrategic picture, whose ingredients are key drivers for nuclear fuel-cycle and weaponization activities in certain countries. The same situation is reflected in the IAEA's mandate with respect to its safeguards verification activities. The activities that are allowed to be executed are those authorized by the IAEA's Board of Governors and focus largely on technical assessments of a country's nuclear activities. The same approach does not account for the political or economic factors involved, even with an enhancement of the physical model analysis to feed the improved state-level approach. Initial steps have been taken to broaden the picture (and thus improve understanding) for IAEA analysts to draw their safeguards conclusions. What is crucially missing or not always visible is the country level analysis of a state's intentions as well as its capabilities to undertake certain activities along critical pathways on the physical model, based on its economic and geopolitical situation. This chapter does not argue that this analysis should be part of the IAEA's mandate; nonetheless, the international community should develop an approach where such issues can be assessed and preventive and corrective action can be discussed. Although partially covered during NPT review cycles and in meetings of the G–7, G–77, NATO, World Economic Forum, or even the UN General Assembly, none of these events can provide comprehensive pictures that account for a state's current situation, its history, its mistakes, and its unsolved issues in this domain. Such an account would allow the international community to propose a way forward that takes stock of current realities, but at the same time formulates a vision for a sustainable future. A variety of individual, limited-scope analyses, and recommendations have been put forward by academics or at dedicated international and nongovernmental activities such as the Proliferation Security Institute and the Global Initiative for Combatting Nuclear Terrorism. However, even when these efforts are sound and agreeable at global level, their conclusions will remain without concrete effects if they are not enshrined in a valid international comprehensive treaty and corresponding commitment.

Another challenge that has global relevance, but a slightly lower political resonance level, is control over sensitive and strategic goods, technologies, materials, and knowledge. Early on, a number of countries recognized that verification of nuclear materials and related fuel-cycle activities is not sufficient to have a full picture of the proliferation risk in certain countries or regions. In particular, those who joined under different export control arrangements were aware of this predicament. After some near-misses using the traditional verification process, the international community recognized that a more comprehensive verification process is required and thus designed the Additional Protocol, known as the IAEA's current gold standard for verification basis—though unfortunately, not yet adhered to by all countries. In addition to the reporting and verification requirements imposed by the Additional Protocol, further capabilities for analysis may bring additional insights, such as the trade analysis of dual-use goods and commodities. These items have both military and civil use, but go beyond the direct-use items or "trigger lists" embedded in the Additional Protocol. The fact, for example, that the Joint Comprehensive Plan of Action (JCPOA) was complemented with a Procurement Channel Mechanism to come to grips with the potential proliferation challenges confirms the relevance of this issue. The area of strategic trade control is both complex and sensitive. It touches upon industrial and country competitiveness, trade patterns, underlying financing schemes, and the loopholes for control present in the global market (such as free-trade zones, tax paradises, and the use of bitcoin, which makes financial transaction traceability much more challenging). Despite these challenges, more can be done to address the risks posed by strategic trade. For instance, the UN Security Council Resolution 1540 Committee tries to tackle this concern by requesting that countries develop more effective and efficient control systems, but in fact the committee has no role, opportunity, or budget to intervene or otherwise correct loopholes and weaknesses.

On a more practical level, internal IAEA challenges include the human resources policies deployed, which may affect continuity of approach (with relatively short-term contracts in a number of vital areas), as well as the risk of stovepiping between the departments. This is not a new finding, and some actions have been undertaken in a workable direction, including how to tackle cyber threats and security concerns across the whole Secretariat. However, more can be done. Especially when addressing newcomer states in nuclear technology, an integrated approach between the different departments of IAEA to promote synergies among nuclear energy development, safety, security, and safeguards is encouraged.

The way forward

In the current unstable international environment of nuclear engagements, agreements, and ambitions, the IAEA's role of providing solid, verified, and comprehensive technical safeguards evaluations is all the more important. Political boundary conditions can change and alliances between countries may be volatile, but the IAEA's contributions with respect to its internationally accepted mandate and special role toward both its Board of Governors and the UN Security Council need to be absolutely safeguarded.

With the rise of interest in nuclear technology in areas not previously involved in nuclear developments, lacking the experience of operating independent safety and security authorities, the international community has a huge potential task for capacity building and support that is best channeled through the IAEA. This goes far beyond the safe and secure management of radioactive sources—an activity that has been ongoing for years, due to the widespread use of these sources in various applications—and requires the provision of education, training, in-field capacity building, legal assistance, and the fostering of regional networking and collaboration. A large number of IAEA Member States are not operating nuclear reactors, but are looking toward the benefits that can be obtained from working closely with the IAEA. The Agency's technical cooperation dimension is steadily increasing. The IAEA Director General attaches key importance to fostering this dimension and profiling the IAEA more in this direction as an organization providing assistance and support, rather than only "policing" or "verification."

It is felt that in fact these roles do not necessarily need to be fully separated. In the areas of safeguards and nonproliferation, in states (or regions, as in the case of Euratom) where there is a high willingness for collaboration, there can be a positive return from capacity building in verification capabilities. When the quality and reliability of the reporting increases, the IAEA can seek to materialize these positive signals and strive to maintain or even increase its safeguards effectiveness and efficiency, while at the same time possibly saving on outlay such as inspector resources and equipment costs. This idea, which is at the foundation of the integrated safeguards approach, merits further pursuit, as it is in cases where the IAEA is drawing broader safeguards conclusions. At the same time, vigilance needs to remain high, and it should be analyzed how to "behave" when broader conclusions would need to be withdrawn for one or another reasons. In line with the above reasoning, it also should be reiterated that for safeguards, the IAEA has a most impressive set of tools—including complementary access and limited unannounced inspections—but some of these tools might not be utilized to the full extent. A more comprehensive application of available tools is recommended.

Notes

1. "Remarks by President Barack Obama in Prague As Delivered," Office of the Press Secretary, The White House, April 5, 2009, https://obamawhitehouse.archives.gov/the-press-office/remarks-president-barack-obama-prague-delivered.
2. Mercedita Balbuena and Ania Hryniewicz, "EC-IAEA Cooperation on its Action Plan on Nuclear Safety Continues," IAEA, January 25, 2017, https://www.iaea.org/newscenter/news/ec-iaea-cooperation-on-its-action-plan-on-nuclear-safety-continues.
3. See the STRESA website at https://stresa.jrc.ec.europa.eu/.

Appendix
Keynote address to the Conference on the International Atomic Energy Agency at 60, held at the Woodrow Wilson International Center for Scholars, Washington, DC, on November 6–7, 2017

Sixty years of Atoms for Peace and development

Yukiya Amano

The origins of the International Atomic Energy Agency (IAEA) are usually traced back to U.S. president Dwight D. Eisenhower's Atoms for Peace speech to the United Nations General Assembly on December 8, 1953. Concerned about the postwar nuclear arms race between the United States and the Soviet Union, Eisenhower expressed hope that "this greatest of destructive forces can be developed into a great boon, for the benefit of all mankind." He proposed that governments should make contributions of uranium and fissionable materials to a new International Atomic Energy Agency, whose responsibility would be to ensure that the material was allocated "to serve the peaceful pursuits of mankind."[1]

When the IAEA came into existence in 1957, its role was somewhat different from that outlined by Eisenhower. His initial idea—that the new agency should take control of some stocks of nuclear material from the two superpowers of the time—did not materialize. But the president's fundamental goal of an organization focused on "atoms for peace" was achieved. His suggestion that experts be mobilized to apply atomic energy to the needs of agriculture, medicine, and other peaceful activities is reflected in the IAEA Statute. Article II of the Statute states: "The Agency shall seek to accelerate and enlarge the contribution of atomic energy to peace, health and prosperity throughout the world."[2] Eisenhower's proposal on peaceful activities has been embodied in a concrete way in the IAEA technical cooperation program. His suggestion that a special purpose of the new agency would be "to provide abundant electrical energy in the power-starved areas of the world" has been partially fulfilled. With assistance from the IAEA, 30 countries have introduced nuclear power and nearly 30 more, mainly in the developing world, are considering introducing it.

From technical assistance to cooperation

In listing the Agency's functions, the IAEA Statute highlights nuclear energy, nuclear safety, safeguards, and the transfer of nuclear technology. Although the range of the IAEA's activities has broadened considerably in 60 years—for example, nuclear security is now one of the most important, and growing, areas of our work—these four original objectives remain at the heart of our activities today. In the early years, the IAEA's "technical assistance" program, as it then was known, was modest. Early projects were small in scale and short in duration. The focus was on helping countries to build up capacity in nuclear science and technology and establish relevant institutions and facilities. In the late 1970s, as contributions to the Technical Cooperation Fund increased and the benefits of having larger projects became evident, the Agency introduced multiyear projects. By the end of the 1980s, significant progress had been made in building capacity and infrastructure in Member States.

The Agency has helped to improve the health and prosperity of millions of people by making nuclear science and technology available in healthcare, food and agriculture, industry, and many other areas. Countries are using nuclear technology not just to generate electricity but to produce more food, treat diseases such as cancer, manage water supplies, protect the seas and oceans, and monitor climate change. Countries determine their own priorities. They decide in what areas they wish to benefit from nuclear science and technology. We then do our best to provide the support they seek.

That support is not primarily about handing over equipment. We focus on transferring knowledge and expertise. High-quality technical training helps developing countries to build future generations of nuclear specialists. Many developing countries have already acquired a high level of expertise in nuclear technology, and there are many excellent examples of South-South cooperation. This makes a vital contribution to helping the Agency deliver its technical cooperation program. Since 2015, helping countries to achieve the United Nations Sustainable Development Goals (SDGs), using relevant nuclear technology, has been an important part of our work. In fact, the IAEA helps countries to use nuclear science and technology to meet at least 9 of the 17 SDGs directly, including those aimed at ending hunger, improving human health, and increasing the availability of clean water and, of course, energy. A few examples will illustrate the broad range of activities supported by the IAEA.

Food and nutrition

The IAEA helps countries to grow more food by developing new varieties of crops such as rice and barley, using a technique known as radiation-induced mutation. These plants have higher yields and are more resistant to drought and disease. By applying radiation in the laboratory, scientists accelerate the spontaneous mutation process that occurs in nature all the time. They can quickly develop new varieties of plants with desirable characteristics. This does not involve genetic modification of the plants. As a result, farmers in Peru are growing abundant crops of new varieties of barley at high altitudes, while farmers in Myanmar are growing more rice. Producing the new plants involves sophisticated science, but farmers do not have to change traditional growing methods.

Nuclear techniques also help to protect food sources on both land and sea. Pollutants and biotoxins in the seas and oceans pose a threat to fish and shellfish, which are key sources of food for millions of people around the world. Nuclear and isotopic tools provide insights into the movement of pollutants and toxins in the seas, their transfer to marine organisms, and their increasing concentrations as they move up the food chain to end on our plates. The IAEA Environment Laboratories in Monaco help countries to detect and measure such contamination so they can take the necessary measures to protect consumers. On land, the IAEA contributed to the eradication of the cattle disease rinderpest by helping to develop nuclear technologies that could be used in the field to diagnose and control the disease.

The IAEA also has had a role to play in responding to national disasters and public health crises. After devastating earthquakes in Ecuador and Nepal, the Agency sent experts in nondestructive testing techniques, including radiography, to assess the safety of hospitals and schools in danger of collapse. It also was able to respond promptly to emergencies such as the Ebola and Zika viruses, supplying affected countries with simple kits derived from nuclear materials so that they could detect the diseases quickly and accurately in the field.

The IAEA is unique within the United Nations system in having eight specialist nuclear applications laboratories near Vienna. These laboratories train scientists; support research in human health, food, and other areas; and provide analytical services to national laboratories. At the time of writing, a long-overdue modernization of the laboratories is nearing completion.

Cancer

Improving access to radiotherapy and nuclear medicine is a priority for many of our 170 Member States, especially for developing countries. Cancer diagnosis and treatment is therefore a particular focus of our work.

Cancer used to be regarded as a disease primarily of prosperous, developed countries. But it is now reaching alarming proportions in developing countries, and many are ill-equipped to deal with it. It is estimated that, by 2030, some 60 percent of all new cancer cases will be recorded in developing countries, and that is where around 70 percent of cancer-related deaths will occur. In many of those countries, prevention, screening, early diagnosis, and treatment services are either nonexistent or totally inadequate. In Africa, for example, nearly 30 countries do not have a single radiotherapy machine. The IAEA is working to change that. It has helped countries plan and build nuclear medicine and radiotherapy facilities and has arranged education and training for oncologists, radiologists, medical physicists, and other specialists. The IAEA is an active partner in the United Nations Joint Global Programme on Cervical Cancer Prevention and Control, which aims to reduce cervical cancer mortality in participating countries by 25 percent by 2025.

In early 2018 I was in the Ugandan capital, Kampala, for the inauguration of a new Cobalt 60 radiotherapy machine. Uganda had no radiotherapy services at all for two years after its old machine—the only one in the country—broke down. The IAEA helped the government to buy the new equipment, installed it safely at the Uganda Cancer Institute, and decommissioned the old machine. It also provided training for the institute's specialist staff. Likewise, in Ghana, the Agency provided diagnostic equipment for child cancers. It helped Lesotho to plan its first radiotherapy center and arranged specialist training in radiation oncology so that local doctors will be ready to start treating patients as soon as the new facility opens.

The IAEA helps governments to put national plans in place to offer comprehensive cancer care to their people. IAEA expert missions assess the level of nuclear medicine and radiotherapy services in a country and offer recommendations on improvements, and the Agency also supports important research projects. It works closely with Member States on nuclear safety, helping to ensure that both patients and staff are protected from harmful exposure to radiation. The Agency's Dosimetry Laboratory near Vienna provides dosimetry auditing services for radiotherapy centers throughout the world, free of charge. This helps to ensure that patients receiving radiotherapy get exactly the right radiation dose.

The IAEA's work in the cancer field undoubtedly helps to save lives, yet developing countries' needs in this area remain great. There is an estimated shortage of 5,000 radiotherapy machines throughout the world. To meet the cancer needs of developing countries, many thousands of radiation oncologists, medical physicists, dosimetrists, and radiation therapists need to be trained. This is a daunting challenge. But I believe much can be achieved if cancer in developing countries is given its rightful place at the top of the global development agenda and if governments, organizations such as ours, professional associations, and nongovernmental organizations work together. In my meetings with government leaders, I constantly stress the importance of cancer control as a development issue. We work hard to build productive cooperation with relevant partners such as the World Health Organization and the International Agency for Research on Cancer. I also have encouraged leading doctors, academics, and technical specialists in developed countries to share their expertise with developing countries, such as by inviting researchers from developing countries to spend time at their facilities.

Safe and secure nuclear power

Under Article III of the IAEA Statute, the Agency is authorized "[t]o make provision, in accordance with this Statute, for materials, services, equipment, and facilities to meet the needs of research on, and development and practical application of, atomic energy for peaceful purposes, including the production of electric power, with due consideration for the needs of the under-developed areas of the world."[3] Many countries believe that nuclear power can help them to obtain secure, reliable supplies of energy and to mitigate the impact of climate change. At the time of writing, 30 countries are using nuclear power. It is likely to make a growing contribution to sustainable development in the coming decades. Today, 70 percent of the world's electricity comes from fossil fuels; 11 percent comes from nuclear power, which is one of the lowest-carbon emitting technologies for generating electricity. But when it comes to low-carbon electricity, nuclear power generates almost one-third of the global total.

By 2050, if climate change goals set under the Paris Agreement are to be met, around 80 percent of electricity will need to be low-carbon. Nuclear power plants produce virtually no greenhouse gas emissions or air pollutants during their operation, and emissions over their entire lifecycle are very low. The use of nuclear power reduces carbon dioxide emissions by about two gigatons per year: the equivalent of taking more than 400 million cars off the road every year. Renewable sources of power such as wind and solar undoubtedly will play an increasingly important role globally in the coming decades, but by nature they are intermittent, and modern economies require stable, dependable power sources. It is difficult to see how the world will be able to meet the challenge of securing sufficient energy, and mitigating the impact of climate change, without making more use of nuclear power. It is up to each country to decide whether to introduce nuclear power. The IAEA does not attempt to influence a country's decision. But if countries opt for nuclear power, the Agency's job is to help them use it safely, securely, and sustainably.

Nuclear safety and security are national responsibilities, but the IAEA serves as the global platform for cooperation in these areas. For example, we establish international nuclear safety standards. These are not legally binding, but they are used voluntarily by almost all countries to protect people and the environment from harmful effects of ionizing radiation. The IAEA coordinated the international response to the most serious accidents at nuclear power plants at Chernobyl in 1986 and Fukushima Dai-ichi in 2011. As far as security is concerned, the IAEA helps countries to prevent nuclear and other radioactive material from falling into the hands of terrorists. We train police and border guards, provide radiation detection equipment, and advise on nuclear security at major events such as the Olympic Games and World Cup soccer championships.

Nuclear safeguards

Article III of the IAEA Statute authorizes the Agency to apply safeguards to any of a state's activities in the field of atomic power, at the request of the state. Under the Treaty on the Non-proliferation of Nuclear Weapons, nonnuclear-weapon states are required to conclude a comprehensive safeguards agreement with the IAEA. They must declare all nuclear facilities and other locations where nuclear material and activities exist. The IAEA analyzes the declarations and sends inspectors to verify that the declarations are correct. We may install cameras, tamper-proof seals, and other equipment so that we know what is happening when our inspectors are not physically present. After this initial stage, we continue to monitor the facilities and locations to verify that facilities are not being misused and that nuclear material is not being diverted from peaceful activities.

Since the end of the 20th century, the IAEA has been strongly encouraging states to conclude an Additional Protocol, a powerful verification tool introduced in 1997 after the serious difficulties encountered in verification of the Iraqi and North Korean nuclear programs. The Additional Protocol requires countries to submit extensive, detailed declarations about their activities related to the nuclear fuel cycle, and to update them at least once a year. The Agency analyzes the declarations and, if necessary, seeks clarifications and access to specific locations. Countries have an obligation to provide both clarifications and access. The important thing for the Agency is to gain a full understanding of a country's entire nuclear fuel cycle, from the mining of uranium all the way through to the final disposal of spent fuel and radioactive waste. This enables us to spot any anomalies or possible diversion of nuclear material from peaceful activities. Our interest is in locations with nuclear material, nuclear fuel-cycle related equipment, and expertise or combinations of these elements. For the Agency, the civilian or military status of a particular location is not relevant.

We presently implement safeguards in 181 countries in the same rigorous, impartial, and objective manner, in accordance with each country's safeguards agreements and Additional Protocol, and with standards and practices established over decades. The IAEA has a legal obligation to protect confidential information that countries share with us, and we do not disclose information about the facilities and locations we inspect. The safeguards conclusions drawn by the IAEA, based on our independent verification and findings, provide credible assurance to the international community that states are abiding by their safeguards obligations.

Iran

The best-known safeguards issue on the IAEA's agenda in the past decade-and-a-half has been the Iranian nuclear program. Given the long and complex history of this issue, it is worth considering in some detail for the light it sheds on the IAEA approach to nuclear verification.

In 2002, an Iranian opposition group claimed that Iran had been building nuclear facilities at Natanz and Arak, and had not declared this new construction. The IAEA began looking into the matter. The first IAEA report, delivered in June 2003, indicated that Iran was building uranium enrichment facilities at Natanz and a heavy-water production plant at Arak. It also found that Iran had failed to meet a number of its obligations under its safeguards agreement. The Agency began a process of trying to clarify safeguards issues in Iran, and this process continued for well over a decade. IAEA reports often stated that Iran was not forthcoming in clarifying unresolved issues. In August 2003, the IAEA stated that it had found highly enriched uranium particles at Natanz, and that this finding was "not consistent with the nuclear material declarations made by Iran."[4]

In September 2005, the IAEA Board of Governors adopted a resolution in which it found Iran to be in noncompliance with its safeguards obligations. In February 2006, the Board (of which I was chairman) decided to report Iran's noncompliance to the United Nations Security Council. In July that year the Security Council adopted its first resolution on Iran, demanding that Iran should suspend all enrichment-related and reprocessing activities within one month. In December 2006, the Security Council adopted a second resolution that required Iran to suspend work on all heavy-water-related projects and imposed sanctions on Iran. In the following years, despite additional resolutions by the Security Council and the IAEA Board, Iran continued its enrichment-related activities and its work on heavy-water-related projects. The Agency continued to work hard to resolve the Iran nuclear issue. It participated in a number of initiatives, which ultimately delivered little, and the situation gradually deteriorated. International tension over Iran rose, at times to dangerous levels.

When I became Director General in December 2009, I felt it important to spell out our assessment of the situation in light of relevant safeguards rules, the facts that we had established through many years of verification efforts, and our concerns. In my first report to the Board in February 2010, I said that the information available to the Agency raised concerns about the possible existence in Iran of past or current undisclosed activities related to the development of a nuclear payload for a missile. I also stated that Iran had not provided the necessary cooperation to permit the Agency to confirm that all nuclear material in Iran was being used in peaceful activities. In my view, this was a logical conclusion based on the facts and the rules, but many commentators characterized it as "blunt."[5]

In my first few years in office, little headway was made in our talks with Iran. In the hope of achieving a breakthrough, in November 2011 I presented a detailed report to our Board of Governors in which I identified 12 areas of concern on what had become known as the "possible military dimensions" of Iran's nuclear program. Our information indicated that Iran had carried out activities relevant to the development of a nuclear explosive device. It also indicated that, before the end of 2003, these activities had taken place under a structured program, and that some activities might still be ongoing. I did not say that the information was correct. But I did say that our information was broadly consistent and credible in terms of technical detail. I asked Iran to clarify the 12 areas. In response, the Board asked Iran and the IAEA to cooperate to resolve the issues. Looking back, I see the release of this report as one of the turning points in the Iran nuclear issue. It showed the path to a possible solution by identifying the areas that needed clarification.

In the next two years some progress was made in our discussions, but no agreement was reached. Mostly, we were going around in circles. Then, in late 2013, after the election of President Hassan Rouhani in Iran, we started to see a change in both atmosphere and substance, and there was some movement in the right direction. The IAEA and Iran agreed on a Framework for Cooperation. We started to work with Iran to resolve all the outstanding issues, including the possible military dimensions, through strengthened cooperation and a step-by-step approach. Separately, Iran and the P5+1 countries (China, France, Germany, Russia, the United Kingdom, and the United States) agreed on a Joint Plan of Action and began talks aimed at achieving a mutually agreed, long-term comprehensive solution to ensure Iran's nuclear program would be exclusively peaceful.

This dual-track approach succeeded in moving things forward. In July 2015, I signed a roadmap with Iran aimed at clarifying the possible military dimensions by the end of that year. On the same day, Iran and the abovementioned six countries, plus the European Union, agreed on a Joint Comprehensive Plan of Action (JCPOA). The Security Council endorsed the agreement and asked the IAEA to verify and monitor Iran's nuclear-related commitments under the JCPOA. Our Board authorized us to do so.

In September 2015, I traveled to Iran for high-level meetings with Iranian leaders. I visited a location at the Parchin site to which the Agency had long requested access. This visit was an important milestone because Parchin had been seen as a litmus test of Iran's willingness to cooperate with the IAEA to clarify the possible military dimensions. Implementation of the roadmap enabled us to obtain a much better understanding of Iran's nuclear activities. As a result, I was able to present a final assessment on past and present outstanding issues regarding Iran's nuclear program to our Board in December 2015. In that report, I stated that Iran had conducted a range of activities relevant to the development of a nuclear explosive device before the end of 2003. However, these activities did not advance beyond feasibility and scientific studies, and the acquisition of certain relevant technical competences and capabilities. Based on my report, the IAEA Board noted that all activities under the roadmap had been implemented as agreed and declared that its consideration of this issue was closed. This report paved the way for implementation of the JCPOA to begin on January 16, 2016.

In my quarterly reports to the IAEA Board of Governors since then, I have stated that the nuclear-related commitments made by Iran under the JCPOA are being implemented. Iran is now subject to the world's most robust nuclear verification regime. Our inspectors have expanded access to locations and have more information about Iran's nuclear program, which is smaller than it was before the agreement came into effect. To date, the U.S. withdrawal from the JCPOA has not affected the agreement or the IAEA's role in implementing it.

North Korea

As far as the other major safeguards issue on the IAEA agenda is concerned—the North Korean nuclear program—it has not been possible to make comparable progress. The Agency started to encounter difficulties in its verification activities almost immediately after the entry into force of the comprehensive safeguards agreement with North Korea in 1992. North Korea was found to be noncompliant with its Safeguards Agreement in 1993, and since 1994 the Agency has not been able to conduct all necessary safeguards activities in the country.

Agency inspectors conducted certain verification and monitoring activities in North Korea from 1994 to 2002 in the context of the Agreed Framework between the United States and North Korea, and from 2007 to 2009 in relation to the agreement in the Six-Party Talks. However, the inspectors were required to leave North Korea in April 2009, and since then the Agency has had no presence on the ground. We have continued to monitor North Korea's nuclear program to the extent of our abilities, including through the use of satellite imagery. We also have been working to maintain and enhance our readiness to return to North Korea when political developments make this possible.

I have expressed serious concern about North Korea's nuclear program and called upon the country to comply fully with its obligations under all relevant resolutions of the Security Council and the IAEA. At the time of writing, we are following political developments concerning North Korea's nuclear program with great interest. The IAEA stands ready to contribute to the peaceful resolution of this nuclear issue by resuming verification activities in the country if requested by the countries concerned.

Other developments in nuclear verification

The world in which the IAEA implements safeguards today is markedly different from that of 1957, the year in which the Agency was established, and so are the challenges we face. New technology and modern communications have made it easier to access knowledge, materials, and expertise that would have been much more restricted back then—and this makes nuclear proliferation easier.

Important new legal instruments, such as the Additional Protocol, have been developed. One hundred and thirty-two countries have brought Additional Protocols into force, giving the Agency greater access to locations and information. We also have made increasing use of modern technology such as remote monitoring and satellite imagery. Advanced equipment and methods enable us to detect even minute particles of nuclear material. We have dramatically improved our analytical capabilities by building new state-of-the-art safeguards laboratories near Vienna, which analyze samples of material brought back by our inspectors. Wherever possible, we monitor nuclear facilities remotely, in real time, using permanently installed cameras and other sensors. We are also making progress in using advanced information technology to collect and analyze a huge volume of safeguards-relevant information.

The number of nuclear facilities coming under IAEA safeguards continues to grow. So does the amount of nuclear material to be safeguarded. Nevertheless, IAEA resources are limited, demand from Member States for our services has been rising, and our budget is being squeezed. That means we must constantly find ways of working more effectively and more efficiently in all areas of our work, including safeguards. But, in turn, Member States need to provide us with adequate resources to do our job.

Conclusion

The IAEA at 60 has a remarkably broad mandate, and it needs to be implemented in a balanced manner. From the 26 countries that ratified the IAEA Statute in 1957, we have grown to an organization with 170 Member States that spans the globe. Our membership continues to expand.

Our work is unique. No other international organization offers the range of services related to nuclear science and technology that we do. In the coming decades, we will continue to focus on delivering concrete results for our Member States and improving the well-being and prosperity of the people of the world through the use of relevant nuclear technology. We will continue to contribute to international peace and security by verifying that nuclear material stays in peaceful uses.

As we celebrated our 60th anniversary in 2016–2017, we amended our motto to "Atoms for Peace and Development." Delivering concrete results for all our Member States in pursuit of that objective remains the primary goal of the IAEA.

Notes

1. "Atoms for Peace Speech [December 8, 1953]," International Atomic Energy Agency (IAEA), https://www.iaea.org/about/history/atoms-for-peace-speech.
2. Statute of the IAEA, Article II, https://www.iaea.org/about/statute#a1-2.
3. Statute of the IAEA, Article III, https://www.iaea.org/about/statute#a1-3.
4. IAEA Board of Governors, "Implementation of the NPT Safeguards Agreement in the Islamic Republic of Iran," GOV/2003/63, August 26, 2003, 2, https://www.iaea.org/sites/default/files/gov2003-63.pdf.
5. IAEA Board of Governors, "Implementation of the NPT Safeguards Agreement and Relevant Provisions of Security Council Resolutions 1737 (2006), 1747 (2007), 1803 (2008) and 1835 (2008) in the Islamic Republic of Iran," GOV/2010/10, February 18, 2010, https://www.iaea.org/sites/default/files/gov2010-10.pdf.

Index

Figures are indicated by italic page numbers. Notes are indicated by "n" following the page number.